CAPTAIN BLOOD

His Odyssey

BY

RAFAEL SABATINI

BOSTON AND NEW YORK

HOUGHTON MIFFLIN COMPANY

The Riverside Press Cambridge

1924

COPYRIGHT, 1922, BY RAFAEL SABATINI

COPYRIGHT, 1924, BY HOUGHTON MIFFLIN COMPANY

ALL RIGHTS RESERVED

The Riverside Press

CAMBRIDGE · MASSACHUSETTS

PRINTED IN THE U.S.A.

CONTENTS

ILLUSTRATIONS

From drawings by Clyde O. Deland

CAPTAIN BLOOD

His Odyssey

CAPTAIN BLOOD
His Odyssey

• •

CHAPTER I

THE MESSENGER

PETER BLOOD, bachelor of medicine and several other things besides, smoked a pipe and tended the geraniums boxed on the sill of his window above Water Lane in the town of Bridgewater.

Sternly disapproving eyes considered him from a window opposite, but went disregarded. Mr. Blood's attention was divided between his task and the stream of humanity in the narrow street below; a stream which poured for the second time that day towards Castle Field, where earlier in the afternoon Ferguson, the Duke's chaplain, had preached a sermon containing more treason than divinity.

These straggling, excited groups were mainly composed of men with green boughs in their hats and the most ludicrous of weapons in their hands. Some, it is true, shouldered fowling pieces, and here and there a sword was brandished; but more of them were armed with clubs, and most of them trailed the mammoth pikes fashioned out of scythes, as formidable to the eye as they were clumsy to the hand. There were weavers, brewers, carpenters, smiths, masons, brick-

layers, cobblers, and representatives of every other of
the trades of peace among these improvised men of
war. Bridgewater, like Taunton, had yielded so gen-
erously of its manhood to the service of the bastard
Duke that for any to abstain whose age and strength
admitted of his bearing arms was to brand himself a
coward or a papist.

Yet Peter Blood, who was not only able to bear
arms, but trained and skilled in their use, who was
certainly no coward, and a papist only when it so
suited him, tended his geraniums and smoked his pipe
on that warm July evening as indifferently as if
nothing were afoot. One other thing he did. He flung
after those war-fevered enthusiasts a line of Horace
— a poet for whose work he had early conceived an
inordinate affection:

"Quo, quo, scelesti, ruitis?"

And now perhaps you guess why the hot, intrepid
blood inherited from the roving sires of his Somersetshire mother remained cool amidst all this frenzied
fanatical heat of rebellion; why the turbulent spirit
which had forced him once from the sedate academi-
cal bonds his father would have imposed upon him,
should now remain quiet in the very midst of turbu-
lence. You realize how he regarded these men who
were rallying to the banners of liberty — the banners
woven by the virgins of Taunton, the girls from the
seminaries of Miss Blake and Mrs. Musgrove, who —
as the ballad runs — had ripped open their silk petticoats to make colours for King Monmouth's army.
That Latin line, contemptuously flung after them as
they clattered down the cobbled street, reveals his

mind. To him they were fools rushing in wicked frenzy upon their ruin.

You see, he knew too much about this fellow Monmouth and the pretty brown slut who had borne him, to be deceived by the legend of legitimacy, on the strength of which this standard of rebellion had been raised. He had read the absurd proclamation posted at the Cross at Bridgewater — as it had been posted also at Taunton and elsewhere — setting forth that "upon the decease of our Sovereign Lord Charles the Second, the right of succession to the Crown of England, Scotland, France, and Ireland, with the dominions and territories thereunto belonging, did legally descend and devolve upon the most illustrious and high-born Prince James, Duke of Monmouth, son and heir apparent to the said King Charles the Second."

It had moved him to laughter, as had the further announcement that "James Duke of York did first cause the said late King to be poysoned, and immediately thereupon did usurp and invade the Crown."

He knew not which was the greater lie. For Mr. Blood had spent a third of his life in the Netherlands, where this same James Scott — who now proclaimed himself James the Second, by the grace of God, King, et cætera — first saw the light some six-and-thirty years ago, and he was acquainted with the story current there of the fellow's real paternity. Far from being legitimate — by virtue of a pretended secret marriage between Charles Stuart and Lucy Walter — it was possible that this Monmouth who now proclaimed himself King of England was not even the illegitimate child of the late sovereign. What but ruin and disaster could be the end of this grotesque pretension? How could it be hoped that England would ever swallow such a Perkin? And it was on his behalf, to uphold his fantastic claim, that these West Country clods, led by a few armigerous Whigs, had been seduced into rebellion!

> "Quo, quo, scelesti, ruitis?"

He laughed and sighed in one; but the laugh dominated the sigh, for Mr. Blood was unsympathetic, as are most self-sufficient men; and he was very self-sufficient; adversity had taught him so to be. A more tender-hearted man, possessing his vision and his knowledge, might have found cause for tears in the contemplation of these ardent, simple, Nonconformist sheep going forth to the shambles — escorted to the rallying ground on Castle Field by wives and daughters, sweethearts and mothers, sustained by the delusion that they were to take the field in defence of Right, of Liberty, and of Religion. For he knew, as all Bridgewater knew and had known now for some hours, that it was Monmouth's intention to deliver battle that same night. The Duke was to lead a surprise attack upon the Royalist army under Feversham that was now encamped on Sedgemoor. Mr. Blood assumed that Lord Feversham would be equally well-informed, and if in this assumption he was wrong, at least he was justified of it. He was not to suppose the Royalist commander so indifferently skilled in the trade he followed.

Mr. Blood knocked the ashes from his pipe, and drew back to close his window. As he did so, his glance travelling straight across the street met at last the glance of those hostile eyes that watched him.

There were two pairs, and they belonged to the Misses Pitt, two amiable, sentimental maiden ladies who yielded to none in Bridgewater in their worship of the handsome Monmouth.

Mr. Blood smiled and inclined his head, for he was on friendly terms with these ladies, one of whom, indeed, had been for a little while his patient. But there was no response to his greeting. Instead, the eyes gave him back a stare of cold disdain. The smile on his thin lips grew a little broader, a little less pleasant. He understood the reason of that hostility, which had been daily growing in this past week since Monmouth had come to turn the brains of women of all ages. The Misses Pitt, he apprehended, contemned him that he, a young and vigorous man, of a military training which might now be valuable to the Cause, should stand aloof; that he should placidly smoke his pipe and tend his geraniums on this evening of all evenings, when men of spirit were rallying to the Protestant Champion, offering their blood to place him on the throne where he belonged.

If Mr. Blood had condescended to debate the matter with these ladies, he might have urged that having had his fill of wandering and adventuring, he was now embarked upon the career for which he had been originally intended and for which his studies had equipped him; that he was a man of medicine and not of war; a healer, not a slayer. But they would have answered him, he knew, that in such a cause it behooved every man who deemed himself a man to take up arms. They would have pointed out that their own nephew Jeremiah, who was by trade a sailor, the master of a ship — which by an ill-chance for that young man had come to anchor at this season in Bridgewater Bay — had quitted the helm to snatch up a musket in defence of Right. But Mr. Blood was not of those who argue. As I have said, he was a self-sufficient man.

He closed the window, drew the curtains, and turned to the pleasant, candle-lighted room, and the table on which Mrs. Barlow, his housekeeper, was in the very act of spreading supper. To her, however, he spoke aloud his thought.

"It's out of favour I am with the vinegary virgins over the way."

He had a pleasant, vibrant voice, whose metallic ring was softened and muted by the Irish accent which in all his wanderings he had never lost. It was a voice that could woo seductively and caressingly, or command in such a way as to compel obedience. Indeed, the man's whole nature was in that voice of his. For the rest of him, he was tall and spare, swarthy of tint as a gipsy, with eyes that were startlingly blue in that dark face and under those level black brows. In their glance those eyes, flanking a high-bridged, intrepid nose, were of singular penetration and of a steady haughtiness that went well with his firm lips. Though dressed in black as became his calling, yet it was with an elegance derived from the love of clothes that is peculiar to the adventurer he had been, rather than to the staid medicus he now was. His coat was of fine camlet, and it was laced with silver; there were ruffles of Mechlin at his wrists and a Mechlin cravat encased his throat. His great black periwig was as sedulously curled as any at Whitehall.

Seeing him thus, and perceiving his real nature, which was plain upon him, you might have been tempted to speculate how long such a man would be content to lie by in this little backwater of the world into which chance had swept him some six months ago; how long he would continue to pursue the trade for which he had qualified himself before he had begun to live. Difficult of belief though it may be when you know his history, previous and subsequent, yet it is possible that but for the trick that Fate was about to play him, he might have continued this peaceful existence, settling down completely to the life of a doctor in this Somersetshire haven. It is possible, but not probable.

He was the son of an Irish medicus, by a Somersetshire lady in whose veins ran the rover blood of the Frobishers, which may account for a certain wildness that had early manifested itself in his disposition. This wildness had profoundly alarmed his father, who for an Irishman was of a singularly peace-loving nature. He had early resolved that the boy should follow his own honourable profession, and Peter Blood, being quick to learn and oddly greedy of knowledge, had satisfied his parent by receiving at the age of twenty the degree of baccalaureus medicinæ at Trinity College, Dublin. His father survived that satisfaction by three months only. His mother had then been dead some years already. Thus Peter Blood came into an inheritance of some few hundred pounds, with which he had set out to see the world and give for a season a free rein to that restless spirit by which he was imbued. A set of curious chances led him to take service with the Dutch, then at war with France; and a predilection for the sea made him elect that this service should be upon that element. He had the

advantage of a commission under the famous de Ruyter, and fought in the Mediterranean engagement in
which that great Dutch admiral lost his life.

After the Peace of Nimeguen his movements are
obscure. But we know that he spent two years in a
Spanish prison, though we do not know how he contrived to get there. It may be due to this that upon
his release he took his sword to France, and saw service with the French in their warring upon the Spanish
Netherlands. Having reached, at last, the age of
thirty-two, his appetite for adventure surfeited, his
health having grown indifferent as the result of a neglected wound, he was suddenly overwhelmed by
homesickness. He took ship from Nantes with intent
to cross to Ireland. But the vessel being driven by
stress of weather into Bridgewater Bay, and Blood's
health having grown worse during the voyage, he decided to go ashore there, additionally urged to it by
the fact that it was his mother's native soil.

Thus in January of that year 1685 he had come to
Bridgewater, possessor of a fortune that was approximately the same as that with which he had originally
set out from Dublin eleven years ago.

Because he liked the place, in which his health was
rapidly restored to him, and because he conceived
that he had passed through adventures enough for a
man's lifetime, he determined to settle there, and
take up at last the profession of medicine from which
he had, with so little profit, broken away.

That is all his story, or so much of it as matters up
to that night, six months later, when the battle of
Sedgemoor was fought.

Deeming the impending action no affair of his, as

indeed it was not, and indifferent to the activity with which Bridgewater was that night agog, Mr. Blood closed his ears to the sounds of it, and went early to bed. He was peacefully asleep long before eleven o'clock, at which hour, as you know, Monmouth rode out with his rebel host along the Bristol Road, circuitously to avoid the marshland that lay directly between himself and the Royal Army. You also know that his numerical advantage — possibly counterbalanced by the greater steadiness of the regular troops on the other side — and the advantages he derived from falling by surprise upon an army that was more or less asleep, were all lost to him by blundering and bad leadership before ever he was at grips with Feversham.

The armies came into collision in the neighbourhood of two o'clock in the morning. Mr. Blood slept undisturbed through the distant boom of cannon. Not until four o'clock, when the sun was rising to dispel the last wisps of mist over that stricken field of battle, did he awaken from his tranquil slumbers.

He sat up in bed, rubbed the sleep from his eyes, and collected himself. Blows were thundering upon the door of his house, and a voice was calling incoherently. This was the noise that had aroused him. Conceiving that he had to do with some urgent obstetrical case, he reached for bedgown and slippers, to go below. On the landing he almost collided with Mrs. Barlow, new-risen and unsightly, in a state of panic. He quieted her cluckings with a word of reassurance, and went himself to open.

There in slanting golden light of the new-risen sun

stood a breathless, wild-eyed man and a steaming horse. Smothered in dust and grime, his clothes in disarray, the left sleeve of his doublet hanging in rags, this young man opened his lips to speak, yet for a long moment remained speechless.

In that moment Mr. Blood recognized him for the young shipmaster, Jeremiah Pitt, the nephew of the maiden ladies opposite, one who had been drawn by the general enthusiasm into the vortex of that rebellion. The street was rousing, awakened by the sailor's noisy advent; doors were opening, and lattices were being unlatched for the protrusion of anxious, inquisitive heads.

"Take your time, now," said Mr. Blood. "I never knew speed made by overhaste."

But the wild-eyed lad paid no heed to the admonition. He plunged, headlong, into speech, gasping, breathless.

"It is Lord Gildoy," he panted. "He is sore wounded . . . at Oglethorpe's Farm by the river. I bore him thither . . . and . . . and he sent me for you. Come away! Come away!"

He would have clutched the doctor, and haled him forth by force in bedgown and slippers as he was. But the doctor eluded that too eager hand.

"To be sure, I'll come," said he. He was distressed. Gildoy had been a very friendly, generous patron to him since his settling in these parts. And Mr. Blood was eager enough to do what he now could to discharge the debt, grieved that the occasion should have arisen, and in such a manner — for he knew quite well that the rash young nobleman had been an active agent of the Duke's. "To be sure, I'll come. But first give me leave to get some clothes and other things that I may need."

"There's no time to lose."

"Be easy now. I'll lose none. I tell ye again, ye'll go quickest by going leisurely. Come in ... take a chair ..." He threw open the door of a parlour.

Young Pitt waved aside the invitation.

"I'll wait here. Make haste, in God's name."

Mr. Blood went off to dress and to fetch a case of instruments.

Questions concerning the precise nature of Lord Gildoy's hurt could wait until they were on their way. Whilst he pulled on his boots, he gave Mrs. Barlow instructions for the day, which included the matter of a dinner he was not destined to eat.

When at last he went forth again, Mrs. Barlow clucking after him like a disgruntled fowl, he found young Pitt smothered in a crowd of scared, half-dressed townsfolk — mostly women — who had come hastening for news of how the battle had sped. The news he gave them was to be read in the lamentations with which they disturbed the morning air.

At sight of the doctor, dressed and booted, the case of instruments tucked under his arm, the messenger disengaged himself from those who pressed about, shook off his weariness and the two tearful aunts that clung most closely, and seizing the bridle of his horse, he climbed to the saddle.

"Come along, sir," he cried. "Mount behind me."

Mr. Blood, without wasting words, did as he was bidden. Pitt touched the horse with his spur. The little crowd gave way, and thus, upon the crupper of that doubly-laden horse, clinging to the belt of his companion, Peter Blood set out upon his Odyssey. For this Pitt, in whom he beheld no more than the messenger of a wounded rebel gentleman, was indeed the very messenger of Fate.

CHAPTER II

OGLETHORPE'S FARM stood a mile or so to the south of Bridgewater on the right bank of the river. It was a straggling Tudor building showing grey above the ivy that clothed its lower parts. Approaching it now, through the fragrant orchards amid which it seemed to drowse in Arcadian peace beside the waters of the Parrett, sparkling in the morning sunlight, Mr. Blood might have had a difficulty in believing it part of a world tormented by strife and bloodshed.

On the bridge, as they had been riding out of Bridgewater, they had met a vanguard of fugitives from the field of battle, weary, broken men, many of them wounded, all of them terror-stricken, staggering in speedless haste with the last remnants of their strength into the shelter which it was their vain illusion the town would afford them. Eyes glazed with lassitude and fear looked up piteously out of haggard faces at Mr. Blood and his companion as they rode forth; hoarse voices cried a warning that merciless pursuit was not far behind. Undeterred, however, young Pitt rode amain along the dusty road by which these poor fugitives from that swift rout on Sedgemoor came flocking in ever-increasing numbers. Presently he swung aside, and quitting the road took to a pathway that crossed the dewy meadowlands. Even here they met odd groups of these human derelicts, who were scattering in all directions, looking fearfully behind them as they came through the long grass, expecting at every moment to see the red coats of the dragoons.

But as Pitt's direction was a southward one, bringing them ever nearer to Feversham's headquarters, they were presently clear of that human flotsam and jetsam of the battle, and riding through the peaceful orchards heavy with the ripening fruit that was soon to make its annual yield of cider.

At last they alighted on the kidney stones of the courtyard, and Baynes, the master of the homestead, grave of countenance and flustered of manner, gave them welcome.

In the spacious, stone-flagged hall, the doctor found Lord Gildoy — a very tall and dark young gentleman, prominent of chin and nose — stretched on a cane day-bed under one of the tall mullioned windows, in the care of Mrs. Baynes and her comely daughter. His cheeks were leaden-hued, his eyes closed, and from his blue lips came with each laboured breath a faint, moaning noise.

Mr. Blood stood for a moment silently considering his patient. He deplored that a youth with such bright hopes in life as Lord Gildoy's should have risked all, perhaps existence itself, to forward the ambition of a worthless adventurer. Because he had liked and honoured this brave lad he paid his case the tribute of a sigh. Then he knelt to his task, ripped away doublet and underwear to lay bare his lordship's mangled side, and called for water and linen and what else he needed for his work.

He was still intent upon it a half-hour later when

the dragoons invaded the homestead. The clatter of
hooves and hoarse shouts that heralded their approach disturbed him not at all. For one thing, he
was not easily disturbed; for another, his task absorbed him. But his lordship, who had now recovered consciousness, showed considerable alarm, and
the battle-stained Jeremy Pitt sped to cover in a
clothes-press. Baynes was uneasy, and his wife and
daughter trembled. Mr. Blood reassured them.

"Why, what's the fear?" he said. "It's a Christian
country, this, and Christian men do not make war
upon the wounded, nor upon those who harbour
them." He still had, you see, illusions about Chris-
tians. He held a glass of cordial, prepared under his
directions, to his lordship's lips. "Give your mind
peace, my lord. The worst is done."

And then they came rattling and clanking into the
stone-flagged hall — a round dozen jack-booted,
lobster-coated troopers of the Tangiers Regiment, led
by a sturdy, black-browed fellow with a deal of gold
lace about the breast of his coat.

Baynes stood his ground, his attitude half-defiant,
whilst his wife and daughter shrank away in renewed
fear. Mr. Blood, at the head of the day-bed, looked
over his shoulder to take stock of the invaders.

The officer barked an order, which brought his men
to an attentive halt, then swaggered forward, his
gloved hand bearing down the pummel of his sword,
his spurs jingling musically as he moved. He announced his authority to the yeoman.

"I am Captain Hobart, of Colonel Kirke's dragoons. What rebels do you harbour?"

The yeoman took alarm at that ferocious truculence. It expressed itself in his trembling voice. "I ... I am no harbourer of rebels, sir. This wounded gentleman ..."

"I can see for myself." The Captain stamped forward to the day-bed, and scowled down upon the grey-faced sufferer.

"No need to ask how he came in this state and by his wounds. A damned rebel, and that's enough for me." He flung a command at his dragoons. "Out with him, my lads."

Mr. Blood got between the day-bed and the troopers. "In the name of humanity, sir!" said he, on a note of anger. "This is England, not Tangiers. The gentleman is in sore case. He may not be moved without peril to his life."

Captain Hobart was amused.

"Oh, I am to be tender of the lives of these rebels! Odds blood! Do you think it's to benefit his health we're taking him? There's gallows being planted along the road from Weston to Bridgewater, and he'll serve for one of them as well as another. Colonel Kirke'll learn these nonconforming oafs something they'll not forget in generations."

"You're hanging men without trial? Faith, then, it's mistaken I am. We're in Tangiers, after all, it seems, where your regiment belongs."

The Captain considered him with a kindling eye. He looked him over from the soles of his riding-boots to the crown of his periwig. He noted the spare, active frame, the arrogant poise of the head, the air of authority that invested Mr. Blood, and soldier recognized soldier. The Captain's eyes narrowed. Recognition went further.

"Who the hell may you be?" he exploded.

"My name is Blood, sir — Peter Blood, at your service."

"Aye — aye! Codso! That's the name. You were in French service once, were you not?"

If Mr. Blood was surprised, he did not betray it.

"I was."

"Then I remember you — five years ago, or more, you were in Tangiers."

"That is so. I knew your colonel."

"Faith, you may be renewing the acquaintance." The Captain laughed unpleasantly. "What brings you here, sir?"

"This wounded gentleman. I was fetched to attend him. I am a medicus."

"A doctor — you?" Scorn of that lie — as he conceived it — rang in the heavy, hectoring voice.

"Medicinæ baccalaureus," said Mr. Blood.

"Don't fling your French at me, man," snapped Hobart. "Speak English!"

Mr. Blood's smile annoyed him.

"I am a physician practising my calling in the town of Bridgewater."

The Captain sneered. "Which you reached by way of Lyme Regis in the following of your bastard Duke."

It was Mr. Blood's turn to sneer. "If your wit were as big as your voice, my dear, it's the great man you'd be by this."

For a moment the dragoon was speechless. The colour deepened in his face.

"You may find me great enough to hang you."

"Faith, yes. Ye've the look and the manners of a hangman. But if you practise your trade on my pa-

tient here, you may be putting a rope round your own
neck. He's not the kind you may string up and no
questions asked. He has the right to trial, and the
right to trial by his peers."

"By his peers?"

The Captain was taken aback by these three words,
which Mr. Blood had stressed.

"Sure, now, any but a fool or a savage would have
asked his name before ordering him to the gallows.
The gentleman is my Lord Gildoy."

And then his lordship spoke for himself, in a weak
voice.

"I make no concealment of my association with
the Duke of Monmouth. I'll take the consequences.
But, if you please, I'll take them after trial — by my
peers, as the doctor has said."

The feeble voice ceased, and was followed by a
moment's silence. As is common in many blustering
men, there was a deal of timidity deep down in Hobart. The announcement of his lordship's rank had
touched those depths. A servile upstart, he stood in
awe of titles. And he stood in awe of his colonel.
Percy Kirke was not lenient with blunderers.

By a gesture he checked his men. He must consider. Mr. Blood, observing his pause, added further
matter for his consideration.

"Ye'll be remembering, Captain, that Lord Gildoy
will have friends and relatives on the Tory side, who'll
have something to say to Colonel Kirke if his lordship
should be handled like a common felon. You'll go
warily, Captain, or, as I've said, it's a halter for your
neck ye'll be weaving this morning."

Captain Hobart swept the warning aside with a

bluster of contempt, but he acted upon it none the less. "Take up the day-bed," said he, "and convey him on that to Bridgewater. Lodge him in the gaol until I take order about him."

"He may not survive the journey," Blood remonstrated. "He's in no case to be moved."

"So much the worse for him. My affair is to round up rebels." He confirmed his order by a gesture. Two of his men took up the day-bed, and swung to depart with it.

Gildoy made a feeble effort to put forth a hand towards Mr. Blood. "Sir," he said, "you leave me in your debt. If I live I shall study how to discharge it."

Mr. Blood bowed for answer; then to the men: "Bear him steadily," he commanded. "His life depends on it."

As his lordship was carried out, the Captain became brisk. He turned upon the yeoman.

"What other cursed rebels do you harbour?"

"None other, sir. His lordship . . ."

"We've dealt with his lordship for the present. We'll deal with you in a moment when we've searched your house. And, by God, if you've lied to me . . ." He broke off, snarling, to give an order. Four of his dragoons went out. In a moment they were heard moving noisily in the adjacent room. Meanwhile, the Captain was questing about the hall, sounding the wainscoting with the butt of a pistol.

Mr. Blood saw no profit to himself in lingering.

"By your leave, it's a very good day I'll be wishing you," said he.

"By my leave, you'll remain awhile," the Captain ordered him.

Mr. Blood shrugged, and sat down. "You're tiresome," he said. "I wonder your colonel hasn't discovered it yet."

But the Captain did not heed him. He was stooping to pick up a soiled and dusty hat in which there was pinned a little bunch of oak leaves. It had been lying near the clothes-press in which the unfortunate Pitt had taken refuge. The Captain smiled malevolently. His eyes raked the room, resting first sardonically on the yeoman, then on the two women in the background, and finally on Mr. Blood, who sat with one leg thrown over the other in an attitude of indifference that was far from reflecting his mind.

Then the Captain stepped to the press, and pulled open one of the wings of its massive oaken door. He took the huddled inmate by the collar of his doublet, and lugged him out into the open.

"And who the devil's this?" quoth he. "Another nobleman?"

Mr. Blood had a vision of those gallows of which Captain Hobart had spoken, and of this unfortunate young shipmaster going to adorn one of them, strung up without trial, in the place of the other victim of whom the Captain had been cheated. On the spot he invented not only a title but a whole family for the young rebel.

"Faith, ye've said it, Captain. This is Viscount Pitt, first cousin to Sir Thomas Vernon, who's married to that slut Moll Kirke, sister to your own colonel, and sometime lady in waiting upon King James's queen."

Both the Captain and his prisoner gasped. But whereas thereafter young Pitt discreetly held his peace, the Captain rapped out a nasty oath. He considered his prisoner again.

"He's lying, is he not?" he demanded, seizing the lad by the shoulder, and glaring into his face. "He's rallying me, by God!"

"If ye believe that," said Blood, "hang him, and see what happens to you."

The dragoon glared at the doctor and then at his prisoner. "Pah!" He thrust the lad into the hands of his men. "Fetch him along to Bridgewater. And make fast that fellow also," he pointed to Baynes. "We'll show him what it means to harbour and comfort rebels."

There was a moment of confusion. Baynes struggled in the grip of the troopers, protesting vehemently. The terrified women screamed until silenced by a greater terror. The Captain strode across to them. He took the girl by the shoulders. She was a pretty, golden-headed creature, with soft blue eyes that looked up entreatingly, piteously into the face of the dragoon. He leered upon her, his eyes aglow, took her chin in his hand, and set her shuddering by his brutal kiss.

"It's an earnest," he said, smiling grimly. "Let that quiet you, little rebel, till I've done with these rogues."

And he swung away again, leaving her faint and trembling in the arms of her anguished mother. His men stood, grinning, awaiting orders, the two prisoners now fast pinioned.

"Take them away. Let Cornet Drake have charge of them." His smouldering eye again sought the cowering girl. "I'll stay awhile — to search out this place.

There may be other rebels hidden here." As an afterthought, he added: "And take this fellow with you."
He pointed to Mr. Blood. "Bestir!"

Mr. Blood started out of his musings. He had been
considering that in his case of instruments there was a
lancet with which he might perform on Captain Hobart a beneficial operation. Beneficial, that is, to humanity. In any case, the dragoon was obviously ple-
thoric and would be the better for a blood-letting.
The difficulty lay in making the opportunity. He was
beginning to wonder if he could lure the Captain aside
with some tale of hidden treasure, when this untimely
interruption set a term to that interesting specula-
tion.

He sought to temporize.

"Faith it will suit me very well," said he. "For
Bridgewater is my destination, and but that ye detained me I'd have been on my way thither now."

"Your destination there will be the gaol."

"Ah, bah! Ye're surely joking!"

"There's a gallows for you if you prefer it. It's
merely a question of now or later."

Rude hands seized Mr. Blood, and that precious
lancet was in the case on the table out of reach. He
twisted out of the grip of the dragoons, for he was
strong and agile, but they closed with him again immediately, and bore him down. Pinning him to the
ground, they tied his wrists behind his back, then
roughly pulled him to his feet again.

"Take him away," said Hobart shortly, and turned
to issue his orders to the other waiting troopers. "Go
search the house, from attic to cellar; then report to
me here."

The soldiers trailed out by the door leading to the interior. Mr. Blood was thrust by his guards into the courtyard, where Pitt and Baynes already waited. From the threshold of the hall, he looked back at Captain Hobart, and his sapphire eyes were blazing. On his lips trembled a threat of what he would do to Hobart if he should happen to survive this business. Betimes he remembered that to utter it were probably to extinguish his chance of living to execute it. For to-day the King's men were masters in the West, and the West was regarded as enemy country, to be subjected to the worst horror of war by the victorious side. Here a captain of horse was for the moment lord of life and death.

Under the apple-trees in the orchard Mr. Blood and his companions in misfortune were made fast each to a trooper's stirrup leather. Then at the sharp order of the cornet, the little troop started for Bridgewater. As they set out there was the fullest confirmation of Mr. Blood's hideous assumption that to the dragoons this was a conquered enemy country. There were sounds of rending timbers, of furniture smashed and overthrown, the shouts and laughter of brutal men, to announce that this hunt for rebels was no more than a pretext for pillage and destruction. Finally above all other sounds came the piercing screams of a woman in acutest agony.

Baynes checked in his stride, and swung round writhing, his face ashen. As a consequence he was jerked from his feet by the rope that attached him to the stirrup leather, and he was dragged helplessly a yard or two before the trooper reined in, cursing him foully, and striking him with the flat of his sword.

It came to Mr. Blood, as he trudged forward under the laden apple-trees on that fragrant, delicious July morning, that man — as he had long suspected — was the vilest work of God, and that only a fool would set himself up as a healer of a species that was best exterminated.

CHAPTER III

THE LORD CHIEF JUSTICE

IT was not until two months later — on the 19th of September, if you must have the actual date — that Peter Blood was brought to trial, upon a charge of high treason. We know that he was not guilty of this; but we need not doubt that he was quite capable of it by the time he was indicted. Those two months of inhuman, unspeakable imprisonment had moved his mind to a cold and deadly hatred of King James and his representatives. It says something for his fortitude that in all the circumstances he should still have had a mind at all. Yet, terrible as was the position of this entirely innocent man, he had cause for thankfulness on two counts. The first of these was that he should have been brought to trial at all; the second, that his trial took place on the date named, and not a day earlier. In the very delay which exacerbated him lay — although he did not realize it — his only chance of avoiding the gallows.

Easily, but for the favour of Fortune, he might have been one of those haled, on the morrow of the battle, more or less haphazard from the overflowing gaol at Bridgewater to be summarily hanged in the market-place by the bloodthirsty Colonel Kirke. There was about the Colonel of the Tangiers Regiment a deadly despatch which might have disposed in like fashion of all those prisoners, numerous as they were, but for the vigorous intervention of Bishop

Mews, which put an end to the drumhead courts-martial.

Even so, in that first week after Sedgemoor, Kirke and Feversham contrived between them to put to death over a hundred men after a trial so summary as to be no trial at all. They required human freights for the gibbets with which they were planting the countryside, and they little cared how they procured them or what innocent lives they took. What, after all, was the life of a clod? The executioners were kept busy with rope and chopper and cauldrons of pitch. I spare you the details of that nauseating picture. It is, after all, with the fate of Peter Blood that we are concerned rather than with that of the Monmouth rebels.

He survived to be included in one of those melancholy droves of prisoners who, chained in pairs, were marched from Bridgewater to Taunton. Those who were too sorely wounded to march were conveyed in carts, into which they were brutally crowded, their wounds undressed and festering. Many were fortunate enough to die upon the way. When Blood insisted upon his right to exercise his art so as to relieve some of this suffering, he was accounted importunate and threatened with a flogging. If he had one regret now it was that he had not been out with Monmouth. That, of course, was illogical; but you can hardly expect logic from a man in his position.

His chain companion on that dreadful march was the same Jeremy Pitt who had been the agent of his present misfortunes. The young shipmaster had remained his close companion after their common arrest. Hence, fortuitously, had they been chained together in the crowded prison, where they were almost suffocated by the heat and the stench during those days of July, August, and September.

Scraps of news filtered into the gaol from the outside world. Some may have been deliberately allowed to penetrate. Of these was the tale of Monmouth's execution. It created profoundest dismay amongst those men who were suffering for the Duke and for the religious cause he had professed to champion. Many refused utterly to believe it. A wild story began to circulate that a man resembling Monmouth had offered himself up in the Duke's stead, and that Monmouth survived to come again in glory to deliver Zion and make war upon Babylon.

Mr. Blood heard that tale with the same indifference with which he had received the news of Monmouth's death. But one shameful thing he heard in connection with this which left him not quite so unmoved, and served to nourish the contempt he was forming for King James. His Majesty had consented to see Monmouth. To have done so unless he intended to pardon him was a thing execrable and damnable beyond belief; for the only other object in granting that interview could be the evilly mean satisfaction of spurning the abject penitence of his unfortunate nephew.

Later they heard that Lord Grey, who after the Duke — indeed, perhaps, before him — was the main leader of the rebellion, had purchased his own pardon for forty thousand pounds. Peter Blood found this of a piece with the rest. His contempt for King James blazed out at last.

"Why, here's a filthy mean creature to sit on a

throne. If I had known as much of him before as I know to-day, I don't doubt I should have given cause to be where I am now." And then on a sudden thought: "And where will Lord Gildoy be, do you suppose?" he asked.

Young Pitt, whom he addressed, turned towards him a face from which the ruddy tan of the sea had faded almost completely during those months of captivity. His grey eyes were round and questioning. Blood answered him.

"Sure, now, we've never seen his lordship since that day at Oglethorpe's. And where are the other gentry that were taken? — the real leaders of this plaguey rebellion. Grey's case explains their absence, I think. They are wealthy men that can ransom themselves. Here awaiting the gallows are none but the unfortunates who followed; those who had the honour to lead them go free. It's a curious and instructive reversal of the usual way of these things. Faith, it's an uncertain world entirely!"

He laughed, and settled down into that spirit of scorn, wrapped in which he stepped later into the great hall of Taunton Castle to take his trial. With him went Pitt and the yeoman Baynes. The three of them were to be tried together, and their case was to open the proceedings of that ghastly day.

The hall, even to the galleries — thronged with spectators, most of whom were ladies — was hung in scarlet; a pleasant conceit, this, of the Lord Chief Justice's, who naturally enough preferred the colour that should reflect his own bloody mind.

At the upper end, on a raised dais, sat the Lords Commissioners, the five judges in their scarlet robes and heavy dark periwigs, Baron Jeffreys of Wem enthroned in the middle place.

The prisoners filed in under guard. The crier called for silence under pain of imprisonment, and as the hum of voices gradually became hushed, Mr. Blood considered with interest the twelve good men and true that composed the jury. Neither good nor true did they look. They were scared, uneasy, and hang-dog as any set of thieves caught with their hands in the pockets of their neighbours. They were twelve shaken men, each of whom stood between the sword of the Lord Chief Justice's recent bloodthirsty charge and the wall of his own conscience.

From them Mr. Blood's calm, deliberate glance passed on to consider the Lords Commissioners, and particularly the presiding judge, that Lord Jeffreys, whose terrible fame had come ahead of him from Dorchester.

He beheld a tall, slight man on the young side of forty, with an oval face that was delicately beautiful. There were dark stains of suffering or sleeplessness under the low-lidded eyes, heightening their brilliance and their gentle melancholy. The face was very pale, save for the vivid colour of the full lips and the hectic flush on the rather high but inconspicuous cheek-bones. It was something in those lips that marred the perfection of that countenance; a fault, elusive but undeniable, lurked there to belie the fine sensitiveness of those nostrils, the tenderness of those dark, liquid eyes and the noble calm of that pale brow.

The physician in Mr. Blood regarded the man with peculiar interest knowing as he did the agonizing malady from which his lordship suffered, and the amazingly irregular, debauched life that he led in spite of it — perhaps because of it.

"Peter Blood, hold up your hand!"

Abruptly he was recalled to his position by the harsh voice of the clerk of arraigns. His obedience was mechanical, and the clerk droned out the wordy indictment which pronounced Peter Blood a false traitor against the Most Illustrious and Most Excellent Prince, James the Second, by the grace of God, of England, Scotland, France, and Ireland King, his supreme and natural lord. It informed him that, having no fear of God in his heart, but being moved and seduced by the instigation of the Devil, he had failed in the love and true and due natural obedience towards his said lord the King, and had moved to disturb the peace and tranquillity of the kingdom and to stir up war and rebellion to depose his said lord the King from the title, honour, and the regal name of the imperial crown — and much more of the same kind, at the end of all of which he was invited to say whether he was guilty or not guilty.

He answered more than was asked.

"It's entirely innocent I am."

A small, sharp-faced man at a table before and to the right of him bounced up. It was Mr. Pollexfen, the Judge-Advocate.

"Are you guilty or not guilty?" snapped this peppery gentleman. "You must take the words."

"Words, is it?" said Peter Blood. "Oh — not guilty." And he went on, addressing himself to the bench. "On this same subject of words, may it please your lordships, I am guilty of nothing to justify any of those words I have heard used to describe me, unless it be of a want of patience at having been closely confined for two months and longer in a fœtid gaol with great peril to my health and even life."

Being started, he would have added a deal more; but at this point the Lord Chief Justice interposed in a gentle, rather plaintive voice.

"Look you, sir: because we must observe the common and usual methods of trial, I must interrupt you now. You are no doubt ignorant of the forms of law?"

"Not only ignorant, my lord, but hitherto most happy in that ignorance. I could gladly have forgone this acquaintance with them."

A pale smile momentarily lightened the wistful countenance.

"I believe you. You shall be fully heard when you come to your defence. But anything you say now is altogether irregular and improper."

Enheartened by that apparent sympathy and consideration, Mr. Blood answered thereafter, as was required of him, that he would be tried by God and his country. Whereupon, having prayed to God to send him a good deliverance, the clerk called upon Andrew Baynes to hold up his hand and plead.

From Baynes, who pleaded not guilty, the clerk passed on to Pitt, who boldly owned his guilt. The Lord Chief Justice stirred at that.

"Come; that's better," quoth he, and his four scarlet brethren nodded. "If all were as obstinate as his two fellow-rebels, there would never be an end."

After that ominous interpolation, delivered with an inhuman iciness that sent a shiver through the court, Mr. Pollexfen got to his feet. With great prolixity he stated the general case against the three men, and the particular case against Peter Blood, whose indictment was to be taken first.

The only witness called for the King was Captain Hobart. He testified briskly to the manner in which he had found and taken the three prisoners, together with Lord Gildoy. Upon the orders of his colonel he would have hanged Pitt out of hand, but was restrained by the lies of the prisoner Blood, who led him to believe that Pitt was a peer of the realm and a person of consideration.

As the Captain's evidence concluded, Lord Jeffreys looked across at Peter Blood.

"Will the prisoner Blood ask the witness any questions?"

"None, my lord. He has correctly related what occurred."

"I am glad to have your admission of that without any of the prevarications that are usual in your kind. And I will say this, that here prevarication would avail you little. For we always have the truth in the end. Be sure of that."

Baynes and Pitt similarly admitted the accuracy of the Captain's evidence, whereupon the scarlet figure of the Lord Chief Justice heaved a sigh of relief.

"This being so, let us get on, in God's name; for we have much to do." There was now no trace of gentleness in his voice. It was brisk and rasping, and the lips through which it passed were curved in scorn. "I take it, Mr. Pollexfen, that the wicked treason of these three rogues being established — indeed, admitted by them — there is no more to be said."

Peter Blood's voice rang out crisply, on a note that almost seemed to contain laughter.

"May it please your lordship, but there's a deal more to be said."

His lordship looked at him, first in blank amazement at his audacity, then gradually with an expression of dull anger. The scarlet lips fell into unpleasant, cruel lines that transfigured the whole countenance.

"How now, rogue? Would you waste our time with idle subterfuge?"

"I would have your lordship and the gentlemen of the jury hear me on my defence, as your lordship promised that I should be heard."

"Why, so you shall, villain; so you shall." His lordship's voice was harsh as a file. He writhed as he spoke, and for an instant his features were distorted. A delicate dead-white hand, on which the veins showed blue, brought forth a handkerchief with which he dabbed his lips and then his brow. Observing him with his physician's eye, Peter Blood judged him a prey to the pain of the disease that was destroying him. "So you shall. But after the admission made, what defence remains?"

"You shall judge, my lord."

"That is the purpose for which I sit here."

"And so shall you, gentlemen." Blood looked from judge to jury. The latter shifted uncomfortably under the confident flash of his blue eyes. Lord Jeffreys's bullying charge had whipped the spirit out of them. Had they, themselves, been prisoners accused of treason, he could not have arraigned them more ferociously.

Peter Blood stood boldly forward, erect, self-possessed, and saturnine. He was freshly shaven, and his periwig, if out of curl, was at least carefully combed and dressed.

"Captain Hobart has testified to what he knows — that he found me at Oglethorpe's Farm on the Monday morning after the battle at Weston. But he has not told you what I did there."

Again the Judge broke in. "Why, what should you have been doing there in the company of rebels, two of whom — Lord Gildoy and your fellow there — have already admitted their guilt?"

"That is what I beg leave to tell your lordship."

"I pray you do, and in God's name be brief, man. For if I am to be troubled with the say of all you traitor dogs, I may sit here until the Spring Assizes."

"I was there, my lord, in my quality as a physician, to dress Lord Gildoy's wounds."

"What's this? Do you tell us that you are a physician?"

"A graduate of Trinity College, Dublin."

"Good God!" cried Lord Jeffreys, his voice suddenly swelling, his eyes upon the jury. "What an impudent rogue is this! You heard the witness say that he had known him in Tangiers some years ago, and that he was then an officer in the French service. You heard the prisoner admit that the witness had spoken the truth?"

"Why, so he had. Yet what I am telling you is also true, so it is. For some years I was a soldier; but before that I was a physician, and I have been one again since January last, established in Bridgewater, as I can bring a hundred witnesses to prove."

"There's not the need to waste our time with that. I will convict you out of your own rascally mouth. I will ask you only this: How came you, who represent yourself as a physician peacefully following your calling in the town of Bridgewater, to be with the army of the Duke of Monmouth?"

"I was never with that army. No witness has sworn to that, and I dare swear that no witness will. I never was attracted to the late rebellion. I regarded the adventure as a wicked madness. I take leave to ask your lordship" (his brogue became more marked than ever) "what should I, who was born and bred a papist, be doing in the army of the Protestant Champion?"

"A papist thou?" The Judge gloomed on him a moment. "Art more like a snivelling, canting Jack Presbyter. I tell you, man, I can smell a Presbyterian forty miles."

"Then I'll take leave to marvel that with so keen a nose your lordship can't smell a papist at four paces."

There was a ripple of laughter in the galleries, instantly quelled by the fierce glare of the Judge and the voice of the crier.

Lord Jeffreys leaned forward farther upon his desk. He raised that delicate white hand, still clutching its handkerchief, and sprouting from a froth of lace.

"We'll leave your religion out of account for the moment, friend," said he. "But mark what I say to you." With a minatory forefinger he beat the time of his words. "Know, friend, that there is no religion a man can pretend to can give a countenance to lying. Thou hast a precious immortal soul, and there is nothing in the world equal to it in value. Consider that the great God of Heaven and Earth, before Whose tribunal thou and we and all persons are to stand at the last day, will take vengeance on thee for every falsehood, and justly strike thee into eternal flames, make thee drop into the bottomless pit of fire and brimstone, if thou offer to deviate the least from the truth and nothing but the truth. For I tell thee God is not mocked. On that I charge you to answer truthfully. How came you to be taken with these rebels?"

Peter Blood gaped at him a moment in consternation. The man was incredible, unreal, fantastic, a nightmare judge. Then he collected himself to answer.

"I was summoned that morning to succour Lord Gildoy, and I conceived it to be the duty imposed upon me by my calling to answer that summons."

"Did you so?" The Judge, terrible now of aspect — his face white, his twisted lips red as the blood for which they thirsted — glared upon him in evil mockery. Then he controlled himself as if by an effort. He sighed. He resumed his earlier gentle plaintiveness.

"Lord! How you waste our time. But I'll have patience with you. Who summoned you?"

"Master Pitt there, as he will testify."

"Oh! Master Pitt will testify — he that is himself a traitor self-confessed. Is that your witness?"

"There is also Master Baynes here, who can answer to it."

"Good Master Baynes will have to answer for himself; and I doubt not he'll be greatly exercised to save his own neck from a halter. Come, come, sir; are these your only witnesses?"

"I could bring others from Bridgewater, who saw me set out that morning upon the crupper of Master Pitt's horse."

His lordship smiled. "It will not be necessary. For, mark me, I do not intend to waste more time on you. Answer me only this: When Master Pitt, as you pretend, came to summon you, did you know that he had been, as you have heard him confess, of Monmouth's following?"

"I did, my lord."

"You did! Ha!" His lordship looked at the cringing jury and uttered a short, stabbing laugh. "Yet in spite of that you went with him?"

"To succour a wounded man, as was my sacred duty."

"Thy sacred duty, sayest thou?" Fury blazed out of him again. "Good God! What a generation of vipers do we live in! Thy sacred duty, rogue, is to thy King and to God. But let it pass. Did he tell you whom it was that you were desired to succour?"

"Lord Gildoy — yes."

"And you knew that Lord Gildoy had been wounded in the battle, and on what side he fought?"

"I knew."

"And yet, being, as you would have us believe, a true and loyal subject of our Lord the King, you went to succour him?"

Peter Blood lost patience for a moment. "My business, my lord, was with his wounds, not with his politics."

A murmur from the galleries and even from the jury approved him. It served only to drive his terrible judge into a deeper fury.

"Jesus God! Was there ever such an impudent villain in the world as thou?" He swung, white-faced, to the jury. "I hope, gentlemen of the jury, you take notice of the horrible carriage of this traitor rogue, and withal you cannot but observe the spirit of this sort of people, what a villainous and devilish one it is. Out of his own mouth he has said enough to hang him a dozen times. Yet is there more. Answer me this, sir: When you cozened Captain Hobart with your lies concerning the station of this other traitor Pitt, what was your business then?"

"To save him from being hanged without trial, as was threatened."

"What concern was it of yours whether or how the wretch was hanged?"

"Justice is the concern of every loyal subject, for an injustice committed by one who holds the King's commission is in some sense a dishonour to the King's majesty."

It was a shrewd, sharp thrust aimed at the jury, and it reveals, I think, the alertness of the man's mind, his self-possession ever steadiest in moments of dire peril. With any other jury it must have made the impression that he hoped to make. It may even have made its impression upon these poor pusillanimous sheep. But the dread judge was there to efface it.

He gasped aloud, then flung himself violently forward.

"Lord of Heaven!" he stormed. "Was there ever such a canting, impudent rascal? But I have done with you. I see thee, villain, I see thee already with a halter round thy neck."

Having spoken so, gloatingly, evilly, he sank back again, and composed himself. It was as if a curtain fell. All emotion passed again from his pale face. Back to invest it again came that gentle melancholy. Speaking after a moment's pause, his voice was soft, almost tender, yet every word of it carried sharply through that hushed court.

"If I know my own heart it is not in my nature to desire the hurt of anybody, much less to delight in his eternal perdition. It is out of compassion for you that I have used all these words — because I would have you have some regard for your immortal soul, and not ensure its damnation by obdurately persisting in falsehood and prevarication. But I see that all the pains in the world, and all compassion and charity are lost upon you, and therefore I will say no more to you." He turned again to the jury that countenance of wistful beauty. "Gentlemen, I must tell you for law, of which we are the judges, and not you, that if any person be in actual rebellion against the King, and another person — who really and actually was not in rebellion — does knowingly receive, harbour, comfort, or succour him, such a person is as much a traitor as he who indeed bore arms. We are bound by our oaths and consciences to declare to you what is law; and you are bound by your oaths and your consciences to deliver and to declare to us by your verdict the truth of the facts."

. Upon that he proceeded to his summing-up, showing how Baynes and Blood were both guilty of treason, the first for having harboured a traitor, the second for having succoured that traitor by dressing his wounds. He interlarded his address by sycophantic allusions to his natural lord and lawful sovereign, the King, whom God had set over them, and with vituperations of Nonconformity and of Monmouth, of whom — in his own words — he dared boldly affirm that the meanest subject within the kingdom that was of legitimate birth had a better title to the crown.

"Jesus God! That ever we should have such a generation of vipers among us," he burst out in rhetorical frenzy. And then he sank back as if exhausted by the violence he had used. A moment he was still, dabbing his lips again; then he moved uneasily; once more his features were twisted by pain, and in a few snarling, almost incoherent words he dismissed the jury to consider the verdict.

Peter Blood had listened to the intemperate, the blasphemous, and almost obscene invective of that tirade with a detachment that afterwards, in retrospect, surprised him. He was so amazed by the man, by the reactions taking place in him between mind and body, and by his methods of bullying and coercing the jury into bloodshed, that he almost forgot that his own life was at stake.

The absence of that dazed jury was a brief one. The verdict found the three prisoners guilty. Peter Blood looked round the scarlet-hung court. For an instant that foam of white faces seemed to heave before him. Then he was himself again, and a voice was asking him what he had to say for himself, why sentence of death should not be passed upon him, being convicted of high treason.

He laughed, and his laugh jarred uncannily upon the deathly stillness of the court. It was all so grotesque, such a mockery of justice administered by that wistful-eyed jack-pudding in scarlet, who was himself a mockery — the venal instrument of a brutally spiteful and vindictive king. His laughter shocked the austerity of that same jack-pudding.

"Do you laugh, sirrah, with the rope about your neck, upon the very threshold of that eternity you are so suddenly to enter into?"

And then Blood took his revenge.

"Faith, it's in better case I am for mirth than your lordship. For I have this to say before you deliver judgment. Your lordship sees me — an innocent man whose only offence is that I practised charity — with a halter round my neck. Your lordship, being the justiciar, speaks with knowledge of what is to come to me. I, being a physician, may speak with knowledge of what is to come to your lordship. And I tell you that I would not now change places with you — that I would not exchange this halter that you fling about my neck for the stone that you carry in your body. The death to which you may doom me is a light pleasantry by contrast with the death to which your lordship has been doomed by that Great Judge with whose name your lordship makes so free."

The Lord Chief Justice sat stiffly upright, his face ashen, his lips twitching, and whilst you might have counted ten there was no sound in that paralyzed court after Peter Blood had finished speaking. All those who knew Lord Jeffreys regarded this as the lull before the storm, and braced themselves for the explosion. But none came. Slowly, faintly, the colour crept back into that ashen face. The scarlet figure lost its rigidity, and bent forward. His lordship began to speak. In a muted voice and briefly —

much more briefly than his wont on such occasions and in a manner entirely mechanical, the manner of a man whose thoughts are elsewhere while his lips are speaking — he delivered sentence of death in the prescribed form, and without the least allusion to what Peter Blood had said. Having delivered it, he sank back exhausted, his eyes half-closed, his brow agleam with sweat.

The prisoners filed out.

Mr. Pollexfen — a Whig at heart despite the position of Judge-Advocate which he occupied — was overheard by one of the jurors to mutter in the ear of a brother counsel:

"On my soul, that swarthy rascal has given his lordship a scare. It's a pity he must hang. For a man who can frighten Jeffreys should go far."

CHAPTER IV

HUMAN MERCHANDISE

MR. POLLEXFEN was at one and the same time right and wrong — a condition much more common than is generally supposed.

He was right in his indifferently expressed thought that a man whose mien and words could daunt such a lord of terror as Jeffreys, should by the dominance of his nature be able to fashion himself a considerable destiny. He was wrong — though justifiably so — in his assumption that Peter Blood must hang.

I have said that the tribulations with which he was visited as a result of his errand of mercy to Oglethorpe's Farm contained — although as yet he did not perceive it, perhaps — two sources of thankfulness: one that he was tried at all; the other that his trial took place on the 19th of September. Until the 18th, the sentences passed by the court of the Lords Commissioners had been carried out literally and expeditiously.

But on the morning of the 19th there arrived at Taunton a courier from Lord Sunderland, the Secretary of State, with a letter for Lord Jeffreys wherein he was informed that His Majesty had been graciously pleased to command that eleven hundred rebels should be furnished for transportation to some of His Majesty's southern plantations, Jamaica, Barbados, or any of the Leeward Islands.

You are not to suppose that this command was

dictated by any sense of mercy. Lord Churchill was no more than just when he spoke of the King's heart as being as insensible as marble. It had been realized that in these wholesale hangings there was taking place a reckless waste of valuable material. Slaves were urgently required in the plantations, and a healthy, vigorous man could be reckoned worth at least from ten to fifteen pounds. Then, there were at court many gentlemen who had some claim or other upon His Majesty's bounty. Here was a cheap and ready way to discharge these claims. From amongst the convicted rebels a certain number might be set aside to be bestowed upon those gentlemen, so that they might dispose of them to their own profit.

My Lord Sunderland's letter gives precise details of the royal munificence in human flesh. A thousand prisoners were to be distributed among some eight courtiers and others, whilst a postscriptum to his lordship's letter asked for a further hundred to be held at the disposal of the Queen. These prisoners were to be transported at once to His Majesty's southern plantations, and to be kept there for the space of ten years before being restored to liberty, the parties to whom they were assigned entering into security to see that transportation was immediately effected.

We know from Lord Jeffreys's secretary how the Chief Justice inveighed that night in drunken frenzy against this misplaced clemency to which His Majesty had been persuaded. We know how he attempted by letter to induce the King to reconsider his decision. But James adhered to it. It was — apart from the indirect profit he derived from it — a clemency full worthy of him. He knew that to spare lives in this fashion was to convert them into living deaths. Many must succumb in torment to the horrors of West Indian slavery, and so be the envy of their surviving companions.

Thus it happened that Peter Blood, and with him Jeremy Pitt and Andrew Baynes, instead of being hanged, drawn, and quartered as their sentences directed, were conveyed to Bristol and there shipped with some fifty others aboard the *Jamaica Merchant.* From close confinement under hatches, ill-nourishment and foul water, a sickness broke out amongst them, of which eleven died. Amongst these was the unfortunate yeoman from Oglethorpe's Farm, brutally torn from his quiet homestead amid the fragrant cider orchards for no other sin but that he had practised mercy.

The mortality might have been higher than it was but for Peter Blood. At first the master of the *Jamaica Merchant* had answered with oaths and threats the doctor's expostulations against permitting men to perish in this fashion, and his insistence that he should be made free of the medicine chest and given leave to minister to the sick. But presently Captain Gardner came to see that he might be brought to task for these too heavy losses of human merchandise, and because of this he was belatedly glad to avail himself of the skill of Peter Blood. The doctor went to work zealously and zestfully, and wrought so ably that, by his ministrations and by improving the condition of his fellow-captives, he checked the spread of the disease.

Towards the middle of December the *Jamaica*

Merchant dropped anchor in Carlisle Bay, and put ashore the forty-two surviving rebels-convict.

If these unfortunates had imagined — as many of them appear to have done — that they were coming into some wild, savage country, the prospect, of which they had a glimpse before they were hustled over the ship's side into the waiting boats, was enough to correct the impression. They beheld a town of sufficiently imposing proportions composed of houses built upon European notions of architecture, but without any of the huddle usual in European cities. The spire of a church rose dominantly above the red roofs, a fort guarded the entrance of the wide harbour, with guns thrusting their muzzles between the crenels, and the wide façade of Government House revealed itself dominantly placed on a gentle hill above the town. This hill was vividly green as is an English hill in April, and the day was such a day as April gives to England, the season of heavy rains being newly ended.

On a wide cobbled space on the sea front they found a guard of red-coated militia drawn up to receive them, and a crowd — attracted by their arrival — which in dress and manner differed little from a crowd in a seaport at home save that it contained fewer women and a great number of negroes.

To inspect them, drawn up there on the mole, came Governor Steed, a short, stout, red-faced gentleman, in blue taffetas burdened by a prodigious amount of gold lace, who limped a little and leaned heavily upon a stout ebony cane. After him, in the uniform of a colonel of the Barbados Militia, rolled a tall, corpulent man who towered head and shoulders

above the Governor, with malevolence plainly
written on his enormous yellowish countenance. At
his side, and contrasting oddly with his grossness,
moving with an easy stripling grace, came a slight
young lady in a modish riding-gown. The broad
brim of a grey hat with a scarlet sweep of ostrich
plume shaded an oval face upon which the climate of
the Tropic of Cancer had made no impression, so delicately fair was its complexion. Ringlets of red-brown
hair hung to her shoulders. Frankness looked out
from her hazel eyes which were set wide; commiseration repressed now the mischievousness that normally inhabited her fresh young mouth.

Peter Blood caught himself staring in a sort of
amazement at that piquant face, which seemed here
so out of place, and finding his stare returned, he
shifted uncomfortably. He grew conscious of the
sorry figure that he cut. Unwashed, with rank and
matted hair and a disfiguring black beard upon his
face, and the erstwhile splendid suit of black camlet
in which he had been taken prisoner now reduced to
rags that would have disgraced a scarecrow, he was
in no case for inspection by such dainty eyes as these.
Nevertheless, they continued to inspect him with
round-eyed, almost childlike wonder and pity. Their
owner put forth a hand to touch the scarlet sleeve
of her companion, whereupon with an ill-tempered
grunt the man swung his great bulk round so that he
directly confronted her.

Looking up into his face, she was speaking to him
earnestly, but the Colonel plainly gave her no more
than the half of his attention. His little beady eyes,
closely flanking a fleshly, pendulous nose, had passed

from her and were fixed upon fair-haired, sturdy young Pitt, who was standing beside Blood.

The Governor had also come to a halt, and for a moment now that little group of three stood in conversation. What the lady said, Peter could not hear at all, for she lowered her voice; the Colonel's reached him in a confused rumble, but the Governor was neither considerate nor indistinct; he had a high-pitched voice which carried far, and believing himself witty, he desired to be heard by all.

"But, my dear Colonel Bishop, it is for you to take first choice from this dainty nosegay, and at your own price. After that we'll send the rest to auction."

Colonel Bishop nodded his acknowledgment. He raised his voice in answering. "Your excellency is very good. But, faith, they're a weedy lot, not likely to be of much value in the plantation." His beady eyes scanned them again, and his contempt of them deepened the malevolence of his face. It was as if he were annoyed with them for being in no better condition. Then he beckoned forward Captain Gardner, the master of the *Jamaica Merchant*, and for some minutes stood in talk with him over a list which the latter produced at his request.

Presently he waved aside the list and advanced alone towards the rebels-convict, his eyes considering them, his lips pursed. Before the young Somersetshire shipmaster he came to a halt, and stood an instant pondering him. Then he fingered the muscles of the young man's arm, and bade him open his mouth that he might see his teeth. He pursed his coarse lips again and nodded.

He spoke to Gardner over his shoulder.

"Fifteen pounds for this one."

The Captain made a face of dismay. "Fifteen pounds! It isn't half what I meant to ask for him."

"It is double what I had meant to give," grunted the Colonel.

"But he would be cheap at thirty pounds, your honour."

"I can get a negro for that. These white swine don't live. They're not fit for the labour."

Gardner broke into protestations of Pitt's health, youth, and vigour. It was not a man he was discussing; it was a beast of burden. Pitt, a sensitive lad, stood mute and unmoving. Only the ebb and flow of colour in his cheeks showed the inward struggle by which he maintained his self-control.

Peter Blood was nauseated by the loathsome haggle.

In the background, moving slowly away down the line of prisoners, went the lady in conversation with the Governor, who smirked and preened himself as he limped beside her. She was unconscious of the loathly business the Colonel was transacting. Was she, wondered Blood, indifferent to it?

Colonel Bishop swung on his heel to pass on.

"I'll go as far as twenty pounds. Not a penny more, and it's twice as much as you are like to get from Crabston."

Captain Gardner, recognizing the finality of the tone, sighed and yielded. Already Bishop was moving down the line. For Mr. Blood, as for a weedy youth on his left, the Colonel had no more than a glance of contempt. But the next man, a middle-aged Colossus named Wolverstone, who had lost an eye at Sedgemoor, drew his regard, and the haggling was recommenced.

Peter Blood stood there in the brilliant sunshine and inhaled the fragrant air, which was unlike any air that he had ever breathed. It was laden with a strange perfume, blend of logwood flower, pimento, and aromatic cedars. He lost himself in unprofitable speculations born of that singular fragrance. He was in no mood for conversation, nor was Pitt, who stood dumbly at his side, and who was afflicted mainly at the moment by the thought that he was at last about to be separated from this man with whom he had stood shoulder to shoulder throughout all these troublous months, and whom he had come to love and depend upon for guidance and sustenance. A sense of loneliness and misery pervaded him by contrast with which all that he had endured seemed as nothing. To Pitt, this separation was the poignant climax of all his sufferings.

Other buyers came and stared at them, and passed on. Blood did not heed them. And then at the end of the line there was a movement. Gardner was speaking in a loud voice, making an announcement to the general public of buyers that had waited until Colonel Bishop had taken his choice of that human merchandise. As he finished, Blood, looking in his direction, noticed that the girl was speaking to Bishop, and pointing up the line with a silver-hilted riding-whip she carried. Bishop shaded his eyes with his hand to look in the direction in which she was pointing. Then slowly, with his ponderous, rolling gait, he approached again accompanied by Gardner, and followed by the lady and the Governor.

On they came until the Colonel was abreast of Blood. He would have passed on, but that the lady tapped his arm with her whip.

"But this is the man I meant," she said.

"This one?" Contempt rang in the voice. Peter Blood found himself staring into a pair of beady brown eyes sunk into a yellow, fleshly face like currants into a dumpling. He felt the colour creeping into his face under the insult of that contemptuous inspection. "Bah! A bag of bones. What should I do with him?"

He was turning away when Gardner interposed.

"He may be lean, but he's tough; tough and healthy. When half of them was sick and the other half sickening, this rogue kept his legs and doctored his fellows. But for him there'd ha' been more deaths than there was. Say fifteen pounds for him, Colonel. That's cheap enough. He's tough, I tell your honour — tough and strong, though he be lean. And he's just the man to bear the heat when it comes. The climate'll never kill him."

There came a chuckle from Governor Steed. "You hear, Colonel. Trust your niece. Her sex knows a man when it sees one." And he laughed, well pleased with his wit.

But he laughed alone. A cloud of annoyance swept across the face of the Colonel's niece, whilst the Colonel himself was too absorbed in the consideration of this bargain to heed the Governor's humour. He twisted his lip a little, stroking his chin with his hand the while. Jeremy Pitt had almost ceased to breathe.

"I'll give you ten pounds for him," said the Colonel at last.

Peter Blood prayed that the offer might be rejected. For no reason that he could have given you, he was taken with repugnance at the thought of becoming the property of this gross animal, and in some sort the property of that hazel-eyed young girl. But it would need more than repugnance to save him from his destiny. A slave is a slave, and has no power to shape his fate. Peter Blood was sold to Colonel Bishop — a disdainful buyer — for the ignominious sum of ten pounds.

CHAPTER V

ARABELLA BISHOP

ONE sunny morning in January, about a month after the arrival of the *Jamaica Merchant* at Bridgetown, Miss Arabella Bishop rode out from her uncle's fine house on the heights to the northwest of the city. She was attended by two negroes who trotted after her at a respectful distance, and her destination was Government House, whither she went to visit the Governor's lady, who had lately been ailing. Reaching the summit of a gentle, grassy slope, she met a tall, lean man dressed in a sober, gentlemanly fashion, who was walking in the opposite direction. He was a stranger to her, and strangers were rare enough in the island. And yet in some vague way he did not seem quite a stranger.

Miss Arabella drew rein, affecting to pause that she might admire the prospect, which was fair enough to warrant it. Yet out of the corner of those hazel eyes she scanned this fellow very attentively as he came nearer. She corrected her first impression of his dress. It was sober enough, but hardly gentlemanly. Coat and breeches were of plain homespun; and if the former sat so well upon him it was more by virtue of his natural grace than by that of tailoring. His stockings were of cotton, harsh and plain, and the broad castor, which he respectfully doffed as he came up with her, was an old one unadorned by band or feather. What had seemed to be a periwig at a little distance was now revealed for the man's own lustrous coiling black hair.

Out of a brown, shaven, saturnine face two eyes that were startlingly blue considered her gravely. The man would have passed on but that she detained him.

"I think I know you, sir," said she.

Her voice was crisp and boyish, and there was something of boyishness in her manner — if one can apply the term to so dainty a lady. It arose perhaps from an ease, a directness, which disdained the artifices of her sex, and set her on good terms with all the world. To this it may be due that Miss Arabella had reached the age of five and twenty not merely unmarried but unwooed. She used with all men a sisterly frankness which in itself contains a quality of aloofness, rendering it difficult for any man to become her lover.

Her negroes had halted at some distance in the rear, and they squatted now upon the short grass until it should be her pleasure to proceed upon her way.

The stranger came to a standstill upon being addressed.

"A lady should know her own property," said he.

"My property?"

"Your uncle's, leastways. Let me present myself. I am called Peter Blood, and I am worth precisely ten pounds. I know it because that is the sum your uncle paid for me. It is not every man has the same opportunities of ascertaining his real value."

She recognized him then. She had not seen him since that day upon the mole a month ago, and that she should not instantly have known him again despite the interest he had then aroused in her is not surprising, considering the change he had wrought in his appearance, which now was hardly that of a slave.

"My God!" said she. "And you can laugh!"

"It's an achievement," he admitted. "But then, I have not fared as ill as I might."

"I have heard of that," said she.

What she had heard was that this rebel-convict had been discovered to be a physician. The thing had come to the ears of Governor Steed, who suffered damnably from the gout, and Governor Steed had borrowed the fellow from his purchaser. Whether by skill or good fortune, Peter Blood had afforded the Governor that relief which his excellency had failed to obtain from the ministrations of either of the two physicians practising in Bridgetown. Then the Governor's lady had desired him to attend her for the megrims. Mr. Blood had found her suffering from nothing worse than peevishness — the result of a natural petulance aggravated by the dulness of life in Barbados to a lady of her social aspirations. But he had prescribed for her none the less, and she had conceived herself the better for his prescription. After that the fame of him had gone through Bridgetown, and Colonel Bishop had found that there was more profit to be made out of this new slave by leaving him to pursue his profession than by setting him to work on the plantations, for which purpose he had been originally acquired.

"It is yourself, madam, I have to thank for my comparatively easy and clean condition," said Mr. Blood, "and I am glad to take this opportunity of doing so."

The gratitude was in his words rather than in his tone. Was he mocking, she wondered, and looked at him with the searching frankness that another might have found disconcerting. He took the glance for a question, and answered it.

"If some other planter had bought me," he explained, "it is odds that the facts of my shining abilities might never have been brought to light, and I should be hewing and hoeing at this moment like the poor wretches who were landed with me."

"And why do you thank me for that? It was my uncle who bought you."

"But he would not have done so had you not urged him. I perceived your interest. At the time I resented it."

"You resented it?" There was a challenge in her boyish voice.

"I have had no lack of experiences of this mortal life; but to be bought and sold was a new one, and I was hardly in the mood to love my purchaser."

"If I urged you upon my uncle, sir, it was that I commiserated you." There was a slight severity in her tone, as if to reprove the mixture of mockery and flippancy in which he seemed to be speaking.

She proceeded to explain herself. "My uncle may appear to you a hard man. No doubt he is. They are all hard men, these planters. It is the life, I suppose. But there are others here who are worse. There is Mr. Crabston, for instance, up at Speightstown. He was there on the mole, waiting to buy my uncle's leavings, and if you had fallen into his hands...A dreadful man. That is why."

He was a little bewildered.

"This interest in a stranger . . ." he began. Then changed the direction of his probe. "But there were others as deserving of commiseration."

"You did not seem quite like the others."

"I am not," said he.

"Oh!" She stared at him, bridling a little. "You have a good opinion of yourself."

"On the contrary. The others are all worthy rebels. I am not. That is the difference. I was one who had not the wit to see that England requires purifying. I was content to pursue a doctor's trade in Bridgewater whilst my betters were shedding their blood to drive out an unclean tyrant and his rascally crew."

"Sir!" she checked him. "I think you are talking treason."

"I hope I am not obscure," said he.

"There are those here who would have you flogged if they heard you."

"The Governor would never allow it. He has the gout, and his lady has the megrims."

"Do you depend upon that?" She was frankly scornful.

"You have certainly never had the gout; probably not even the megrims," said he.

She made a little impatient movement with her hand, and looked away from him a moment, out to sea. Quite suddenly she looked at him again; and now her brows were knit.

"But if you are not a rebel, how come you here?"

He saw the thing she apprehended, and he laughed. 'Faith, now, it's a long story," said he.

"And one perhaps that you would prefer not to tell?"

Briefly on that he told it her.

"My God! What an infamy!" she cried, when he had done.

"Oh, it's a sweet country England under King James! There's no need to commiserate me further. All things considered I prefer Barbados. Here at least one can believe in God."

He looked first to right, then to left as he spoke, from the distant shadowy bulk of Mount Hillbay to the limitless ocean ruffled by the winds of heaven. Then, as if the fair prospect rendered him conscious of his own littleness and the insignificance of his woes, he fell thoughtful.

"Is that so difficult elsewhere?" she asked him, and she was very grave.

"Men make it so."

"I see." She laughed a little, on a note of sadness, it seemed to him. "I have never deemed Barbados the earthly mirror of heaven," she confessed. "But no doubt you know your world better than I." She touched her horse with her little silver-hilted whip. "I congratulate you on this easing of your misfortunes."

He bowed, and she moved on. Her negroes sprang up, and went trotting after her.

Awhile Peter Blood remained standing there, where she left him, conning the sunlit waters of Carlisle Bay below, and the shipping in that spacious haven about which the gulls were fluttering noisily.

It was a fair enough prospect, he reflected, but it was a prison, and in announcing that he preferred it to England, he had indulged that almost laudable form of boasting which lies in belittling our misadventures.

He turned, and resuming his way, went off in long, swinging strides towards the little huddle of huts built of mud and wattles — a miniature village enclosed in a stockade which the plantation slaves inhabited, and where he, himself, was lodged with them.

Through his mind sang the line of Lovelace:

> "Stone walls do not a prison make,
> Nor iron bars a cage."

But he gave it a fresh meaning, the very converse of that which its author had intended. A prison, he reflected, was a prison, though it had neither walls nor bars, however spacious it might be. And as he realized it that morning so he was to realize it increasingly as time sped on. Daily he came to think more of his clipped wings, of his exclusion from the world, and less of the fortuitous liberty he enjoyed. Nor did the contrasting of his comparatively easy lot with that of his unfortunate fellow-convicts bring him the satisfaction a differently constituted mind might have derived from it. Rather did the contemplation of their misery increase the bitterness that was gathering in his soul.

Of the forty-two who had been landed with him from the *Jamaica Merchant*, Colonel Bishop had purchased no less than twenty-five. The remainder had gone to lesser planters, some of them to Speightstown, and others still farther north. What may have been the lot of the latter he could not tell, but amongst Bishop's slaves Peter Blood came and went freely, sleeping in their quarters, and their lot he knew to be a brutalizing misery. They toiled in the sugar plantations from sunrise to sunset, and if their labours flagged, there were the whips of the overseer and his men to quicken them. They went in rags, some almost naked; they dwelt in squalor, and they were ill-nourished on salted meat and maize dumplings — food which to many of them was for a season at least so nauseating that two of them sickened and died before Bishop remembered that their lives had a certain value in labour to him and yielded to Blood's intercessions for a better care of such as fell ill. To curb insubordination, one of them who had rebelled against Kent, the brutal overseer, was lashed to death by negroes under his comrades' eyes, and another who had been so misguided as to run away into the woods was tracked, brought back, flogged, and then branded on the forehead with the letters "F. T.," that all might know him for a fugitive traitor as long as he lived. Fortunately for him the poor fellow died as a consequence of the flogging.

After that a dull, spiritless resignation settled down upon the remainder. The most mutinous were quelled, and accepted their unspeakable lot with the tragic fortitude of despair.

Peter Blood alone, escaping these excessive sufferings, remained outwardly unchanged, whilst inwardly the only change in him was a daily deeper hatred of his kind, a daily deeper longing to escape from this place where man defiled so foully the lovely work of his Creator. It was a longing too vague to amount to a hope. Hope here was inadmissible. And yet he did not yield to despair. He set a mask of laughter on his saturnine countenance and went his way, treating the sick to the profit of Colonel Bishop, and encroaching further and further upon the preserves of the two other men of medicine in Bridge-town.

Immune from the degrading punishments and privations of his fellow-convicts, he was enabled to keep his self-respect, and was treated without harshness even by the soulless planter to whom he had been sold. He owed it all to gout and megrims. He had won the esteem of Governor Steed, and — what is even more important — of Governor Steed's lady, whom he shamelessly and cynically flattered and humoured.

Occasionally he saw Miss Bishop, and they seldom met but that she paused to hold him in conversation for some moments, evincing her interest in him. Himself, he was never disposed to linger. He was not, he told himself, to be deceived by her delicate exterior, her sapling grace, her easy, boyish ways and pleasant, boyish voice. In all his life — and it had been very varied — he had never met a man whom he accounted more beastly than her uncle, and he could not dissociate her from the man. She was his niece, of his own blood, and some of the vices of it, some of the remorseless cruelty of the wealthy planter must, he argued, inhabit that pleasant body of hers. He argued this very often to himself, as if answering and convincing some instinct that pleaded otherwise, and arguing it he avoided her when it was possible, and was frigidly civil when it was not.

Justifiable as his reasoning was, plausible as it may seem, yet he would have done better to have trusted the instinct that was in conflict with it. Though the same blood ran in her veins as in those of Colonel Bishop, yet hers was free of the vices that tainted her

uncle's, for these vices were not natural to that blood;
they were, in his case, acquired. Her father, Tom
Bishop — that same Colonel Bishop's brother —
had been a kindly, chivalrous, gentle soul who,
broken-hearted by the early death of a young wife,
had abandoned the Old World and sought an anodyne
for his grief in the New. He had come out to the
Antilles, bringing with him his little daughter, then
five years of age, and had given himself up to the life
of a planter. He had prospered from the first, as men
sometimes will who care nothing for prosperity.
Prospering, he had bethought him of his younger
brother, a soldier at home reputed somewhat wild.
He had advised him to come out to Barbados; and
the advice, which at another season William Bishop
might have scorned, reached him at a moment when
his wildness was beginning to bear such fruit that a
change of climate was desirable. William came, and
was admitted by his generous brother to a partnership in the prosperous plantation. Some six years
later, when Arabella was fifteen, her father died,
leaving her in her uncle's guardianship. It was perhaps his one mistake. But the goodness of his own
nature coloured his views of other men; moreover,
himself, he had conducted the education of his
daughter, giving her an independence of character
upon which perhaps he counted unduly. As things
were, there was little love between uncle and niece.
But she was dutiful to him, and he was circumspect
in his behaviour before her. All his life, and for all his
wildness, he had gone in a certain awe of his brother
whose worth he had the wit to recognize; and now it
was almost as if some of that awe was transferred to

his brother's child, who was also, in a sense, his partner, although she took no active part in the business of the plantations.

Peter Blood judged her — as we are all too prone to judge — upon insufficient knowledge.

He was very soon to have cause to correct that judgment.

One day towards the end of May, when the heat was beginning to grow oppressive, there crawled into Carlisle Bay a wounded, battered English ship, the *Pride of Devon*, her freeboard scarred and broken, her coach a gaping wreck, her mizzen so shot away that only a jagged stump remained to tell the place where it had stood. She had been in action off Martinique with two Spanish treasure ships, and although her captain swore that the Spaniards had beset him without provocation, it is difficult to avoid a suspicion that the encounter had been brought about quite otherwise. One of the Spaniards had fled from the combat, and if the *Pride of Devon* had not given chase it was probably because she was by then in no case to do so. The other had been sunk, but not before the English ship had transferred to her own hold a good deal of the treasure aboard the Spaniard. It was, in fact, one of those piratical affrays which were a perpetual source of trouble between the courts of St. James's and the Escurial, complaints emanating now from one and now from the other side.

Steed, however, after the fashion of most Colonial governors, was willing enough to dull his wits to the extent of accepting the English seaman's story, disregarding any evidence that might belie it. He shared the hatred so richly deserved by arrogant, overbearing Spain that was common to men of every other nation from the Bahamas to the Main. Therefore he gave the *Pride of Devon* the shelter she sought in his harbour and every facility to careen and carry out repairs.

But before it came to this, they fetched from her hold over a score of English seamen as battered and broken as the ship herself, and together with these some half-dozen Spaniards in like case, the only survivors of a boarding party from the Spanish galleon that had invaded the English ship and found itself unable to retreat. These wounded men were conveyed to a long shed on the wharf, and the medical skill of Bridgetown was summoned to their aid. Peter Blood was ordered to bear a hand in this work, and partly because he spoke Castilian — and he spoke it as fluently as his own native tongue — partly because of his inferior condition as a slave, he was given the Spaniards for his patients.

Now Blood had no cause to love Spaniards. His two years in a Spanish prison and his subsequent campaigning in the Spanish Netherlands had shown him a side of the Spanish character which he had found anything but admirable. Nevertheless he performed his doctor's duties zealously and painstakingly, if emotionlessly, and even with a certain superficial friendliness towards each of his patients. These were so surprised at having their wounds healed instead of being summarily hanged that they manifested a docility very unusual in their kind. They were shunned, however, by all those charitably disposed inhabitants of Bridgetown who flocked to the improvised hospital with gifts of fruit and flowers and delicacies for the injured English seamen. Indeed, had the wishes of some of these inhabitants been regarded, the Spaniards would have been left to die like vermin, and of this Peter Blood had an example almost at the very outset.

With the assistance of one of the negroes sent to the shed for the purpose, he was in the act of setting a broken leg, when a deep, gruff voice, that he had come to know and dislike as he had never disliked the voice of living man, abruptly challenged him.

"What are you doing there?"

Blood did not look up from his task. There was not the need. He knew the voice, as I have said.

"I am setting a broken leg," he answered, without pausing in his labours.

"I can see that, fool." A bulky body interposed between Peter Blood and the window. The half-naked man on the straw rolled his black eyes to stare up fearfully out of a clay-coloured face at this intruder. A knowledge of English was unnecessary to inform him that here came an enemy. The harsh, minatory note of that voice sufficiently expressed the fact. "I can see that, fool; just as I can see what the rascal is. Who gave you leave to set Spanish legs?"

"I am a doctor, Colonel Bishop. The man is wounded. It is not for me to discriminate. I keep to my trade."

"Do you, by God! If you'd done that, you wouldn't now be here."

"On the contrary, it is because I did it that I am here."

"Aye, I know that's your lying tale." The Colonel sneered; and then, observing Blood to continue his work unmoved, he grew really angry. "Will you cease that, and attend to me when I am speaking?"

Peter Blood paused, but only for an instant. "The man is in pain," he said shortly, and resumed his work.

"In pain, is he? I hope he is, the damned piratical dog. But will you heed me, you insubordinate knave?"

The Colonel delivered himself in a roar, infuriated by what he conceived to be defiance, and expressing itself in the most unruffled disregard of himself. His long bamboo cane was raised to strike. Peter Blood's blue eyes caught the flash of it, and he spoke quickly to arrest the blow.

"Not insubordinate, sir, whatever I may be. I am acting upon the express orders of Governor Steed."

The Colonel checked, his great face empurpling. His mouth fell open.

"Governor Steed!" he echoed. Then he lowered his cane, swung round, and without another word to Blood rolled away towards the other end of the shed where the Governor was standing at the moment.

Peter Blood chuckled. But his triumph was dictated less by humanitarian considerations than by the reflection that he had baulked his brutal owner.

The Spaniard, realizing that in this altercation, whatever its nature, the doctor had stood his friend, ventured in a muted voice to ask him what had happened. But the doctor shook his head in silence, and pursued his work. His ears were straining to catch the words now passing between Steed and Bishop. The Colonel was blustering and storming, the great bulk of him towering above the wizened little overdressed figure of the Governor. But the little fop was not to be browbeaten. His excellency was conscious that he had behind him the force of public opinion to support him. Some there might be, but they were not many, who held such ruthless views as Colonel Bishop. His excellency asserted his authority. It was by his orders that Blood had devoted himself to the wounded Spaniards, and his orders were to be carried out. There was no more to be said.

Colonel Bishop was of another opinion. In his view there was a great deal to be said. He said it, with great circumstance, loudly, vehemently, obscenely — for he could be fluently obscene when moved to anger.

"You talk like a Spaniard, Colonel," said the Governor, and thus dealt the Colonel's pride a wound that was to smart resentfully for many a week. At the moment it struck him silent, and sent him stamping out of the shed in a rage for which he could find no words.

It was two days later when the ladies of Bridgetown, the wives and daughters of her planters and merchants, paid their first visit of charity to the wharf, bringing their gifts to the wounded seamen.

Again Peter Blood was there, ministering to the sufferers in his care, moving among those unfortunate Spaniards whom no one heeded. All the charity, all the gifts were for the members of the crew of the *Pride of Devon*. And this Peter Blood accounted natural enough. But rising suddenly from the re-dressing of a wound, a task in which he had been absorbed for some moments, he saw to his surprise that one lady, detached from the general throng, was placing some plantains and a bundle of succulent sugar cane on the cloak that served one of his patients for a coverlet. She was elegantly dressed in lavender silk and was followed by a half-naked negro carrying a basket.

Peter Blood, stripped of his coat, the sleeves of his coarse shirt rolled to the elbow, and holding a bloody rag in his hand, stood at gaze a moment. The lady, turning now to confront him, her lips parting in a smile of recognition, was Arabella Bishop.

"The man's a Spaniard," said he, in the tone of one who corrects a misapprehension, and also tinged never so faintly by something of the derision that was in his soul.

The smile with which she had been greeting him withered on her lips. She frowned and stared at him a moment, with increasing haughtiness.

"So I perceive. But he's a human being none the less," said she.

That answer, and its implied rebuke, took him by surprise.

"Your uncle, the Colonel, is of a different opinion," said he, when he had recovered. "He regards them as vermin to be left to languish and die of their festering wounds."

She caught the irony now more plainly in his voice. She continued to stare at him.

"Why do you tell me this?"

"To warn you that you may be incurring the Colonel's displeasure. If he had had his way, I should never have been allowed to dress their wounds."

"And you thought, of course, that I must be of my uncle's mind?" There was a crispness about her voice, an ominous challenging sparkle in her hazel eyes.

"I'd not willingly be rude to a lady even in my thoughts," said he. "But that you should bestow gifts on them, considering that if your uncle came to hear of it . . ." He paused, leaving the sentence unfinished. "Ah, well — there it is!" he concluded.

But the lady was not satisfied at all.

"First you impute to me inhumanity, and then cowardice. Faith! For a man who would not willingly be rude to a lady even in his thoughts, it's none so bad." Her boyish laugh trilled out, but the note of it jarred his ears this time.

He saw her now, it seemed to him, for the first time, and saw how he had misjudged her.

"Sure, now, how was I to guess that . . . that Colonel Bishop could have an angel for his niece?" said he recklessly, for he was reckless as men often are in sudden penitence.

"You wouldn't, of course. I shouldn't think you often guess aright." Having withered him with that and her glance, she turned to her negro and the basket that he carried. From this she lifted now the fruits and delicacies with which it was laden, and piled them in such heaps upon the beds of the six Spaniards that by the time she had so served the last of them her basket was empty, and there was nothing left for her own fellow-countrymen. These, indeed, stood in no need of her bounty — as she no doubt observed — since they were being plentifully supplied by others.

Having thus emptied her basket, she called her negro, and without another word or so much as another glance at Peter Blood, swept out of the place with her head high and chin thrust forward.

Peter watched her departure. Then he fetched a sigh.

It startled him to discover that the thought that he had incurred her anger gave him concern. It could not have been so yesterday. It became so only since he had been vouchsafed this revelation of her true nature. "Bad cess to it now, it serves me right. It seems I know nothing at all of human nature. But how the devil was I to guess that a family that can breed a devil like Colonel Bishop should also breed a saint like this?"

CHAPTER VI

PLANS OF ESCAPE

AFTER that Arabella Bishop went daily to the shed on the wharf with gifts of fruit, and later of money and of wearing apparel for the Spanish prisoners. But she contrived so to time her visits that Peter Blood never again met her there. Also his own visits were growing shorter in a measure as his patients healed. That they all throve and returned to health under his care, whilst fully one third of the wounded in the care of Whacker and Bronson — the two other surgeons — died of their wounds, served to increase the reputation in which this rebel-convict stood in Bridgetown. It may have been no more than the fortune of war. But the townsfolk did not choose so to regard it. It led to a further dwindling of the practices of his free colleagues and a further increase of his own labours and his owner's profit. Whacker and Bronson laid their heads together to devise a scheme by which this intolerable state of things should be brought to an end. But that is to anticipate.

One day, whether by accident or design, Peter Blood came striding down the wharf a full half-hour earlier than usual, and so met Miss Bishop just issuing from the shed. He doffed his hat and stood aside to give her passage. She took it, chin in the air, and eyes which disdained to look anywhere where the sight of him was possible.

"Miss Arabella," said he, on a coaxing, pleading note.

She grew conscious of his presence, and looked him over with an air that was faintly, mockingly searching.

"La!" said she. "It's the delicate-minded gentleman!"

Peter groaned. "Am I so hopelessly beyond forgiveness? I ask it very humbly."

"What condescension!"

"It is cruel to mock me," said he, and adopted mock-humility. "After all, I am but a slave. And you might be ill one of these days."

"What, then?"

"It would be humiliating to send for me if you treat me like an enemy."

"You are not the only doctor in Bridgetown."

"But I am the least dangerous."

She grew suddenly suspicious of him, aware that he was permitting himself to rally her, and in a measure she had already yielded to it. She stiffened, and looked him over again.

"You make too free, I think," she rebuked him.

"A doctor's privilege."

"I am not your patient. Please to remember it in future." And on that, unquestionably angry, she departed.

"Now is she a vixen or am I a fool, or is it both?" he asked the blue vault of heaven, and then went into the shed.

It was to be a morning of excitements. As he was leaving an hour or so later, Whacker, the younger of the other two physicians, joined him — an unprece-

dented condescension this, for hitherto neither of
them had addressed him beyond an occasional and
surly "good-day!"

: "If you are for Colonel Bishop's, I'll walk with you
a little way, Doctor Blood," said he. He was a short,
broad man of five-and-forty with pendulous cheeks
and hard blue eyes.

Peter Blood was startled. But he dissembled it.

"I am for Government House," said he.

"Ah! To be sure! The Governor's lady." And he
laughed; or perhaps he sneered. Peter Blood was not
quite certain. "She encroaches a deal upon your
time, I hear. Youth and good looks, Doctor Blood!
Youth and good looks! They are inestimable advantages in our profession as in others — particularly
where the ladies are concerned."

Peter stared at him. "If you mean what you seem
to mean, you had better say it to Governor Steed. It
may amuse him."

"You surely misapprehend me."

"I hope so."

"You're so very hot, now!" The doctor linked
his arm through Peter's. "I protest I desire to be
your friend — to serve you. Now, listen." Instinctively his voice grew lower. "This slavery in which
you find yourself must be singularly irksome to a man
of parts such as yourself."

"What intuitions!" cried sardonic Mr. Blood. But
the doctor took him literally.

"I am no fool, my dear doctor. I know a man when
I see one, and often I can tell his thoughts."

"If you can tell me mine, you'll persuade me of it,"
said Mr. Blood.

Dr. Whacker drew still closer to him as they stepped along the wharf. He lowered his voice to a still more confidential tone. His hard blue eyes peered up into the swart, sardonic face of his companion, who was a head taller than himself.

"How often have I not seen you staring out over the sea, your soul in your eyes! Don't I know what you are thinking? If you could escape from this hell of slavery, you could exercise the profession of which you are an ornament as a free man with pleasure and profit to yourself. The world is large. There are many nations besides England where a man of your parts would be warmly welcomed. There are many colonies besides these English ones." Lower still came the voice until it was no more than a whisper. Yet there was no one within earshot. "It is none so far now to the Dutch settlement of Curaçao. At this time of the year the voyage may safely be undertaken in a light craft. And Curaçao need be no more than a stepping-stone to the great world, which would lie open to you once you were delivered from this bondage."

Dr. Whacker ceased. He was pale and a little out of breath. But his hard eyes continued to study his impassive companion. "Well?" he said after a pause. "What do you say to that?"

Yet Blood did not immediately answer. His mind was heaving in tumult, and he was striving to calm it that he might take a proper survey of this thing flung into it to create so monstrous a disturbance. He began where another might have ended.

"I have no money. And for that a handsome sum would be necessary."

"Did I not say that I desired to be your friend?"

"Why?" asked Peter Blood at point-blank range.

But he never heeded the answer. Whilst Dr. Whacker was professing that his heart bled for a brother doctor languishing in slavery, denied the opportunity which his gifts entitled him to make for himself, Peter Blood pounced like a hawk upon the obvious truth. Whacker and his colleague desired to be rid of one who threatened to ruin them. Sluggishness of decision was never a fault of Blood's. He leapt where another crawled. And so this thought of evasion never entertained until planted there now by Dr. Whacker sprouted into instant growth.

"I see, I see," he said, whilst his companion was still talking, explaining, and to save Dr. Whacker's face he played the hypocrite. "It is very noble in you — very brotherly, as between men of medicine. It is what I myself should wish to do in like case."

The hard eyes flashed, the husky voice grew tremulous as the other asked almost too eagerly:

"You agree, then? You agree?"

"Agree?" Blood laughed. "If I should be caught and brought back, they'd clip my wings and brand me for life."

"Surely the thing is worth a little risk?" More tremulous than ever was the tempter's voice.

"Surely," Blood agreed. "But it asks more than courage. It asks money. A sloop might be bought for twenty pounds, perhaps."

"It shall be forthcoming. It shall be a loan, which you shall repay us — repay me, when you can."

That betraying "us" so hastily retrieved completed Blood's understanding. The other doctor was also in the business.

They were approaching the peopled part of the mole. Quickly, but eloquently, Blood expressed his thanks, where he knew that no thanks were due.

"We will talk of this again, sir — to-morrow," he concluded. "You have opened for me the gates of hope."

In that at least he uttered no more than the bare truth, and expressed it very baldly. It was, indeed, as if a door had been suddenly flung open to the sunlight for escape from a dark prison in which a man had thought to spend his life.

He was in haste now to be alone, to straighten out his agitated mind and plan coherently what was to be done. Also he must consult another. Already he had hit upon that other. For such a voyage a navigator would be necessary, and a navigator was ready to his hand in Jeremy Pitt. The first thing was to take counsel with the young shipmaster, who must be associated with him in this business if it were to be undertaken. All that day his mind was in turmoil with this new hope, and he was sick with impatience for night and a chance to discuss the matter with his chosen partner. As a result Blood was betimes that evening in the spacious stockade that enclosed the huts of the slaves together with the big white house of the overseer, and he found an opportunity of a few words with Pitt, unobserved by the others.

"To-night when all are asleep, come to my cabin. I have something to say to you."

The young man stared at him, roused by Blood's pregnant tone out of the mental lethargy into which

he had of late been lapsing as a result of the dehuman-
izing life he lived. Then he nodded understanding
and assent, and they moved apart.

The six months of plantation life in Barbados had
made an almost tragic mark upon the young seaman.
His erstwhile bright alertness was all departed. His
face was growing vacuous, his eyes were dull and
lack-lustre, and he moved in a cringing, furtive manner, like an over-beaten dog. He had survived the
ill-nourishment, the excessive work on the sugar
plantation under a pitiless sun, the lashes of the
overseer's whip when his labours flagged, and the
deadly, unrelieved animal life to which he was condemned. But the price he was paying for survival
was the usual price. He was in danger of becoming
no better than an animal, of sinking to the level of
the negroes who sometimes toiled beside him. The
man, however, was still there, not yet dormant, but
merely torpid from a surfeit of despair; and the man
in him promptly shook off that torpidity and awoke
at the first words Blood spoke to him that night —
awoke and wept.

"Escape?" he panted. "O God!" He took his
head in his hands, and fell to sobbing like a child.

"Sh! Steady now! Steady!" Blood admonished
him in a whisper, alarmed by the lad's blubbering.
He crossed to Pitt's side, and set a restraining hand
upon his shoulder. "For God's sake, command yourself. If we're overheard we shall both be flogged for
this."

Among the privileges enjoyed by Blood was that of
a hut to himself, and they were alone in this. But,
after all, it was built of wattles thinly plastered with

mud, and its door was composed of bamboos, through
which sound passed very easily. Though the stockade
was locked for the night, and all within it asleep by
now — it was after midnight — yet a prowling overseer was not impossible, and a sound of voices must
lead to discovery. Pitt realized this, and controlled
his outburst of emotion.

Sitting close thereafter they talked in whispers for
an hour or more, and all the while those dulled wits of
Pitt's were sharpening themselves anew upon this
precious whetstone of hope. They would need to recruit others into their enterprise, a half-dozen at
least, a half-score if possible, but no more than that.
They must pick the best out of that score of survivors
of the Monmouth men that Colonel Bishop had acquired. Men who understood the sea were desirable.
But of these there were only two in that unfortunate
gang, and their knowledge was none too full. They
were Hagthorpe, a gentleman who had served in the
Royal Navy, and Nicholas Dyke, who had been a
petty officer in the late king's time, and there was
another who had been a gunner, a man named Ogle.

It was agreed before they parted that Pitt should
begin with these three and then proceed to recruit
some six or eight others. He was to move with the utmost caution, sounding his men very carefully before
making anything in the nature of a disclosure, and
even then avoid rendering that disclosure so full that
its betrayal might frustrate the plans which as yet
had to be worked out in detail. Labouring with them
in the plantations, Pitt would not want for opportunities of broaching the matter to his fellow-
slaves.

"Caution above everything," was Blood's last recommendation to him at parting. "Who goes slowly,
goes safely, as the Italians have it. And remember
that if you betray yourself, you ruin all, for you are
the only navigator amongst us, and without you
there is no escaping."

Pitt reassured him, and slunk off back to his own
hut, and the straw that served him for a bed.

Coming next morning to the wharf, Blood found
Dr. Whacker in a generous mood. Having slept on
the matter, he was prepared to advance the convict
any sum up to thirty pounds that would enable him
to acquire a boat capable of taking him away from
the settlement. Blood expressed his thanks becom-
ingly, betraying no sign that he saw clearly into the
true reason of the other's munificence.

"It's not money I'll require," said he, "but the
boat itself. For who will be selling me a boat and incurring the penalties in Governor Steed's proclamation? Ye'll have read it, no doubt?"

Dr. Whacker's heavy face grew overcast. Thoughtfully he rubbed his chin. "I've read it — yes. And
I dare not procure the boat for you. It would be discovered. It must be. And the penalty is a fine of two
hundred pounds besides imprisonment. It would
ruin me. You'll see that?"

The high hopes in Blood's soul began to shrink.
And the shadow of his despair overcast his face.

"But then . . ." he faltered. "There is nothing to
be done."

"Nay, nay: things are not so desperate." Dr.
Whacker smiled a little with tight lips. "I've
thought of it. You will see that the man who buys

the boat must be one of those who goes with you —
so that he is not here to answer questions afterwards."

"But who is to go with me save men in my own
case? What I cannot do, they cannot."

"There are others detained on the island besides
slaves. There are several who are here for debt, and
would be glad enough to spread their wings. There's
a fellow Nuttall, now, who follows the trade of a shipwright, whom I happen to know would welcome such
a chance as you might afford him."

"But how should a debtor come with money to buy
a boat? The question will be asked."

"To be sure it will. But if you contrive shrewdly,
you'll all be gone before that happens."

Blood nodded understanding, and the doctor, setting a hand upon his sleeve, unfolded the scheme he
had conceived.

"You shall have the money from me at once.
Having received it, you'll forget that it was I who
supplied it to you. You have friends in England —
relatives, perhaps — who sent it out to you through
the agency of one of your Bridgetown patients, whose
name as a man of honour you will on no account di-
vulge lest you bring trouble upon him. That is your
tale if there are questions."

He paused, looking hard at Blood. Blood nodded
understanding and assent. Relieved, the doctor continued: "But there should be no questions if you go
carefully to work. You concert matters with Nuttall.
You enlist him as one of your companions — and a
shipwright should be a very useful member of your
crew. You engage him to discover a likely sloop whose
owner is disposed to sell. Then let your preparations

all be made before the purchase is effected, so that your escape may follow instantly upon it before the inevitable questions come to be asked. You take me?"

So well did Blood take him that within an hour he contrived to see Nuttall, and found the fellow as disposed to the business as Dr. Whacker had predicted. When he left the shipwright, it was agreed that Nuttall should seek the boat required, for which Blood would at once produce the money.

The quest took longer than was expected by Blood, who waited impatiently with the doctor's gold concealed about his person. But at the end of some three weeks, Nuttall — whom he was now meeting daily — informed him that he had found a serviceable wherry, and that its owner was disposed to sell it for twenty-two pounds. That evening, on the beach, remote from all eyes, Peter Blood handed that sum to his new associate, and Nuttall went off with instructions to complete the purchase late on the following day. He was to bring the boat to the wharf, where under cover of night Blood and his fellow-convicts would join him and make off.

Everything was ready. In the shed, from which all the wounded men had now been removed and which had since remained untenanted, Nuttall had concealed the necessary stores: a hundredweight of bread, a quantity of cheese, a cask of water and some few bottles of Canary, a compass, quadrant, chart, half-hour glass, log and line, a tarpaulin, some carpenter's tools, and a lantern and candles. And in the stockade, all was likewise in readiness. Hagthorpe, Dyke, and Ogle had agreed to join the venture, and eight others had been carefully recruited. In Pitt's hut, which he shared with five other rebels-convict, all of whom were to join in this bid for liberty, a ladder had been constructed in secret during those nights of waiting. With this they were to surmount the stockade and gain the open. The risk of detection, so that they made little noise, was negligible. Beyond locking them all into that stockade at night, there was no great precaution taken. Where, after all, could any so foolish as to attempt escape hope to conceal himself in that island? The chief risk lay in discovery by those of their companions who were to be left behind. It was because of these that they must go cautiously and in silence.

The day that was to have been their last in Barbados was a day of hope and anxiety to the twelve associates in that enterprise, no less than to Nuttall in the town below.

Towards sunset, having seen Nuttall depart to purchase and fetch the sloop to the prearranged moorings at the wharf, Peter Blood came sauntering towards the stockade, just as the slaves were being driven in from the fields. He stood aside at the entrance to let them pass, and beyond the message of hope flashed by his eyes, he held no communication with them.

He entered the stockade in their wake, and as they broke their ranks to seek their various respective huts, he beheld Colonel Bishop in talk with Kent, the overseer. The pair were standing by the stocks, planted in the middle of that green space for the punishment of offending slaves.

As he advanced, Bishop turned to regard him, scowling.

"Where have you been this while?" he bawled, and

although a minatory note was normal to the Colonel's voice, yet Blood felt his heart tightening apprehensively.

"I've been at my work in the town," he answered. "Mrs. Patch has a fever and Mr. Dekker has sprained his ankle."

"I sent for you to Dekker's, and you were not there. You are given to idling, my fine fellow. We shall have to quicken you one of these days unless you cease from abusing the liberty you enjoy. D'ye forget that ye're a rebel-convict?"

"I am not given the chance," said Blood, who never could learn to curb his tongue.

"By God! Will you be pert with me?"

Remembering all that was at stake, growing suddenly conscious that from the huts surrounding the enclosure anxious ears were listening, he instantly practised an unusual submission.

"Not pert, sir. I . . . I am sorry I should have been sought . . ."

"Aye, and you'll be sorrier yet. There's the Governor with an attack of gout, screaming like a wounded horse, and you nowhere to be found. Be off, man — away with you at speed to Government House! You're awaited, I tell you. Best lend him a horse, Kent, or the lout'll be all night getting there."

They bustled him away, choking almost from a reluctance that he dared not show. The thing was unfortunate; but after all not beyond remedy. The escape was set for midnight, and he should easily be back by then.

He mounted the horse that Kent procured him, intending to make all haste.

"How shall I reënter the stockade, sir?" he enquired at parting.

"You'll not reënter it," said Bishop. "When they've done with you at Government House, they may find a kennel for you there until morning."

Peter Blood's heart sank like a stone through water.

"But . . ." he began.

"Be off, I say. Will you stand there talking until dark? His excellency is waiting for you." And with his cane Colonel Bishop slashed the horse's quarters so brutally that the beast bounded forward, all but unseating her rider.

Peter Blood went off in a state of mind bordering on despair. And there was occasion for it. A postponement of the escape at least until to-morrow night was necessary now, and postponement must mean the discovery of Nuttall's transaction and the asking of questions it would be difficult to answer.

It was in his mind to slink back in the night, once his work at Government House were done, and from the outside of the stockade make known to Pitt and the others his presence, and so have them join him that their project might still be carried out. But in this he reckoned without the Governor, whom he found really in the thrall of a severe attack of gout, and almost as severe an attack of temper nourished by Blood's delay.

The doctor was kept in constant attendance upon him until long after midnight, when at last he was able to ease the sufferer a little by a bleeding. Thereupon he would have withdrawn. But Steed would not hear of it. Blood must sleep in his own chamber to be at hand in case of need. It was as if Fate made sport of him. For that night at least the escape must be definitely abandoned.

Not until the early hours of the morning did Peter Blood succeed in making a temporary escape from Government House on the ground that he required certain medicaments which he must, himself, procure from the apothecary.

On that pretext, he made an excursion into the awakening town, and went straight to Nuttall, whom he found in a state of livid panic. The unfortunate debtor, who had sat up waiting through the night, conceived that all was discovered and that his own ruin would be involved. Peter Blood quieted his fears.

"It will be for to-night instead," he said, with more assurance than he felt, "if I have to bleed the Governor to death. Be ready as last night."

"But if there are questions meanwhile?" bleated Nuttall. He was a thin, pale, small-featured man with weak eyes that now blinked desperately.

"Answer as best you can. Use your wits, man. I can stay no longer." And Peter went off to the apothecary for his pretexted drugs.

Within an hour of his going came an officer of the Secretary's to Nuttall's miserable hovel. The seller of the boat had — as by law required since the coming of the rebels-convict — duly reported the sale at the Secretary's office, so that he might obtain the reimbursement of the ten-pound surety into which every keeper of a small boat was compelled to enter. The Secretary's office postponed this reimbursement until it should have obtained confirmation of the transaction.

"We are informed that you have bought a wherry from Mr. Robert Farrell," said the officer.

"That is so," said Nuttall, who conceived that for him this was the end of the world.

"You are in no haste, it seems, to declare the same at the Secretary's office." The emissary had a proper bureaucratic haughtiness.

Nuttall's weak eyes blinked at a redoubled rate.

"To . . . to declare it?"

"Ye know it's the law."

"I . . . I didn't, may it please you."

"But it's in the proclamation published last January."

"I . . . I can't read, sir. I . . . I didn't know."

"Faugh!" The messenger withered him with his disdain. "Well, now you're informed. See to it that you are at the Secretary's office before noon with the ten pounds surety into which you are obliged to enter."

The pompous officer departed, leaving Nuttall in a cold perspiration despite the heat of the morning. He was thankful that the fellow had not asked the question he most dreaded, which was how he, a debtor, should come by the money to buy a wherry. But this he knew was only a respite. The question would presently be asked of a certainty, and then hell would open for him. He cursed the hour in which he had been such a fool as to listen to Peter Blood's chatter of escape. He thought it very likely that the whole plot would be discovered, and that he would probably be hanged, or at least branded and sold into slavery like those other damned rebels-convict, with whom he had been so mad as to associate himself. If only he had the ten pounds for this infernal surety, which until this moment had never entered into their calculations, it was possible that the thing might be done quickly and questions postponed until later. As the Secretary's messenger had overlooked the fact that he was a debtor, so might the others at the Secretary's office, at least for a day or two; and in that time he would, he hoped, be beyond the reach of their questions. But in the meantime what was to be done about this money? And it was to be found before noon!

Nuttall snatched up his hat, and went out in quest of Peter Blood. But where look for him? Wandering aimlessly up the irregular, unpaved street, he ventured to enquire of one or two if they had seen Dr. Blood that morning. He affected to be feeling none so well, and indeed his appearance bore out the deception. None could give him information; and since Blood had never told him of Whacker's share in this business, he walked in his unhappy ignorance past the door of the one man in Barbados who would eagerly have saved him in this extremity.

Finally he determined to go up to Colonel Bishop's plantation. Probably Blood would be there. If he were not, Nuttall would find Pitt, and leave a message with him. He was acquainted with Pitt and knew of Pitt's share in this business. His pretext for seeking Blood must still be that he needed medical assistance.

And at the same time that he set out, insensitive in his anxiety to the broiling heat, to climb the heights to the north of the town, Blood was setting out from Government House at last, having so far eased the

Governor's condition as to be permitted to depart. Being mounted, he would, but for an unexpected delay, have reached the stockade ahead of Nuttall, in which case several unhappy events might have been averted. The unexpected delay was occasioned by Miss Arabella Bishop.

They met at the gate of the luxuriant garden of Government House, and Miss Bishop, herself mounted, stared to see Peter Blood on horseback. It happened that he was in good spirits. The fact that the Governor's condition had so far improved as to restore him his freedom of movement had sufficed to remove the depression under which he had been laboring for the past twelve hours and more. In its rebound the mercury of his mood had shot higher far than present circumstances warranted. He was disposed to be optimistic. What had failed last night would certainly not fail again to-night. What was a day, after all? The Secretary's office might be troublesome, but not really troublesome for another twenty-four hours at least; and by then they would be well away.

This joyous confidence of his was his first misfortune. The next was that his good spirits were also shared by Miss Bishop, and that she bore no rancour. The two things conjoined to make the delay that in its consequences was so deplorable.

"Good-morning, sir," she hailed him pleasantly. "It's close upon a month since last I saw you."

"Twenty-one days to the hour," said he. "I've counted them."

"I vow I was beginning to believe you dead."

"I have to thank you for the wreath."

"The wreath?"

"To deck my grave," he explained.

"Must you ever be rallying?" she wondered, and looked at him gravely, remembering that it was his rallying on the last occasion had driven her away in dudgeon.

"A man must sometimes laugh at himself or go mad," said he. "Few realize it. That is why there are so many madmen in the world."

"You may laugh at yourself all you will, sir. But sometimes I think you laugh at me, which is not civil."

"Then, faith, you're wrong. I laugh only at the comic, and you are not comic at all."

"What am I, then?" she asked him, laughing.

A moment he pondered her, so fair and fresh to behold, so entirely maidenly and yet so entirely frank and unabashed.

"You are," he said, "the niece of the man who owns me his slave." But he spoke lightly. So lightly that she was encouraged to insistence.

"Nay, sir, that is an evasion. You shall answer me truthfully this morning."

"Truthfully? To answer you at all is a labour. But to answer truthfully! Oh, well, now, I should say of you that he'll be lucky who counts you his friend." It was in his mind to add more. But he left it there.

"That's mighty civil," said she. "You've a nice taste in compliments, Mr. Blood. Another in your place . . ."

"Faith, now, don't I know what another would have said? Don't I know my fellow-man at all?"

"Sometimes I think you do, and sometimes I think

you don't. Anyway, you don't know your fellow-woman. There was that affair of the Spaniards."

"Will ye never forget it?"

"Never."

"Bad cess to your memory. Is there no good in me at all that you could be dwelling on instead?"

"Oh, several things."

"For instance, now?" He was almost eager.

"You speak excellent Spanish."

"Is that all?" He sank back into dismay.

"Where did you learn it? Have you been in Spain?"

"That I have. I was two years in a Spanish prison."

"In prison?" Her tone suggested apprehensions in which he had no desire to leave her.

"As a prisoner of war," he explained. "I was taken fighting with the French — in French service, that is."

"But you're a doctor!" she cried.

"That's merely a diversion, I think. By trade I am a soldier — at least, it's a trade I followed for ten years. It brought me no great gear, but it served me better than medicine, which, as you may observe, has brought me into slavery. I'm thinking it's more pleasing in the sight of Heaven to kill men than to heal them. Sure it must be."

"But how came you to be a soldier, and to serve the French?"

"I am Irish, you see, and I studied medicine. Therefore — since it's a perverse nation we are — ... Oh, but it's a long story, and the Colonel will be expecting my return."

She was not in that way to be defrauded of her entertainment. If he would wait a moment they would ride back together. She had but come to enquire of the Governor's health at her uncle's request.

So he waited, and so they rode back together to Colonel Bishop's house. They rode very slowly, at a walking pace, and some whom they passed marvelled to see the doctor-slave on such apparently intimate terms with his owner's niece. One or two may have promised themselves that they would drop a hint to the Colonel. But the two rode oblivious of all others in the world that morning. He was telling her the story of his early turbulent days, and at the end of it he dwelt more fully than hitherto upon the manner of his arrest and trial.

The tale was barely done when they drew up at the Colonel's door, and dismounted, Peter Blood surrendering his nag to one of the negro grooms, who informed them that the Colonel was from home at the moment.

Even then they lingered a moment, she detaining him.

"I am sorry, Mr. Blood, that I did not know before," she said, and there was a suspicion of moisture in those clear hazel eyes. With a compelling friendliness she held out her hand to him.

"Why, what difference could it have made?" he asked.

"Some, I think. You have been very hardly used by Fate."

"Och, now . . ." He paused. His keen sapphire eyes considered her steadily a moment from under his level black brows. "It might have been worse," he said, with a significance which brought a tinge of colour to her cheeks and a flutter to her eyelids.

He stooped to kiss her hand before releasing it, and

she did not deny him. Then he turned and strode off towards the stockade a half-mile away, and a vision of her face went with him, tinted with a rising blush and a sudden unusual shyness. He forgot in that little moment that he was a rebel-convict with ten years of slavery before him; he forgot that he had planned an escape, which was to be carried into effect that night; forgot even the peril of discovery which as a result of the Governor's gout now overhung him.

CHAPTER VII

PIRATES

MR. JAMES NUTTALL made all speed, regardless of the heat, in his journey from Bridgetown to Colonel Bishop's plantation, and if ever man was built for speed in a hot climate that man was Mr. James Nuttall, with his short, thin body, and his long, fleshless legs. So withered was he that it was hard to believe there were any juices left in him, yet juices there must have been, for he was sweating violently by the time he reached the stockade.

At the entrance he almost ran into the overseer Kent, a squat, bow-legged animal with the arms of a Hercules and the jowl of a bulldog.

"I am seeking Doctor Blood," he announced breathlessly.

"You are in a rare haste," growled Kent. "What the devil is it? Twins?"

"Eh? Oh! Nay, nay. I'm not married, sir. It's a cousin of mine, sir."

"What is?"

"He is taken bad, sir," Nuttall lied promptly upon the cue that Kent himself had afforded him. "Is the doctor here?"

"That's his hut yonder." Kent pointed carelessly. "If he's not there, he'll be somewhere else." And he took himself off. He was a surly, ungracious beast at all times, readier with the lash of his whip than with his tongue.

Nuttall watched him go with satisfaction, and even noted the direction that he took. Then he plunged into the enclosure, to verify in mortification that Dr. Blood was not at home. A man of sense might have sat down and waited, judging that to be the quickest and surest way in the end. But Nuttall had no sense. He flung out of the stockade again, hesitated a moment as to which direction he should take, and finally decided to go any way but the way that Kent had gone. He sped across the parched savannah towards the sugar plantation which stood solid as a rampart and gleaming golden in the dazzling June sunshine. Avenues ·intersected the great blocks of ripening amber cane. In the distance down one of these he espied some slaves at work. Nuttall entered the avenue and advanced upon them. They eyed him dully, as he passed them. Pitt was not of their number, and he dared not ask for him. He continued his search for best part of an hour, up one of those lanes and then down another. Once an overseer challenged him, demanding to know his business. He was looking, he said, for Dr. Blood. His cousin was taken ill. The overseer bade him go to the devil, and get out of the plantation. Blood was not there. If he was anywhere he would be in his hut in the stockade.

Nuttall passed on, upon the understanding that he would go. But he went in the wrong direction; he went on towards the side of the plantation farthest from the stockade, towards the dense woods that fringed it there. The overseer was too contemptuous and perhaps too languid in the stifling heat of approaching noontide to correct his course.

Nuttall blundered to the end of the avenue, and

round the corner of it, and there ran into Pitt, alone, toiling with a wooden spade upon an irrigation channel. A pair of cotton drawers, loose and ragged, clothed him from waist to knee; above and below he was naked, save for a broad hat of plaited straw that sheltered his unkempt golden head from the rays of the tropical sun. At sight of him Nuttall returned thanks aloud to his Maker. Pitt stared at him, and the shipwright poured out his dismal news in a dismal tone. The sum of it was that he must have ten pounds from Blood that very morning or they were all undone. And all he got for his pains and his sweat was the condemnation of Jeremy Pitt.

"Damn you for a fool!" said the slave. "If it's Blood you're seeking, why are you wasting your time here?"

"I can't find him," bleated Nuttall. He was indignant at his reception. He forgot the jangled state of the other's nerves after a night of anxious wakefulness ending in a dawn of despair. "I thought that you . . ."

"You thought that I could drop my spade and go and seek him for you? Is that what you thought? My God! that our lives should depend upon such a dummerhead. While you waste your time here, the hours are passing! And if an overseer should catch you talking to me? How'll you explain it?"

For a moment Nuttall was bereft of speech by such ingratitude. Then he exploded.

"I would to Heaven I had never had no hand in this affair. I would so! I wish that . . ."

What else he wished was never known, for at that moment round the block of cane came a big man in biscuit-coloured taffetas followed by two negroes in cotton drawers who were armed with cutlasses. He was not ten yards away, but his approach over the soft, yielding marl had been unheard.

Mr. Nuttall looked wildly this way and that a moment, then bolted like a rabbit for the woods, thus doing the most foolish and betraying thing that in the circumstances it was possible for him to do. Pitt groaned and stood still, leaning upon his spade.

"Hi, there! Stop!" bawled Colonel Bishop after the fugitive, and added horrible threats tricked out with some rhetorical indecencies.

But the fugitive held amain, and never so much as turned his head. It was his only remaining hope that Colonel Bishop might not have seen his face; for the power and influence of Colonel Bishop was quite sufficient to hang any man whom he thought would be better dead.

Not until the runagate had vanished into the scrub did the planter sufficiently recover from his indignant amazement to remember the two negroes who followed at his heels like a brace of hounds. It was a bodyguard without which he never moved in his plantations since a slave had made an attack upon him and all but strangled him a couple of years ago.

"After him, you black swine!" he roared at them. But as they started he checked them. "Wait! Get to heel, damn you!"

It occurred to him that to catch and deal with the fellow there was not the need to go after him, and perhaps spend the day hunting him in that cursed wood. There was Pitt here ready to his hand, and Pitt should tell him the identity of his bashful friend,

and also the subject of that close and secret talk he
had disturbed. Pitt might, of course, be reluctant.
So much the worse for Pitt. The ingenious Colonel
Bishop knew a dozen ways — some of them quite
diverting — of conquering stubbornness in these convict dogs.

He turned now upon the slave a countenance that
was inflamed by heat internal and external, and a
pair of beady eyes that were alight with cruel intelligence. He stepped forward swinging his light bamboo
cane.

"Who was that runagate?" he asked with terrible
suavity.

Leaning over on his spade, Jeremy Pitt hung his
head a little, and shifted uncomfortably on his bare
feet. Vainly he groped for an answer in a mind that
could do nothing but curse the idiocy of Mr. James
Nuttall.

The planter's bamboo cane fell on the lad's naked
shoulders with stinging force.

"Answer me, you dog! What's his name?"

Jeremy looked at the burly planter out of sullen,
almost defiant eyes.

"I don't know," he said, and in his voice there was
a faint note at least of the defiance aroused in him by
a blow which he dared not, for his life's sake, return.
His body had remained unyielding under it, but the
spirit within writhed now in torment.

"You don't know? Well, here's to quicken your
wits." Again the cane descended. "Have you
thought of his name yet?"

"I have not."

"Stubborn, eh?" For a moment the Colonel leered.

Then his passion mastered him. "'Swounds! You impudent dog! D'you trifle with me? D'you think I'm to be mocked?"

Pitt shrugged, shifted sideways on his feet again, and settled into dogged silence. Few things are more provocative; and Colonel Bishop's temper was never one that required much provocation. Brute fury now awoke in him. Fiercely now he lashed those defence-less shoulders, accompanying each blow by blasphemy and foul abuse, until, stung beyond endurance, the lingering embers of his manhood fanned into momentary flame, Pitt sprang upon his tormentor.

But as he sprang, so also sprang the watchful blacks. Muscular bronze arms coiled crushingly about the frail white body, and in a moment the unfortunate slave stood powerless, his wrists pinioned behind him in a leathern thong.

Breathing hard, his face mottled, Bishop pondered him a moment. Then: "Fetch him along," he said.

Down the long avenue between those golden walls of cane standing some eight feet high, the wretched Pitt was thrust by his black captors in the Colonel's wake, stared at with fearful eyes by his fellow-slaves at work there. Despair went with him. What torments might immediately await him he cared little, horrible though he knew they would be. The real source of his mental anguish lay in the conviction that the elaborately planned escape from this unutterable hell was frustrated now in the very moment of execution.

They came out upon the green plateau and headed for the stockade and the overseer's white house. Pitt's eyes looked out over Carlisle Bay, of which this plateau commanded a clear view from the fort on one side to the long sheds of the wharf on the other. Along this wharf a few shallow boats were moored, and Pitt caught himself wondering which of these was the wherry in which with a little luck they might have been now at sea. Out over that sea his glance ranged miserably.

In the roads, standing in for the shore before a gentle breeze that scarcely ruffled the sapphire surface of the Caribbean, came a stately red-hulled frigate, flying the English ensign.

Colonel Bishop halted to consider her, shading his eyes with his fleshly hand. Light as was the breeze, the vessel spread no canvas to it beyond that of her foresail. Furled was her every other sail, leaving a clear view of the majestic lines of her hull, from towering stern castle to gilded beak-head that was aflash in the dazzling sunshine.

So leisurely an advance argued a master indifferently acquainted with these waters, who preferred to creep forward cautiously, sounding his way. At her present rate of progress it would be an hour, perhaps, before she came to anchorage within the harbour. And whilst the Colonel viewed her, admiring, perhaps, the·gracious beauty of her, Pitt was hurried forward into the stockade, and clapped into the stocks that stood there ready for slaves who required correction.

Colonel Bishop followed him presently, with leisurely, rolling gait.

"A mutinous cur that shows his fangs to his master must learn good manners at the cost of a striped hide," was all he said before setting about his executioner's job.

That with his own hands he should do that which most men of his station would, out of self-respect, have relegated to one of the negroes, gives you the measure of the man's beastliness. It was almost as if with relish, as if gratifying some feral instinct of cruelty, that he now lashed his victim about head and shoulders. Soon his cane was reduced to splinters by his violence. You know, perhaps, the sting of a flexible bamboo cane when it is whole. But do you realize its murderous quality when it has been split into several long lithe blades, each with an edge that is of the keenness of a knife?

When, at last, from very weariness, Colonel Bishop flung away the stump and thongs to which his cane had been reduced, the wretched slave's back was bleeding pulp from neck to waist.

As long as full sensibility remained, Jeremy Pitt had made no sound. But in a measure as from pain his senses were mercifully dulled, he sank forward in the stocks, and hung there now in a huddled heap, faintly moaning.

Colonel Bishop set his foot upon the crossbar, and leaned over his victim, a cruel smile on his full, coarse face.

"Let that teach you a proper submission," said he. "And now touching that shy friend of yours, you shall stay here without meat or drink — without meat or drink, d'ye hear me? — until you please to tell me his name and business." He took his foot from the bar. "When you've had enough of this, send me word, and we'll have the branding-irons to you."

On that he swung on his heel, and strode out of the stockade, his negroes following.

Pitt had heard him, as we hear things in our dreams. At the moment so spent was he by his cruel punishment, and so deep was the despair into which he had fallen, that he no longer cared whether he lived or died.

Soon, however, from the partial stupor which pain had mercifully induced, a new variety of pain aroused him. The stocks stood in the open under the full glare of the tropical sun, and its blistering rays streamed down upon that mangled, bleeding back until he felt as if flames of fire were searing it. And, soon, to this was added a torment still more unspeakable. Flies, the cruel flies of the Antilles, drawn by the scent of blood, descended in a cloud upon him.

Small wonder that the ingenious Colonel Bishop, who so well understood the art of loosening stubborn tongues, had not deemed it necessary to have recourse to other means of torture. Not all his fiendish cruelty could devise a torment more cruel, more unendurable than the torments Nature would here procure a man in Pitt's condition.

The slave writhed in his stocks until he was in danger of breaking his limbs, and writhing, screamed in agony.

Thus was he found by Peter Blood, who seemed to his troubled vision to materialize suddenly before him. Mr. Blood carried a large palmetto leaf. Having whisked away with this the flies that were devouring Jeremy's back, he slung it by a strip of fibre from the lad's neck, so that it protected him from further attacks as well as from the rays of the sun. Next, sitting down beside him, he drew the sufferer's head down on his own shoulder, and bathed his face from a pannikin of cold water. Pitt shuddered and moaned on a long, indrawn breath.

"Drink!" he gasped. "Drink, for the love of Christ!"

The pannikin was held to his quivering lips. He drank greedily, noisily, nor ceased until he had drained the vessel. Cooled and revived by the draught, he attempted to sit up.

"My back!" he screamed.

There was an unusual glint in Mr. Blood's eyes; his lips were compressed. But when he parted them to speak, his voice came cool and steady.

"Be easy, now. One thing at a time. Your back's taking no harm at all for the present, since I've covered it up. I'm wanting to know what's happened to you. D'ye think we can do without a navigator that ye go and provoke that beast Bishop until he all but kills you?"

Pitt sat up and groaned again. But this time his anguish was mental rather than physical.

"I don't think a navigator will be needed this time, Peter."

"What's that?" cried Mr. Blood.

Pitt explained the situation as briefly as he could, in a halting, gasping speech. "I'm to rot here until I tell him the identity of my visitor and his business."

Mr. Blood got up, growling in his throat. "Bad cess to the filthy slaver!" said he. "But it must be contrived, nevertheless. To the devil with Nuttall! Whether he gives surety for the boat or not, whether he explains it or not, the boat remains, and we're going, and you're coming with us."

"You're dreaming, Peter," said the prisoner.

"We're not going this time. The magistrates will confiscate the boat since the surety's not paid, even if when they press him Nuttall does not confess the whole plan and get us all branded on the forehead."

Mr. Blood turned away, and with agony in his eyes looked out to sea over the blue water by which he had so fondly hoped soon to be travelling back to freedom.

The great red ship had drawn considerably nearer shore by now. Slowly, majestically, she was entering the bay. Already one or two wherries were putting off from the wharf to board her. From where he stood, Mr. Blood could see the glinting of the brass cannons mounted on the prow above the curving beak-head, and he could make out the figure of a seaman in the forechains on her larboard side, leaning out to heave the lead.

An angry voice aroused him from his unhappy thoughts. "What the devil are you doing here?"

The returning Colonel Bishop came striding into the stockade, his negroes following ever.

Mr. Blood turned to face him, and over that swarthy countenance — which, indeed, by now was tanned to the golden brown of a half-caste Indian — a mask descended.

"Doing?" said he blandly. "Why, the duties of my office."

The Colonel, striding furiously forward, observed two things. The empty pannikin on the seat beside the prisoner, and the palmetto leaf protecting his back. "Have you dared to do this?" The veins on the planter's forehead stood out like cords.

"Of course I have." Mr. Blood's tone was one of faint surprise.

"I said he was to have neither meat nor drink until I ordered it."

"Sure, now, I never heard ye."

"You never heard me? How should you have heard me when you weren't here?"

"Then how did ye expect me to know what orders ye'd given?" Mr. Blood's tone was positively aggrieved. "All that I knew was that one of your slaves was being murthered by the sun and the flies. And I says to myself, this is one of the Colonel's slaves, and I'm the Colonel's doctor, and sure it's my duty to be looking after the Colonel's property. So I just gave the fellow a spoonful of water and covered his back from the sun. And wasn't I right now?"

"Right?" The Colonel was almost speechless.

"Be easy, now, be easy!" Mr. Blood implored him. "It's an apoplexy ye'll be contracting if ye give way to heat like this."

The planter thrust him aside with an imprecation, and stepping forward tore the palmetto leaf from the prisoner's back.

"In the name of humanity, now . . ." Mr. Blood was beginning.

The Colonel swung upon him furiously. "Out of this!" he commanded. "And don't come near him again until I send for you, unless you want to be served in the same way."

He was terrific in his menace, in his bulk, and in the power of him. But Mr. Blood never flinched. It came to the Colonel, as he found himself steadily regarded by those light-blue eyes that looked so arrestingly odd in that tawny face — like pale sapphires set in copper — that this rogue had for some time now been growing presumptuous. It was a matter that he must presently correct. Meanwhile Mr. Blood was speaking again, his tone quietly insistent.

"In the name of humanity," he repeated, "ye'll allow me to do what I can to ease his sufferings, or I swear to you that I'll forsake at once the duties of a doctor, and that it's devil another patient will I attend in this unhealthy island at all."

For an instant the Colonel was too amazed to speak. Then —

"By God!" he roared. "D'ye dare take that tone with me, you dog? D'ye dare to make terms with me?"

"I do that." The unflinching blue eyes looked squarely into the Colonel's, and there was a devil peeping out of them, the devil of recklessness that is born of despair.

Colonel Bishop considered him for a long moment in silence. "I've been too soft with you," he said at last. "But that's to be mended." And he tightened his lips. "I'll have the rods to you, until there's not an inch of skin left on your dirty back."

"Will ye so? And what would Governor Steed do, then?"

"Ye're not the only doctor on the island."

Mr. Blood actually laughed. "And will ye tell that to his excellency, him with the gout in his foot so bad that he can't stand? Ye know very well it's devil another doctor will he tolerate, being an intelligent man that knows what's good for him."

But the Colonel's brute passion thoroughly aroused was not so easily to be baulked. "If you're alive when my blacks have done with you, perhaps you'll come to your senses."

He swung to his negroes to issue an order. But it was never issued. At that moment a terrific rolling thunderclap drowned his voice and shook the very air. Colonel Bishop jumped, his negroes jumped with him, and so even did the apparently imperturbable Mr. Blood. Then the four of them stared together seawards.

Down in the bay all that could be seen of the great ship, standing now within a cable's-length of the fort, were her topmasts thrusting above a cloud of smoke in which she was enveloped. From the cliffs a flight of startled seabirds had risen to circle in the blue, giving tongue to their alarm, the plaintive curlew noisiest of all.

As those men stared from the eminence on which they stood, not yet understanding what had taken place, they saw the British Jack dip from the main truck and vanish into the rising cloud below. A moment more, and up through that cloud to replace the flag of England soared the gold and crimson banner of Castile. And then they understood.

"Pirates!" roared the Colonel, and again, "Pirates!"

Fear and incredulity were blent in his voice. He had paled under his tan until his face was the colour of clay, and there was a wild fury in his beady eyes. His negroes looked at him, grinning idiotically, all teeth and eyeballs.

CHAPTER VIII

SPANIARDS

THE stately ship that had been allowed to sail so leisurely into Carlisle Bay under her false colours was a Spanish privateer, coming to pay off some of the heavy debt piled up by the predaceous Brethren of the Coast, and the recent defeat by the *Pride of Devon* of two treasure galleons bound for Cadiz. It happened that the galleon which escaped in a more or less .crippled condition was commanded by Don Diego de Espinosa y Valdez, who was own brother to the Spanish Admiral Don Miguel de Espinosa, and who was also a very hasty, proud, and hot-tempered gentleman.

Galled by his defeat, and choosing to forget that his own conduct had invited it, he had sworn to teach the English a sharp lesson which they should remember. He would take a leaf out of the book of Morgan and those other robbers of the sea, and make a punitive raid upon an English settlement. Unfortunately for himself and for many others, his brother the Admiral was not at hand to restrain him when for this purpose he fitted out the *Cinco Llagas* at San Juan de Porto Rico. He chose for his objective the island of Barbados, whose natural strength was apt to render her defenders careless. He chose it also because thither had the *Pride of Devon* been tracked by his scouts, and he desired a measure of poetic justice to invest his vengeance. And he chose a moment when

there were no ships of war at anchor in Carlisle Bay.

He had succeeded so well in his intentions that he had aroused no suspicion until he saluted the fort at short range with a broadside of twenty guns.

And now the four gaping watchers in the stockade on the headland beheld the great ship creep forward under the rising cloud of smoke, her mainsail unfurled to increase her steering way, and go about close-hauled to bring her larboard guns to bear upon the unready fort.

With the crashing roar of that second broadside, Colonel Bishop awoke from stupefaction to a recollection of where his duty lay. In the town below drums were beating frantically, and a trumpet was bleating, as if the peril needed further advertising. As commander of the Barbados Militia, the place of Colonel Bishop was at the head of his scanty troops, in that fort which the Spanish guns were pounding into rubble.

Remembering it, he went off at the double, despite his bulk and the heat, his negroes trotting after him.

Mr. Blood turned to Jeremy Pitt. He laughed grimly. "Now that," said he, "is what I call a timely interruption. Though what'll come of it," he added as an afterthought, "the devil himself knows."

As a third broadside was thundering forth, he picked up the palmetto leaf and carefully replaced it on the back of his fellow-slave.

And then into the stockade, panting and sweating, came Kent followed by best part of a score of plantation workers, some of whom were black and all of whom were in a state of panic. He led them into the low white house, to bring them forth again, within a moment, as it seemed, armed now with muskets and hangers and some of them equipped with bandoleers.

By this time the rebels-convict were coming in, in twos and threes, having abandoned their work upon finding themselves unguarded and upon scenting the general dismay.

Kent paused a moment, as his hastily armed guard dashed forth, to fling an order to those slaves.

"To the woods!" he bade them. "Take to the woods, and lie close there, until this is over, and we've gutted these Spanish swine."

On that he went off in haste after his men, who were to be added to those massing in the town, so as to oppose and overwhelm the Spanish landing parties.

The slaves would have obeyed him on the instant but for Mr. Blood.

"What need for haste, and in this heat?" quoth he. He was surprisingly cool, they thought. "Maybe there'll be no need to take to the woods at all, and, anyway, it will be time enough to do so when the Spaniards are masters of the town."

And so, joined now by the other stragglers, and numbering in all a round score — rebels-convict all — they stayed to watch from their vantage-ground the fortunes of the furious battle that was being waged below.

The landing was contested by the militia and by every islander capable of bearing arms with the fierce resoluteness of men who knew that no quarter was to be expected in defeat. The ruthlessness of Spanish soldiery was a byword, and not at his worst had Morgan or L'Ollonais ever perpetrated such horrors as those of which these Castilian gentlemen were capable.

But this Spanish commander knew his business, which was more than could truthfully be said for the Barbados Militia. Having gained the advantage of a surprise blow, which had put the fort out of action, he soon showed them that he was master of the situation. His guns turned now upon the open space behind the mole, where the incompetent Bishop had marshalled his men, tore the militia into bloody rags, and covered the landing parties which were making the shore in their own boats and in several of those which had rashly gone out to the great ship before her identity was revealed.

All through the scorching afternoon the battle went on, the rattle and crack of musketry penetrating ever deeper into the town to show that the defenders were being driven steadily back. By sunset two hundred and fifty Spaniards were masters of Bridgetown, the islanders were disarmed, and at Government House, Governor Steed — his gout forgotten in his panic — supported by Colonel Bishop and some lesser officers, was being informed by Don Diego, with an urbanity that was itself a mockery, of the sum that would be required in ransom.

For a hundred thousand pieces of eight and fifty head of cattle, Don Diego would forbear from reducing the place to ashes. And what time that suave and courtly commander was settling these details with the apoplectic British Governor, the Spaniards were smashing and looting, feasting, drinking, and ravaging after the hideous manner of their kind.

Mr. Blood, greatly daring, ventured down at dusk into the town. What he saw there is recorded by Jeremy Pitt — to whom he subsequently related it —

in that voluminous log from which the greater part of my narrative is derived. I have no intention of repeating any of it here. It is all too loathsome and nauseating, incredible, indeed, that men however abandoned could ever descend such an abyss of bestial cruelty and lust.

What he saw was fetching him in haste and white-faced out of that hell again, when in a narrow street a girl hurtled into him, wild-eyed, her unbound hair streaming behind her as she ran. After her, laughing and cursing in a breath, came a heavy-booted Spaniard. Almost he was upon her, when suddenly Mr. Blood got in his way. The doctor had taken a sword from a dead man's side some little time before and armed himself with it against an emergency.

As the Spaniard checked in anger and surprise, he caught in the dusk the livid gleam of that sword which Mr. Blood had quickly unsheathed.

"Ah, perro inglés!" he shouted, and flung forward to his death.

"It's hoping I am ye're in a fit state to meet your Maker," said Mr. Blood, and ran him through the body. He did the thing skilfully: with the combined skill of swordsman and surgeon. The man sank in a hideous heap without so much as a groan.

Mr. Blood swung to the girl, who leaned panting and sobbing against a wall. He caught her by the wrist.

"Come!" he said.

But she hung back, resisting him by her weight. "Who are you?" she demanded wildly.

"Will ye wait to see my credentials?" he snapped. Steps were clattering towards them from beyond the corner round which she had fled from that Spanish ruffian. "Come," he urged again. And this time, re-assured perhaps by his clear English speech, she went without further questions.

They sped down an alley and then up another, by great good fortune meeting no one, for already they were on the outskirts of the town. They won out of it, and white-faced, physically sick, Mr. Blood dragged her almost at a run up the hill towards Colonel Bishop's house. He told her briefly who and what he was, and thereafter there was no conversation between them until they reached the big white house. It was all in darkness, which at least was reassuring. If the Spaniards had reached it, there would be lights. He knocked, but had to knock again and yet again before he was answered. Then it was by a voice from a window above.

"Who is there?" The voice was Miss Bishop's, a little tremulous, but unmistakably her own.

Mr. Blood almost fainted in relief. He had been imagining the unimaginable. He had pictured her down in that hell out of which he had just come. He had conceived that she might have followed her uncle into Bridgetown, or committed some other impru-dence, and he turned cold from head to foot at the mere thought of what might have happened to her.

"It is I — Peter Blood," he gasped.

"What do you want?"

It is doubtful whether she would have come down to open. For at such a time as this it was no more than likely that the wretched plantation slaves might be in revolt and prove as great a danger as the Spaniards.

But at the sound of her voice, the girl Mr. Blood had rescued peered up through the gloom.

"Arabella!" she called. "It is I, Mary Traill."

"Mary!" The voice ceased above on that exclamation, the head was withdrawn. After a brief pause the door gaped wide. Beyond it in the wide hall stood Miss Arabella, a slim, virginal figure in white, mysteriously revealed in the gleam of a single candle which she carried.

Mr. Blood strode in followed by his distraught companion, who, falling upon Arabella's slender bosom, surrendered herself to a passion of tears. But he wasted no time.

"Whom have you here with you? What servants?" he demanded sharply.

The only male was James, an old negro groom.

"The very man," said Blood. "Bid him get out horses. Then away with you to Speightstown, or even farther north, where you will be safe. Here you are in danger — in dreadful danger."

"But I thought the fighting was over . . ." she was beginning, pale and startled.

"So it is. But the deviltry's only beginning. Miss Traill will tell you as you go. In God's name, madam, take my word for it, and do as I bid you."

"He . . . he saved me," sobbed Miss Traill.

"Saved you?" Miss Bishop was aghast. "Saved you from what, Mary?"

"Let that wait," snapped Mr. Blood almost angrily. "You've all the night for chattering when you're out of this, and away beyond their reach. Will you please call James, and do as I say — and at once!"

"You are very peremptory . . ."

"Oh, my God! I am peremptory! Speak, Miss Traill, tell her whether I've cause to be peremptory."

"Yes, yes," the girl cried, shuddering. "Do as he says — Oh, for pity's sake, Arabella."

Miss Bishop went off, leaving Mr. Blood and Miss Traill alone again.

"I . . . I shall never forget what you did, sir," said she, through her diminishing tears. She was a slight wisp of a girl, a child, no more.

"I've done better things in my time. That's why I'm here," said Mr. Blood, whose mood seemed to be snappy.

She didn't pretend to understand him, and she didn't make the attempt.

"Did you . . . did you kill him?" she asked, fearfully.

He stared at her in the flickering candlelight. "I hope so. It is very probable, and it doesn't matter at all," he said. "What matters is that this fellow James should fetch the horses." And he was stamping off to accelerate these preparations for departure, when her voice arrested him.

"Don't leave me! Don't leave me here alone!" she cried in terror.

He paused. He turned and came slowly back. Standing above her he smiled upon her.

"There, there! You've no cause for alarm. It's all over now. You'll be away soon — away to Speights-town, where you'll be quite safe."

The horses came at last — four of them, for in addition to James who was to act as her guide, Miss Bishop had her woman, who was not to be left behind.

Mr. Blood lifted the slight weight of Mary Traill to

her horse, then turned to say good-bye to Miss Bishop,
who was already mounted. He said it, and seemed to
have something to add. But whatever it was, it remained unspoken.

The horses started, and receded into the sapphire
starlit night, leaving him standing there before
Colonel Bishop's door. The last he heard of them was
Mary Traill's childlike voice calling back on a quaver-
ing note —

"I shall never forget what you did, Mr. Blood. I
shall never forget."

But as it was not the voice he desired to hear, the
assurance brought him little satisfaction. He stood
there in the dark, watching the fireflies amid the rho-
dodendrons, till the hoofbeats had faded. Then he
sighed and roused himself. He had much to do. His
journey into the town had not been one of idle curiosity to see how the Spaniards conducted themselves
in victory. It had been inspired by a very different
purpose, and he had gained in the course of it all the
information he desired. He had an extremely busy
night before him, and must be moving.

He went off briskly in the direction of the stockade,
where his fellow-slaves awaited him in deep anxiety
and some hope.

CHAPTER IX

THE REBELS-CONVICT

THERE were, when the purple gloom of the tropical night descended upon the Caribbean, not more than ten men on guard aboard the *Cinco Llagas*, so confident — and with good reason — were the Spaniards of the complete subjection of the islanders. And when I say that there were ten men on guard, I state rather the purpose for which they were left aboard than the duty which they fulfilled. As a matter of fact, whilst the main body of the Spaniards feasted and rioted ashore, the Spanish gunner and his crew — who had so nobly done their duty and ensured the easy victory of the day — were feasting on the gun-deck upon the wine and the fresh meats fetched out to them from shore. Above, two sentinels only kept vigil, at stem and stern. Nor were they as vigilant as they should have been, or else they must have observed the two wherries that under cover of the darkness came gliding from the wharf, with well-greased rowlocks, to bring up in silence under the great ship's quarter.

From the gallery aft still hung the ladder by which Don Diego had descended to the boat that had taken him ashore. The sentry on guard in the stern, coming presently round this gallery, was suddenly confronted by the black shadow of a man standing before him at the head of the ladder.

"Who's there?" he asked, but without alarm, supposing it one of his fellows.

"It is I," softly answered Peter Blood in the fluent Castilian of which he was master.

"Is it you, Pedro?" The Spaniard came a step nearer.

"Peter is my name; but I doubt I'll not be the Peter you're expecting."

"How?" quoth the sentry, checking.

"This way," said Mr. Blood.

The wooden taffrail was a low one, and the Spaniard was taken completely by surprise. Save for the splash he made as he struck the water, narrowly missing one of the crowded boats that waited under the counter, not a sound announced his misadventure. Armed as he was with corselet, cuissarts, and headpiece, he sank to trouble them no more.

"Whist!" hissed Mr. Blood to his waiting rebels-convict. "Come on, now, and without noise."

Within five minutes they had swarmed aboard, the entire twenty of them overflowing from that narrow gallery and crouching on the quarter-deck itself. Lights showed ahead. Under the great lantern in the prow they saw the black figure of the other sentry, pacing on the forecastle. From below sounds reached them of the orgy on the gun-deck: a rich male voice was singing an obscene ballad to which the others chanted in chorus:

"Y estos son los usos de Castilla y de Leon!"

"From what I've seen to-day I can well believe it," said Mr. Blood, and whispered: "Forward — after me."

Crouching low, they glided, noiseless as shadows, to the quarter-deck rail, and thence slipped without sound down into the waist. Two thirds of them were armed with muskets, some of which they had found in the overseer's house, and others supplied from the secret hoard that Mr. Blood had so laboriously assembled against the day of escape. The remainder were equipped with knives and cutlasses.

In the vessel's waist they hung awhile, until Mr. Blood had satisfied himself that no other sentinel showed above decks but that inconvenient fellow in the prow. Their first attention must be for him. Mr. Blood, himself, crept forward with two companions, leaving the others in the charge of that Nathaniel Hagthorpe whose sometime commission in the King's Navy gave him the best title to this office.

Mr. Blood's absence was brief. When he rejoined his comrades there was no watch above the Spaniards' decks.

Meanwhile the revellers below continued to make merry at their ease in the conviction of complete security. The garrison of Barbados was overpowered and disarmed, and their companions were ashore in complete possession of the town, glutting themselves hideously upon the fruits of victory. What, then, was there to fear? Even when their quarters were invaded and they found themselves surrounded by a score of wild, hairy, half-naked men, who — save that they appeared once to have been white — looked like a horde of savages, the Spaniards could not believe their eyes. Who could have dreamed that a handful of forgotten plantation-slaves would have dared to take so much upon themselves?

The half-drunken Spaniards, their laughter suddenly quenched, the song perishing on their lips, stared, stricken and bewildered, at the levelled muskets by which they were checkmated.

And then, from out of this uncouth pack of savages that beset them, stepped a slim, tall fellow with light-blue eyes in a tawny face, eyes in which glinted the light of a wicked humour. He addressed them in the purest Castilian.

"You will save yourselves pain and trouble by regarding yourselves my prisoners, and suffering yourselves to be quietly bestowed out of harm's way."

"Name of God!" swore the gunner, which did no justice at all to an amazement beyond expression.

"If you please," said Mr. Blood, and thereupon those gentlemen of Spain were induced without further trouble beyond a musket prod or two to drop through a scuttle to the deck below.

After that the rebels–convict refreshed themselves with the good things in the consumption of which they had interrupted the Spaniards. To taste palatable Christian food after months of salt fish and maize dumplings was in itself a feast to these unfortunates. But there were no excesses. Mr. Blood saw to that, although it required all the firmness of which he was capable.

Dispositions were to be made without delay against that which must follow before they could abandon themselves fully to the enjoyment of their victory. This, after all, was no more than a preliminary skirmish, although it was one that afforded them the key to the situation. It remained to dispose so that the utmost profit might be drawn from it. Those dispositions occupied some very considerable portion of the night. But, at least, they were complete before the sun peeped over the shoulder of Mount Hillbay to shed his light upon a day of some surprises.

It was soon after sunrise that the rebel-convict who paced the quarter-deck in Spanish corselet and head-piece, a Spanish musket on his shoulder, announced the approach of a boat. It was Don Diego de Espinosa y Valdez coming aboard with four great treasure-chests, containing each twenty-five thousand pieces of eight, the ransom delivered to him at dawn by Governor Steed. He was accompanied by his son, Don Esteban, and by six men who took the oars.

Aboard the frigate all was quiet and orderly as it should be. She rode at anchor, her larboard to the shore, and the main ladder on her starboard side. Round to this came the boat with Don Diego and his treasure. Mr. Blood had disposed effectively. It was not for nothing that he had served under de Ruyter. The swings were waiting, and the windlass manned. Below, a gun-crew held itself in readiness under the command of Ogle, who — as I have said — had been a gunner in the Royal Navy before he went in for politics and followed the fortunes of the Duke of Monmouth. He was a sturdy, resolute fellow who inspired confidence by the very confidence he displayed in himself.

Don Diego mounted the ladder and stepped upon the deck, alone, and entirely unsuspicious. What should the poor man suspect?

Before he could even look round, and survey this guard drawn up to receive him, a tap over the head with a capstan bar efficiently handled by Hagthorpe put him to sleep without the least fuss.

He was carried away to his cabin, whilst the treasure-chests, handled by the men he had left in the boat, were being hauled to the deck. That being satisfactorily accomplished, Don Esteban and the fellows who had manned the boat came up the ladder, one by one, to be handled with the same quiet efficiency. Peter Blood had a genius for these things, and almost, I suspect, an eye for the dramatic. Dramatic, certainly, was the spectacle now offered to the survivors of the raid.

With Colonel Bishop at their head, and gout-ridden Governor Steed sitting on the ruins of a wall beside him, they glumly watched the departure of the eight boats containing the weary Spanish ruffians who had glutted themselves with rapine, murder, and violences unspeakable.

They looked on, between relief at this departure of their remorseless enemies, and despair at the wild ravages which, temporarily at least, had wrecked the prosperity and happiness of that little colony.

The boats pulled away from the shore, with their loads of laughing, jeering Spaniards, who were still flinging taunts across the water at their surviving victims. They had come midway between the wharf and the ship, when suddenly the air was shaken by the boom of a gun.

A round shot struck the water within a fathom of the foremost boat, sending a shower of spray over its occupants. They paused at their oars, astounded into silence for a moment. Then speech burst from them like an explosion. Angrily voluble they anathematized this dangerous carelessness on the part of their gunner, who should know better than to fire a salute from a cannon loaded with shot. They were still cursing him when a second shot, better aimed than the first, came to crumple one of the boats into splinters, flinging its crew, dead and living, into the water.

But if it silenced these, it gave tongue, still more angry, vehement, and bewildered to the crews of the other seven boats. From each the suspended oars stood out poised over the water, whilst on their feet in the excitement the Spaniards screamed oaths at the ship, begging Heaven and Hell to inform them what madman had been let loose among her guns.

Plump into their middle came a third shot, smashing a second boat with fearful execution. Followed again a moment of awful silence, then among those Spanish pirates all was gibbering and jabbering and splashing of oars, as they attempted to pull in every direction at once. Some were for going ashore, others for heading straight to the vessel and there discovering what might be amiss. That something was very gravely amiss there could be no further doubt, particularly as whilst they discussed and fumed and cursed two more shots came over the water to account for yet a third of their boats.

The resolute Ogle was making excellent practice, and fully justifying his claims to know something of gunnery. In their consternation the Spaniards had simplified his task by huddling their boats together.

After the fourth shot, opinion was no longer divided amongst them. As with one accord they went about, or attempted to do so, for before they had accomplished it two more of their boats had been sunk.

The three boats that remained, without concerning themselves with their more unfortunate fellows, who were struggling in the water, headed back for the wharf at speed.

If the Spaniards understood nothing of all this, the forlorn islanders ashore understood still less, until to help their wits they saw the flag of Spain come down from the mainmast of the *Cinco Llagas*, and the flag of England soar to its empty place. Even then some bewilderment persisted, and it was with fearful eyes that they observed the return of their enemies, who might vent upon them the ferocity aroused by these extraordinary events.

Ogle, however, continued to give proof that his knowledge of gunnery was not of yesterday. After the fleeing Spaniards went his shots. The last of their boats flew into splinters as it touched the wharf, and its remains were buried under a shower of loosened masonry.

That was the end of this pirate crew, which not ten minutes ago had been laughingly counting up the pieces of eight that would fall to the portion of each for his share in that act of villainy. Close upon threescore survivors contrived to reach the shore. Whether they had cause for congratulation, I am unable to say in the absence of any records in which their fate may be traced. That lack of records is in itself eloquent. We know that they were made fast as they landed, and considering the offence they had given I am not disposed to doubt that they had every reason to regret the survival.

The mystery of the succour that had come at the eleventh hour to wreak vengeance upon the Spaniards, and to preserve for the island the extortionate ransom of a hundred thousand pieces of eight, remained yet to be probed. That the *Cinco Llagas* was now in friendly hands could no longer be doubted after the proofs it had given. But who, the people of Bridgetown asked one another, were the men in possession of her, and whence had they come? The only possible assumption ran the truth very closely. A resolute party of islanders must have got aboard during the night, and seized the ship. It remained to ascertain the precise identity of these mysterious saviours, and do them fitting honour.

Upon this errand — Governor Steed's condition not permitting him to go in person — went Colonel Bishop as the Governor's deputy, attended by two officers.

As he stepped from the ladder into the vessel's waist, the Colonel beheld there, beside the main hatch, the four treasure-chests, the contents of one of which had been contributed almost entirely by himself. It was a gladsome spectacle, and his eyes sparkled in beholding it.

Ranged on either side, athwart the deck, stood a score of men in two well-ordered files, with breasts and backs of steel, polished Spanish morions on their heads, overshadowing their faces, and muskets ordered at their sides.

Colonel Bishop could not be expected to recognize at a glance in these upright, furbished, soldierly figures the ragged, unkempt scarecrows that but yesterday had been toiling in his plantations. Still less could he be expected to recognize at once the courtly gentleman who advanced to greet him — a lean, graceful gentleman, dressed in the Spanish fashion, all in black with silver lace, a gold-hilted sword dangling beside him from a gold embroidered baldrick, a broad castor with a sweeping plume set above carefully curled ringlets of deepest black.

"Be welcome aboard the *Cinco Llagas*, Colonel, darling," a voice vaguely familiar addressed the planter. "We've made the best of the Spaniards' wardrobe in honour of this visit, though it was scarcely yourself we had dared hope to expect. You find yourself among friends — old friends of yours, all."

The Colonel stared in stupefaction. Mr. Blood tricked out in all this splendour — indulging therein his natural taste — his face carefully shaven, his hair as carefully dressed, seemed transformed into a younger man. The fact is he looked no more than the thirty-three years he counted to his age.

"Peter Blood!" It was an ejaculation of amazement. Satisfaction followed swiftly. "Was it you, then . . .?"

"Myself it was — myself and these, my good friends and yours." Mr. Blood tossed back the fine lace from his wrist, to wave a hand towards the file of men standing to attention there.

The Colonel looked more closely. "Gad's my life!" he crowed on a note of foolish jubilation. "And it was with these fellows that you took the Spaniard and turned the tables on those dogs! Oddswounds! It was heroic!"

"Heroic, is it? Bedad, it's epic! Ye begin to perceive the breadth and depth of my genius."

Colonel Bishop sat himself down on the hatch-coaming, took off his broad hat, and mopped his brow.

"Y'amaze me!" he gasped. "On my soul, y'amaze me! To have recovered the treasure and to have seized this fine ship and all she'll hold! It will be something to set against the other losses we have suffered. As Gad's my life, you deserve well for this."

"I am entirely of your opinion."

"Damme! You all deserve well, and damme, you shall find me grateful."

"That's as it should be," said Mr. Blood. "The question is how well we deserve, and how grateful shall we find you?"

Colonel Bishop considered him. There was a shadow of surprise in his face.

"Why — his excellency shall write home an account of your exploit, and maybe some portion of your sentences shall be remitted."

"The generosity of King James is well known," sneered Nathaniel Hagthorpe, who was standing by, and amongst the ranged rebels-convict some one ventured to laugh.

Colonel Bishop started up. He was pervaded by the first pang of uneasiness. It occurred to him that all here might not be as friendly as appeared.

"And there's another matter," Mr. Blood resumed. "There's a matter of a flogging that's due to me. Ye're a man of your word in such matters, Colonel — if not perhaps in others — and ye said, I think, that ye'd not leave a square inch of skin on my back."

The planter waved the matter aside. Almost it seemed to offend him.

"Tush! Tush! After this splendid deed of yours, do you suppose I can be thinking of such things?"

"I'm glad ye feel like that about it. But I'm thinking it's mighty lucky for me the Spaniards didn't come to-day instead of yesterday, or it's in the same plight as Jeremy Pitt I'd be this minute. And in that case where was the genius that would have turned the tables on these rascally Spaniards?"

"Why speak of it now?"

"I must, Colonel, darling. Ye've worked a deal of wickedness and cruelty in your time, and I want this to be a lesson to you, a lesson that ye'll remember — for the sake of others who may come after us. There's Jeremy up there in the round-house with a back that's every colour of the rainbow; and the poor lad'll not be himself again for a month. And if it hadn't been for the Spaniards maybe it's dead he'd be by now, and maybe myself with him."

Hagthorpe lounged forward. He was a fairly tall, vigorous man with a clear-cut, attractive face which in itself announced his breeding.

"Why will you be wasting words on the hog?" wondered that sometime officer in the Royal Navy. "Fling him overboard and have done with him."

The Colonel's eyes bulged in his head. "What the devil do you mean?" he blustered.

"It's the lucky man ye are entirely, Colonel, though ye don't guess the source of your good fortune."

And now another intervened — the brawny, one-eyed Wolverstone, less mercifully disposed than his more gentlemanly fellow-convict.

"String him up from the yardarm," he cried, his deep voice harsh and angry, and more than one of the slaves standing to their arms made echo.

Colonel Bishop trembled. Mr. Blood turned. He was quite calm.

"If you please, Wolverstone," said he, "I conduct affairs in my own way. That is the pact. You'll please to remember it." His eyes looked along the ranks, making it plain that he addressed them all. "I desire that Colonel Bishop should have his life. One reason is that I require him as a hostage. If ye insist on hanging him, ye'll have to hang me with him, or in the alternative I'll go ashore."

He paused. There was no answer. But they stood hang-dog and half-mutinous before him, save Hagthorpe, who shrugged and smiled wearily.

Mr. Blood resumed: "Ye'll please to understand that aboard a ship there is one captain. So." He swung again to the startled Colonel. "Though I promise you your life, I must — as you've heard — keep you aboard as a hostage for the good behaviour of Governor Steed and what's left of the fort until we put to sea."

"Until you . . ." Horror prevented Colonel Bishop from echoing the remainder of that incredible speech.

"Just so," said Peter Blood, and he turned to the officers who had accompanied the Colonel. "The boat is waiting, gentlemen. You'll have heard what I said. Convey it with my compliments to his excellency."

"But, sir . . ." one of them began.

"There is no more to be said, gentlemen. My name is Blood — Captain Blood, if you please, of this ship the *Cinco Llagas*, taken as a prize of war from Don Diego de Espinosa y Valdez, who is my prisoner aboard. You are to understand that I have turned the tables on more than the Spaniards. There's the ladder. You'll find it more convenient than being heaved over the side, which is what'll happen if you linger."

They went, though not without some hustling, regardless of the bellowings of Colonel Bishop, whose monstrous rage was fanned by terror at finding himself at the mercy of these men of whose cause to hate him he was very fully conscious.

A half-dozen of them, apart from Jeremy Pitt, who was utterly incapacitated for the present, possessed a superficial knowledge of seamanship. Hagthorpe, although he had been a fighting officer, untrained in navigation, knew how to handle a ship, and under his directions they set about getting under way.

The anchor catted, and the mainsail unfurled, they stood out for the open before a gentle breeze, without interference from the fort.

As they were running close to the headland east of the bay, Peter Blood returned to the Colonel, who, under guard and panic-stricken, had dejectedly resumed his seat on the coamings of the main hatch.

"Can ye swim, Colonel?"

Colonel Bishop looked up. His great face was yellow and seemed in that moment of a preternatural flabbiness; his beady eyes were beadier than ever.

"As your doctor, now, I prescribe a swim to cool the excessive heat of your humours." Blood delivered the explanation pleasantly, and, receiving still no answer from the Colonel, continued: "It's a mercy for you I'm not by nature as bloodthirsty as some of my friends here. And it's the devil's own labour I've had to prevail upon them not to be vindictive. I doubt if ye're worth the pains I've taken for you."

He was lying. He had no doubt at all. Had he followed his own wishes and instincts, he would certainly have strung the Colonel up, and accounted it a meritorious deed. It was the thought of Arabella Bishop that had urged him to mercy, and had led him to oppose the natural vindictiveness of his fellow-slaves until he had been in danger of precipitating a mutiny. It was entirely to the fact that the Colonel was her uncle, although he did not even begin to suspect such a cause, that he owed such mercy as was now being shown him.

"You shall have a chance to swim for it," Peter Blood continued. "It's not above a quarter of a mile to the headland yonder, and with ordinary luck ye should manage it. Faith, you're fat enough to float. Come on! Now, don't be hesitating or it's a long voyage ye'll be going with us, and the devil knows what may happen to you. You're not loved any more than you deserve."

Colonel Bishop mastered himself, and rose. A merciless despot, who had never known the need for restraint in all these years, he was doomed by ironic fate to practise restraint in the very moment when his feelings had reached their most violent intensity.

Peter Blood gave an order. A plank was run out over the gunwale, and lashed down.

"If you please, Colonel," said he, with a graceful flourish of invitation.

The Colonel looked at him, and there was hell in his glance. Then, taking his resolve, and putting the best face upon it, since no other could help him here, he kicked off his shoes, peeled off his fine coat of biscuit-coloured taffetas, and climbed upon the plank.

A moment he paused, steadied by a hand that

clutched the ratlines, looking down in terror at the green water rushing past some five-and-twenty feet below.

"Just take a little walk, Colonel, darling," said a smooth, mocking voice behind him.

Still clinging, Colonel Bishop looked round in hesitation, and saw the bulwarks lined with swarthy faces — the faces of men that as lately as yesterday would have turned pale under his frown, faces that were now all wickedly agrin.

For a moment rage stamped out his fear. He cursed them aloud venomously and incoherently, then loosed his hold and stepped out upon the plank. Three steps he took before he lost his balance and went tumbling into the green depths below.

When he came to the surface again, gasping for air, the *Cinco Llagas* was already some furlongs to leeward. But the roaring cheer of mocking valediction from the rebels-convict reached him across the water, to drive the iron of impotent rage deeper into his soul.

CHAPTER X

DON DIEGO

D ON DIEGO DE ESPINOSA Y VALDEZ awoke, and with languid eyes in aching head, he looked round the cabin, which was flooded with sunlight from the square windows astern. Then he uttered a moan, and closed his eyes again, impelled to this by the monstrous ache in his head. Lying thus, he attempted to think, to locate himself in time and space. But between the pain in his head and the confusion in his mind, he found coherent thought impossible.

An indefinite sense of alarm drove him to open his eyes again, and once more to consider his surroundings.

There could be no doubt that he lay in the great cabin of his own ship, the *Cinco Llagas*, so that his vague disquiet must be, surely, ill-founded. And yet, stirrings of memory coming now to the assistance of reflection, compelled him uneasily to insist that here something was not as it should be. The low position of the sun, flooding the cabin.with golden light from those square ports astern, suggested to him at first that it was early morning, on the assumption that the vessel was headed westward. Then the alternative occurred to him. They might be sailing eastward, in which case the time of day would be late afternoon. That they were sailing he could feel from the gentle forward heave of the vessel under him. But how did they come to be sailing, and he, the master, not to know whether their course lay east or west, not to be able to recollect whither they were bound?

His mind went back over the adventure of yesterday, if of yesterday it was. He was clear on the matter of the easily successful raid upon the Island of Barbados; every detail stood vividly in his memory up to the moment at which, returning aboard, he had stepped on to his own deck again. There memory abruptly and inexplicably ceased.

He was beginning to torture his mind with conjecture, when the door opened, and to Don Diego's increasing mystification he beheld his best suit of clothes step into the cabin. It was a singularly elegant and characteristically Spanish suit of black taffetas with silver lace that had been made for him a year ago in Cadiz, and he knew each detail of it so well that it was impossible he could now be mistaken.

The suit paused to close the door, then advanced towards the couch on which Don Diego was extended, and inside the suit came a tall, slender gentleman of about Don Diego's own height and shape. Seeing the wide, startled eyes of the Spaniard upon him, the gentleman lengthened his stride.

"Awake, eh?" said he in Spanish.

The recumbent man looked up bewildered into a pair of light-blue eyes that regarded him out of a tawny, sardonic face set in a cluster of black ringlets. But he was too bewildered to make any answer.

The stranger's fingers touched the top of Don Diego's head, whereupon Don Diego winced and cried out in pain.

"Tender, eh?" said the stranger. He took Don

Diego's wrist between thumb and second finger. And then, at last, the intrigued Spaniard spoke.

"Are you a doctor?"

"Among other things." The swarthy gentleman continued his study of the patient's pulse. "Firm and regular," he announced at last, and dropped the wrist. "You've taken no great harm."

Don Diego struggled up into a sitting position on the red velvet couch.

"Who the devil are you?" he asked. "And what the devil are you doing in my clothes and aboard my ship?"

The level black eyebrows went up, a faint smile curled the lips of the long mouth.

"You are still delirious, I fear. This is not your ship. This is my ship, and these are my clothes."

"Your ship?" quoth the other, aghast, and still more aghast he added: "Your clothes? But ... Then ..." Wildly his eyes looked about him. They scanned the cabin once again, scrutinizing each familiar object. "Am I mad?" he asked at last. "Surely this ship is the *Cinco Llagas?*"

"The *Cinco Llagas* it is."

"Then ..." The Spaniard broke off. His glance grew still more troubled. "Valga me Dios!" he cried out, like a man in anguish. "Will you tell me also that you are Don Diego de Espinosa?"

"Oh, no, my name is Blood — Captain Peter Blood. This ship, like this handsome suit of clothes, is mine by right of conquest. Just as you, Don Diego, are my prisoner."

Startling as was the explanation, yet it proved soothing to Don Diego, being so much less startling than the things he was beginning to imagine.

"But ... Are you not Spanish, then?"

"You flatter my Castilian accent. I have the honour to be Irish. You were thinking that a miracle had happened. So it has — a miracle wrought by my genius, which is considerable."

Succinctly now Captain Blood dispelled the mystery by a relation of the facts. It was a narrative that painted red and white by turns the Spaniard's countenance. He put a hand to the back of his head, and there discovered, in confirmation of the story, a lump as large as a pigeon's egg. Lastly, he stared wild-eyed at the sardonic Captain Blood.

"And my son? What of my son?" he cried out.
"He was in the boat that brought me aboard."

"Your son is safe; he and the boat's crew together with your gunner and his men are snugly in irons under hatches."

Don Diego sank back on the couch, his glittering dark eyes fixed upon the tawny face above him. He composed himself. After all, he possessed the stoicism proper to his desperate trade. The dice had fallen against him in this venture. The tables had been turned upon him in the very moment of success. He accepted the situation with the fortitude of a fatalist.

With the utmost calm he enquired:

"And now, Señor Capitan?"

"And now," said Captain Blood — to give him the title he had assumed — "being a humane man, I am sorry to find that ye're not dead from the tap we gave you. For it means that you'll be put to the trouble of dying all over again."

"Ah!" Don Diego drew a deep breath. "But is that necessary?" he asked, without apparent perturbation.

Captain Blood's blue eyes approved his bearing. "Ask yourself," said he. "Tell me, as an experienced and bloody pirate, what in my place would you do, yourself?"

"Ah, but there is a difference." Don Diego sat up to argue the matter. "It lies in the fact that you boast yourself a humane man."

Captain Blood perched himself on the edge of the long oak table. "But I am not a fool," said he, "and I'll not allow a natural Irish sentimentality to stand in the way of my doing what is necessary and proper. You and your ten surviving scoundrels are a menace on this ship. More than that, she is none so well found in water and provisions. True, we are fortunately a small number, but you and your party inconveniently increase it. So that on every hand, you see, prudence suggests to us that we should deny ourselves the pleasure of your company, and, steeling our soft hearts to the inevitable, invite you to be so obliging as to step over the side."

"I see," said the Spaniard pensively. He swung his legs from the couch, and sat now upon the edge of it, his elbows on his knees. He had taken the measure of his man, and met him with a mock-urbanity and a suave detachment that matched his own. "I confess," he admitted, "that there is much force in what you say."

"You take a load from my mind," said Captain Blood. "I would not appear unnecessarily harsh, especially since I and my friends owe you so very much.

For, whatever it may have been to others, to us your raid upon Barbados was most opportune. I am glad, therefore, that you agree that I have no choice."

"But, my friend, I did not agree so much."

"If there is any alternative that you can suggest, I shall be most happy to consider it."

Don Diego stroked his pointed black beard.

"Can you give me until morning for reflection? My head aches so damnably that I am incapable of thought. And this, you will admit, is a matter that asks serious thought."

Captain Blood stood up. From a shelf he took a half-hour glass, reversed it so that the bulb containing the red sand was uppermost, and stood it on the table.

"I am sorry to press you in such a matter, Don Diego, but one glass is all that I can give you. If by the time those sands have run out you can propose no acceptable alternative, I shall most reluctantly be driven to ask you to go over the side with your friends."

Captain Blood bowed, went out, and locked the door.

Elbows on his knees and face in his hands, Don Diego sat watching the rusty sands as they filtered from the upper to the lower bulb. And what time he watched, the lines in his lean brown face grew deeper. Punctually as the last grains ran out, the door re-opened.

The Spaniard sighed, and sat upright to face the returning Captain Blood with the answer for which he came.

"I have thought of an alternative, sir captain; but

it depends upon your charity. It is that you put us ashore on one of the islands of this pestilent archipelago, and leave us to shift for ourselves."

Captain Blood pursed his lips. "It has its difficulties," said he slowly.

"I feared it would be so." Don Diego sighed again, and stood up. "Let us say no more."

The light-blue eyes played over him like points of steel.

"You are not afraid to die, Don Diego?"

The Spaniard threw back his head, a frown between his eyes.

"The question is offensive, sir."

"Then let me put it in another way — perhaps more happily: You do not desire to live?"

"Ah, that I can answer. I do desire to live; and even more do I desire that my son may live. But the desire shall not make a coward of me for your amusement, master mocker." It was the first sign he had shown of the least heat or resentment.

Captain Blood did not directly answer. As before he perched himself on the corner of the table.

"Would you be willing, sir, to earn life and liberty — for yourself, your son, and the other Spaniards who are on board?"

"To earn it?" said Don Diego, and the watchful blue eyes did not miss the quiver that ran through him. "To earn it, do you say? Why, if the service you would propose is one that cannot hurt my honour . . ."

"Could I be guilty of that?" protested the Captain. "I realize that even a pirate has his honour." And forthwith he propounded his offer. "If you will look from those windows, Don Diego, you will see what appears to be a cloud on the horizon. That is the island of Barbados well astern. All day we have been sailing east before the wind with but one intent — to set as great a distance between Barbados and ourselves as possible. But now, almost out of sight of land, we are in a difficulty. The only man among us schooled in the art of navigation is fevered, delirious, in fact, as a result of certain ill-treatment he received ashore before we carried him away with us. I can handle a ship in action, and there are one or two men aboard who can assist me; but of the higher mysteries of seamanship and of the art of finding a way over the trackless wastes of ocean, we know nothing. To hug the land, and go blundering about what you so aptly call this pestilent archipelago, is for us to court disaster, as you can perhaps conceive. And so it comes to this: We desire to make for the Dutch settlement of Curaçao as straightly as possible. Will you pledge me your honour, if I release you upon parole, that you will navigate us thither? If so, we will release you and your surviving men upon arrival there."

Don Diego bowed his head upon his breast, and strode away in thought to the stern windows. There he stood looking out upon the sunlit sea and the dead water in the great ship's wake — his ship, which these English dogs had wrested from him; his ship, which he was asked to bring safely into a port where she would be completely lost to him and refitted perhaps to make war upon his kin. That was in one scale; in the other were the lives of sixteen men. Fourteen of them mattered little to him, but the remaining two were his own and his son's.

He turned at length, and his back being to the light, the Captain could not see how pale his face had grown.

"I accept," he said.

CHAPTER X

FILIAL PIETY

BY virtue of the pledge he had given, Don Diego de Espinosa enjoyed the freedom of the ship that had been his, and the navigation which he had undertaken was left entirely in his hands. And because those who manned her were new to the seas of the Spanish Main, and because even the things that had happened in Bridgetown were not enough to teach them to regard every Spaniard as a treacherous, cruel dog to be slain at sight, they used him with the civility which his own suave urbanity invited. He took his meals in the great cabin with Blood and the three officers elected to support him: Hagthorpe, Wolverstone, and Dyke.

They found Don Diego an agreeable, even an amusing companion, and their friendly feeling towards him was fostered by his fortitude and brave equanimity in this adversity.

That Don Diego was not playing fair it was impossible to suspect. Moreover, there was no conceivable reason why he should not. And he had been of the utmost frankness with them. He had denounced their mistake in sailing before the wind upon leaving Barbados. They should have left the island to leeward, heading into the Caribbean and away from the archipelago. As it was, they would now be forced to pass through this archipelago again so as to make

Curaçao, and this passage was not to be accomplished without some measure of risk to themselves. At any point between the islands they might come upon an equal or superior craft; whether she were Spanish or English would be equally bad for them, and being undermanned they were in no case to fight. To lessen this risk as far as possible, Don Diego directed at first a southerly and then a westerly course; and so, taking a line midway between the islands of Tobago and Grenada, they won safely through the danger-zone and came into the comparative security of the Caribbean Sea.

"If this wind holds," he told them that night at supper, after he had announced to them their position, "we should reach Curaçao inside three days."

For three days the wind held, indeed it freshened a little on the second, and yet when the third night descended upon them they had still made no landfall. The *Cinco Llagas* was ploughing through a sea contained on every side by the blue bowl of heaven. Captain Blood uneasily mentioned it to Don Diego.

"It will be for to-morrow morning." he was answered with calm conviction.

"By all the saints, it is always 'to-morrow morning' with you Spaniards; and to-morrow never comes, my friend."

"But this to-morrow is coming, rest assured. However early you may be astir, you shall see land ahead, Don Pedro."

Captain Blood passed on, content, and went to visit Jerry Pitt, his patient, to whose condition Don Diego owed his chance of life. For twenty-four hours now the fever had left the sufferer, and under Peter

Blood's dressings, his lacerated back was beginning to heal satisfactorily. So far, indeed, was he recovered that he complained of his confinement, of the heat in his cabin. To indulge him Captain Blood consented that he should take the air on deck, and so, as the last of the daylight was fading from the sky, Jeremy Pitt came forth upon the Captain's arm.

Seated on the hatch-coamings, the Somersetshire lad gratefully filled his lungs with the cool night air, and professed himself revived thereby. Then with the seaman's instinct his eyes wandered to the darkling vault of heaven, spangled already with a myriad golden points of light. Awhile he scanned it idly, vacantly; then, his attention became sharply fixed. He looked round and up at Captain Blood, who stood beside him.

"D'ye know anything of astronomy, Peter?" quoth he.

"Astronomy, is it? Faith, now, I couldn't tell the Belt of Orion from the Girdle of Venus."

"Ah! And I suppose all the others of this lubberly crew share your ignorance."

"It would be more amiable of you to suppose that they exceed it."

Jeremy pointed ahead to a spot of light in the heavens over the starboard bow. "That is the North Star," said he.

"Is it now? Glory be, I wonder ye can pick it out from the rest."

"And the North Star ahead almost over your starboard bow means that we're steering a course, north, northwest, or maybe north by west, for I doubt if we are standing more than ten degrees westward."

"And why shouldn't we?" wondered Captain Blood.

"You told me — didn't you? — that we came west of the archipelago between Tobago and Grenada, steering for Curaçao. If that were our present course, we should have the North Star abeam, out yonder."

On the instant Mr. Blood shed his laziness. He stiffened with apprehension, and was about to speak when a shaft of light clove the gloom above their heads, coming from the door of the poop cabin which had just been opened. It closed again, and presently there was a step on the companion. Don Diego was approaching. Captain Blood's fingers pressed Jerry's shoulder with significance. Then he called the Don, and spoke to him in English as had become his custom when others were present.

"Will ye settle a slight dispute for us, Don Diego?" said he lightly. "We are arguing, Mr. Pitt and I, as to which is the North Star."

"So?" The Spaniard's tone was easy; there was almost a suggestion that laughter lurked behind it, and the reason for this was yielded by his next sentence. "But you tell me Mr. Pitt he is your navigant?"

"For lack of a better," laughed the Captain, good-humouredly contemptuous. "Now I am ready to wager him a hundred pieces of eight that that is the North Star." And he flung out an arm towards a point of light in the heavens straight abeam. He afterwards told Pitt that had Don Diego confirmed him, he would have run him through upon that instant. Far from that, however, the Spaniard freely expressed his scorn.

"You have the assurance that is of ignorance, Don Pedro; and you lose. The North Star is this one." And he indicated it.

"You are sure?"

"But my dear Don Pedro!" The Spaniard's tone was one of amused protest. "But is it possible that I mistake? Besides, is there not the compass? Come to the binnacle and see there what course we make."

His utter frankness, and the easy manner of one who has nothing to conceal resolved at once the doubt that had leapt so suddenly in the mind of Captain Blood. Pitt was satisfied less easily.

"In that case, Don Diego, will you tell me, since Curaçao is our destination, why our course is what it is?"

Again there was no faintest hesitation on Don Diego's part. "You have reason to ask," said he, and sighed. "I had hope' it would not be observe'. I have been careless — oh, of a carelessness very culpable. I neglect observation. Always it is my way. I make too sure. I count too much on dead reckoning. And so to-day I find when at last I take out the quadrant that we do come by a half-degree too much south, so that Curaçao is now almost due north. That is what cause the delay. But we will be there to-morrow."

The explanation, so completely satisfactory, and so readily and candidly forthcoming, left no room for further doubt that Don Diego should have been false to his parole. And when presently Don Diego had withdrawn again, Captain Blood confessed to Pitt that it was absurd to have suspected him. Whatever his antecedents, he had proved his quality when he announced himself ready to die sooner than enter into any undertaking that could hurt his honour or his country.

New to the seas of the Spanish Main and to the ways of the adventurers who sailed it, Captain Blood still entertained illusions. But the next dawn was to shatter them rudely and for ever.

Coming on deck before the sun was up, he saw land ahead, as the Spaniard had promised them last night. Some ten miles ahead it lay, a long coast-line filling the horizon east and west, with a massive headland jutting forward straight before them. Staring at it, he frowned. He had not conceived that Curaçao was of such considerable dimensions. Indeed, this looked less like an island than the main itself.

Beating out aweather, against the gentle landward breeze he beheld a great ship on their starboard bow, that he conceived to be some three or four miles off, and — as well as he could judge her at that distance — of a tonnage equal if not superior to their own. Even as he watched her she altered her course, and going about came heading towards them, close-hauled.

A dozen of his fellows were astir on the forecastle, looking eagerly ahead, and the sound of their voices and laughter reached him across the length of the stately *Cinco Llagas*.

"There," said a soft voice behind him in liquid Spanish, "is the Promised Land, Don Pedro."

It was something in that voice, a muffled note of exultation, that awoke suspicion in him, and made whole the half-doubt he had been entertaining. He

turned sharply to face Don Diego, so sharply that the
sly smile was not effaced from the Spaniard's countenance before Captain Blood's eyes had flashed
upon it.

"You find an odd satisfaction in the sight of it —
all things considered," said Mr. Blood.

"Of course." The Spaniard rubbed his hands, and
Mr. Blood observed that they were unsteady. "The
satisfaction of a mariner."

"Or of a traitor — which?" Blood asked him
quietly. And as the Spaniard fell back before him
with suddenly altered countenance that confirmed
his every suspicion, he flung an arm out in the direction of the distant shore. "What land is that?"
he demanded. "Will you have the effrontery to tell
me that is the coast of Curaçao?"

He advanced upon Don Diego suddenly, and Don
Diego, step by step, fell back. "Shall I tell you what
land it is? Shall I?" His fierce assumption of knowledge seemed to dazzle and daze the Spaniard. For
still Don Diego made no answer. And then Captain
Blood drew a bow at a venture — or not quite at a
venture. Such a coast-line as that, if not of the main
itself, and the main he knew it could not be, must
belong to either Cuba or Hispaniola. Now knowing
Cuba to lie farther north and west of the two, it followed, he reasoned swiftly, that if Don Diego meant
betrayal he would steer for the nearer of these Spanish territories. "That land, you treacherous, for-
sworn Spanish dog, is the island of Hispaniola."

Having said it, he closely watched the swarthy
face now overspread with pallor, to see the truth or
falsehood of his guess reflected there. But now the

retreating Spaniard had come to the middle of the quarter-deck, where the mizzen sail made a screen to shut them off from the eyes of the Englishmen below. His lips writhed in a snarling smile.

"Ah, perro inglés! You know too much," he said under his breath, and sprang for the Captain's throat.

Tight-locked in each other's arms, they swayed a moment, then together went down upon the deck, the Spaniard's feet jerked from under him by the right leg of Captain Blood. The Spaniard had depended upon his strength, which was considerable. But it proved no match for the steady muscles of the Irishman, tempered of late by the vicissitudes of slavery. He had depended upon choking the life out of Blood, and so gaining the half-hour that might be necessary to bring up that fine ship that was beating towards them — a Spanish ship, perforce, since none other would be so boldly cruising in these Spanish waters off Hispaniola. But all that Don Diego had accomplished was to betray himself completely, and to no purpose. This he realized when he found himself upon his back, pinned down by Blood, who was kneeling on his chest, whilst the men summoned by their Captain's shout came clattering up the companion.

"Will I say a prayer for your dirty soul now, whilst I am in this position?" Captain Blood was furiously mocking him.

But the Spaniard, though defeated, now beyond hope for himself, forced his lips to smile, and gave back mockery for mockery.

"Who will pray for your soul, I wonder, when that galleon comes to lie board and board with you?"

"That galleon!" echoed Captain Blood with sudden and awful realization that already it was too late to avoid the consequences of Don Diego's betrayal of them.

"That galleon," Don Diego repeated, and added with a deepening sneer: "Do you know what ship it is? I will tell you. It is the *Encarnacion*, the flagship of Don Miguel de Espinosa, the Lord Admiral of Castile, and Don Miguel is my brother. It is a very fortunate encounter. The Almighty, you see, watches over the destinies of Catholic Spain."

There was no trace of humour or urbanity now in Captain Blood. His light eyes blazed: his face was set.

He rose, relinquishing the Spaniard to his men. "Make him fast," he bade them. "Truss him, wrist and heel, but don't hurt him — not so much as a hair of his precious head."

The injunction was very necessary. Frenzied by the thought that they were likely to exchange the slavery from which they had so lately escaped for a slavery still worse, they would have torn the Spaniard limb from limb upon the spot. And if they now obeyed their Captain and refrained, it was only because the sudden steely note in his voice promised for Don Diego Valdez something far more exquisite than death.

"You scum! You dirty pirate! You man of honour!" Captain Blood apostrophized his prisoner.

But Don Diego looked up at him and laughed.

"You underrated me." He spoke English, so that all might hear. "I tell you that I was not fear death, and I show you that I was not fear it. You no understand. You just an English dog."

"Irish, if you please," Captain Blood corrected him. "And your parole, you tyke of Spain?"

"You think I give my parole to leave you sons of filth with this beautiful Spanish ship, to go make war upon other Spaniards! Ha!" Don Diego laughed in his throat. "You fool! You can kill me. Pish! It is very well. I die with my work well done. In less than an hour you will be the prisoners of Spain, and the *Cinco Llagas* will go belong to Spain again."

Captain Blood regarded him steadily out of a face which, if impassive, had paled under its deep tan. About the prisoner, clamant, infuriated, ferocious, the rebels-convict surged, almost literally "athirst for his blood."

"Wait," Captain Blood imperiously commanded, and turning on his heel, he went aside to the rail. As he stood there deep in thought, he was joined by Hagthorpe, Wolverstone, and Ogle the gunner. In silence they stared with him across the water at that other ship. She had veered a point away from the wind, and was running now on a line that must in the end converge with that of the *Cinco Llagas*.

"In less than half-an-hour," said Blood presently, "we shall have her athwart our hawse, sweeping our decks with her guns."

"We can fight," said the one-eyed giant with an oath.

"Fight!" sneered Blood. "Undermanned as we are, mustering a bare twenty men, in what case are we to fight? No, there would be only one way. To persuade her that all is well aboard, that we are Spaniards, so that she may leave us to continue on our course."

"And how is that possible?" Hagthorpe asked.

"It isn't possible," said Blood. "If it were . . ." And then he broke off, and stood musing, his eyes upon the green water. Ogle, with a bent for sarcasm, interposed a suggestion bitterly.

"We might send Don Diego de Espinosa in a boat manned by his Spaniards to assure his brother the Admiral that we are all loyal subjects of his Catholic Majesty."

The Captain swung round, and for an instant looked as if he would have struck the gunner. Then his expression changed: the light of inspiration was in his glance.

"Bedad! ye've said it. He doesn't fear death, this damned pirate; but his son may take a different view. Filial piety's mighty strong in Spain." He swung on his heel abruptly, and strode back to the knot of men about his prisoner. "Here!" he shouted to them. "Bring him below." And he led the way down to the waist, and thence by the booby hatch to the gloom of the 'tween-decks, where the air was rank with the smell of tar and spun yarn. Going aft he threw open the door of the spacious ward-room, and went in followed by a dozen of the hands with the pinioned Spaniard. Every man aboard would have followed him but for his sharp command to some of them to remain on deck with Hagthorpe.

In the ward-room the three stern chasers were in position, loaded, their muzzles thrusting through the open ports, precisely as the Spanish gunners had left them.

"Here, Ogle, is work for you," said Blood, and as the burly gunner came thrusting forward through the little throng of gaping men, Blood pointed to the middle chaser: "Have that gun hauled back," he ordered.

When this was done, Blood beckoned those who held Don Diego.

"Lash him across the mouth of it," he bade them, and whilst, assisted by another two, they made haste to obey, he turned to the others. "To the roundhouse, some of you, and fetch the Spanish prisoners. And you, Dyke, go up and bid them set the flag of Spain aloft."

Don Diego, with his body stretched in an arc across the cannon's mouth, legs and arms lashed to the carriage on either side of it, eyeballs rolling in his head, glared maniacally at Captain Blood. A man may not fear to die, and yet be appalled by the form in which death comes to him.

From frothing lips he hurled blasphemies and insults at his tormentor.

"Foul barbarian! Inhuman savage! Accursed heretic! Will it not content you to kill me in some Christian fashion?"

Captain Blood vouchsafed him a malignant smile, before he turned to meet the fifteen manacled Spanish prisoners, who were thrust into his presence.

Approaching, they had heard Don Diego's outcries; at close quarters now they beheld with horror-stricken eyes his plight. From amongst them a comely, olive-skinned stripling, distinguished in bearing and apparel from his companions, started forward with an anguished cry of "Father!"

Writhing in the arms that made haste to seize and hold him, he called upon heaven and hell to avert this horror, and lastly, addressed to Captain Blood an appeal for mercy that was at once fierce and piteous. Considering him, Captain Blood thought with satisfaction that he displayed the proper degree of filial piety.

He afterwards confessed that for a moment he was in danger of weakening, that for a moment his mind rebelled against the pitiless thing it had planned. But to correct the sentiment he evoked a memory of what these Spaniards had performed in Bridgetown. Again he saw the white face of that child Mary Traill as she fled in horror before the jeering ruffian whom he had slain, and other things even more unspeakable seen on that dreadful evening rose now before the eyes of his memory to stiffen his faltering purpose. The Spaniards had shown themselves without mercy or sentiment or decency of any kind; stuffed with religion, they were without a spark of that Christianity, the Symbol of which was mounted on the mainmast of the approaching ship. A moment ago this cruel, vicious Don Diego had insulted the Almighty by his assumption that He kept a specially benevolent watch over the destinies of Catholic Spain. Don Diego should be taught his error.

Recovering the cynicism in which he had approached his task, the cynicism essential to its proper performance, he commanded Ogle to kindle a match and remove the leaden apron from the touchhole of the gun that bore Don Diego. Then, as the younger Espinosa broke into fresh intercessions mingled with imprecations, he wheeled upon him sharply.

"Peace!" he snapped. "Peace, and listen! It is no

part of my intention to blow your father to hell as he deserves, or indeed to take his life at all."

Having surprised the lad into silence by that promise — a promise surprising enough in all the circumstances — he proceeded to explain his aims in that faultless and elegant Castilian of which he was fortunately master — as fortunately for Don Diego as for himself.

"It is your father's treachery that has brought us into this plight and deliberately into risk of capture and death aboard that ship of Spain. Just as your father recognized his brother's flagship, so will his brother have recognized the *Cinco Llagas*. So far, then, all is well. But presently the *Encarnacion* will be sufficiently close to perceive that here all is not as it should be. Sooner or later, she must guess or discover what is wrong, and then she will open fire or lay us board and board. Now, we are in no case to fight, as your father knew when he ran us into this trap. But fight we will, if we are driven to it. We make no tame surrender to the ferocity of Spain."

He laid his hand on the breech of the gun that bore Don Diego.

"Understand this clearly: to the first shot from the *Encarnacion* this gun will fire the answer. I make myself clear, I hope?"

White-faced and trembling, young Espinosa stared into the pitiless blue eyes that so steadily regarded him.

"If it is clear?" he faltered, breaking the utter silence in which all were standing. "But, name of God, how should it be clear? How should I understand? Can you avert the fight? If you know a way, and if I, or these, can help you to it — if that is what you mean — in Heaven's name let me hear it."

"A fight would be averted if Don Diego de Espinosa were to go aboard his brother's ship, and by his presence and assurances inform the Admiral that all is well with the *Cinco Llagas*, that she is indeed still a ship of Spain as her flag now announces. But of course Don Diego cannot go in person, because he is ... otherwise engaged. He has a slight touch of fever — shall we say? — that detains him in his cabin. But you, his son, may convey all this and some other matters together with his homage to your uncle. You shall go in a boat manned by six of these Spanish prisoners, and I — a distinguished Spaniard delivered from captivity in Barbados by your recent raid — will accompany you to keep you in countenance. If I return alive, and without accident of any kind to hinder our free sailing hence, Don Diego shall have his life, as shall every one of you. But if there is the least misadventure, be it from treachery or ill-fortune — I care not which — the battle, as I have had the honour to explain, will be opened on our side by this gun, and your father will be the first victim of the conflict."

He paused a moment. There was a hum of approval from his comrades, an anxious stirring among the Spanish prisoners. Young Espinosa stood before him, the colour ebbing and flowing in his cheeks. He waited for some direction from his father. But none came. Don Diego's courage, it seemed, had sadly waned under that rude test. He hung limply in his fearful bonds, and was silent. Evidently he dared not encourage his son to defiance, and presumably was ashamed to urge him to yield. Thus, he left decision entirely with the youth.

"Come," said Blood. "I have been clear enough, I think. What do you say?"

Don Esteban moistened his parched lips, and with the back of his hand mopped the anguish-sweat from his brow. His eyes gazed wildly a moment upon the shoulders of his father, as if beseeching guidance. But his father remained silent. Something like a sob escaped the boy.

"I . . . I accept," he answered at last, and swung to the Spaniards. "And you — you will accept too," he insisted passionately. "For Don Diego's sake and for your own — for all our sakes. If you do not, this man will butcher us all without mercy."

Since he yielded, and their leader himself counselled no resistance, why should they encompass their own destruction by a gesture of futile heroism? They answered without much hesitation that they would do as was required of them.

Blood turned, and advanced to Don Diego.

"I am sorry to inconvenience you in this fashion, but . . ." For a second he checked and frowned as his eyes intently observed the prisoner. Then, after that scarcely perceptible pause, he continued, ". . . But I do not think that you have anything beyond this inconvenience to apprehend, and you may depend upon me to shorten it as far as possible."

Don Diego made him no answer.

Peter Blood waited a moment, observing him; then he bowed and stepped back.

CHAPTER XII

DON PEDRO SANGRE

THE *Cinco Llagas* and the *Encarnacion*, after a proper exchange of signals, lay hove to within a quarter of a mile of each other, and across the intervening space of gently heaving, sunlit waters sped a boat from the former, manned by six Spanish seamen and bearing in her stern sheets Don Esteban de Espinosa and Captain Peter Blood.

She also bore two treasure-chests containing fifty thousand pieces of eight. Gold has at all times been considered the best of testimonies of good faith, and Blood was determined that in all respects appearances should be entirely on his side. His followers had accounted this a supererogation of pretence. But Blood's will in the matter had prevailed. He carried further a bulky package addressed to a grande of Spain, heavily sealed with the arms of Espinosa — another piece of evidence hastily manufactured in the cabin of the *Cinco Llagas* — and he was spending these last moments in completing his instructions to his young companion.

Don Esteban expressed his last lingering uneasiness:

"But if you should betray yourself?" he cried.

"It will be unfortunate for ... everybody. I advised your father to say a prayer for our success. I depend upon you to help me more materially."

"I will do my best. God knows I will do my best," the boy protested.

Blood nodded thoughtfully, and no more was said until they bumped alongside the towering mass of the *Encarnacion*. Up the ladder went Don Esteban closely followed by Captain Blood. In the waist stood the Admiral himself to receive them, a handsome, self-sufficient man, very tall and stiff, a little older and greyer than Don Diego, whom he closely resembled. He was supported by four officers and a friar in the black and white habit of St. Dominic.

Don Miguel opened his arms to his nephew, whose lingering panic he mistook for pleasurable excitement, and having enfolded him to his bosom turned to greet Don Esteban's companion.

Peter Blood bowed gracefully, entirely at his ease, so far as might be judged from appearances.

"I am," he announced, making a literal translation of his name, "Don Pedro Sangre, an unfortunate gentleman of Leon, lately delivered from captivity by Don Esteban's most gallant father." And in a few words he sketched the imagined conditions of his capture by, and deliverance from, those accursed heretics who held the island of Barbados.

"Benedicamus Domino," said the friar to his tale.

"Ex hoc nunc et usque in seculum," replied Blood, the occasional papist, with lowered eyes.

The Admiral and his attending officers gave him a sympathetic hearing and a cordial welcome. Then came the dreaded question.

"But where is my brother? Why has he not come, himself, to greet me?"

It was young Espinosa who answered this:

"My father is afflicted at denying himself that honour and pleasure. But unfortunately, sir uncle, he is a little indisposed — oh, nothing grave; merely sufficient to make him keep his cabin. It is a little fever, the result of a slight wound taken in the recent raid upon Barbados, which resulted in this gentleman's happy deliverance."

"Nay, nephew, nay," Don Miguel protested with ironic repudiation. "I can have no knowledge of these things. I have the honour to represent upon the seas His Catholic Majesty, who is at peace with the King of England. Already you have told me more than it is good for me to know. I will endeavour to forget it, and I will ask you, sirs," he added, glancing at his officers, "to forget it also." But he winked into the twinkling eyes of Captain Blood; then added matter that at once extinguished that twinkle. "But since Diego cannot come to me, why, I will go across to him."

For a moment Don Esteban's face was a mask of pallid fear. Then Blood was speaking in a lowered, confidential voice that admirably blended suavity, impressiveness, and sly mockery.

"If you please, Don Miguel, but that is the very thing you must not do — the very thing Don Diego does not wish you to do. You must not see him until his wounds are healed. That is his own wish. That is the real reason why he is not here. For the truth is that his wounds are not so grave as to have prevented his coming. It was his consideration of himself and the false position in which you would be placed if you had direct word from him of what has happened. As your excellency has said, there is peace between His

Catholic Majesty and the King of England, and your brother Don Diego . . ." He paused a moment. "I am sure that I need say no more. What you hear from us is no more than a mere rumour. Your excellency understands."

His excellency frowned thoughtfully. "I understand . . . in part," said he.

Captain Blood had a moment's uneasiness. Did the Spaniard doubt his bona fides? Yet in dress and speech he knew himself to be impeccably Spanish, and was not Don Esteban there to confirm him? He swept on to afford further confirmation before the Admiral could say another word.

"And we have in the boat below two chests containing fifty thousand pieces of eight, which we are to deliver to your excellency."

His excellency jumped; there was a sudden stir among his officers.

"They are the ransom extracted by Don Diego from the Governor of . . ."

"Not another word, in the name of Heaven!" cried the Admiral in alarm. "My brother wishes me to assume charge of this money, to carry it to Spain for him? Well, that is a family matter between my brother and myself. So, it can be done. But I must not know . . ." He broke off. "Hum! A glass of Malaga in my cabin, if you please," he invited them, "whilst the chests are being hauled aboard."

He gave his orders touching the embarkation of these chests, then led the way to his regally appointed cabin, his four officers and the friar following by particular invitation.

Seated at table there, with the tawny wine before

them, and the servant who had poured it withdrawn, Don Miguel laughed and stroked his pointed, grizzled beard.

"Virgen santisima! That brother of mine has a mind that thinks of everything. Left to myself, I might have committed a fine indiscretion by venturing aboard his ship at such a moment. I might have seen things which as Admiral of Spain it would be difficult for me to ignore."

Both Esteban and Blood made haste to agree with him, and then Blood raised his glass, and drank to the glory of Spain and the damnation of the besotted James who occupied the throne of England. The latter part of his toast was at least sincere.

The Admiral laughed.

"Sir, sir, you need my brother here to curb your imprudences. You should remember that His Catholic Majesty and the King of England are very good friends. That is not a toast to propose in this cabin. But since it has been proposed, and by one who has such particular personal cause to hate these English hounds, why, we will honour it — but unofficially."

They laughed, and drank the damnation of King James — quite unofficially, but the more fervently on that account. Then Don Esteban, uneasy on the score of his father, and remembering that the agony of Don Diego was being protracted with every moment that they left him in his dreadful position, rose and announced that they must be returning.

"My father," he explained, "is in haste to reach San Domingo. He desired me to stay no longer than necessary to embrace you. If you will give us leave, then, sir uncle."

In the circumstances "sir uncle" did not insist.

As they returned to the ship's side, Blood's eyes anxiously scanned the line of seamen leaning over the bulwarks in idle talk with the Spaniards in the cock-boat that waited at the ladder's foot. But their manner showed him that there was no ground for his anxiety. The boat's crew had been wisely reticent.

The Admiral took leave of them — of Esteban affectionately, of Blood ceremoniously.

"I regret to lose you so soon, Don Pedro. I wish that you could have made a longer visit to the *Encarnacion*."

"I am indeed unfortunate," said Captain Blood politely.

"But I hope that we may meet again."

"That is to flatter me beyond all that I deserve."

They reached the boat, and she cast off from the great ship. As they were pulling away, the Admiral waving to them from the taffrail, they heard the shrill whistle of the bo'sun piping the hands to their stations, and before they had reached the *Cinco Llagas*, they beheld the *Encarnacion* go about under sail. She dipped her flag to them, and from her poop a gun fired a salute.

Aboard the *Cinco Llagas* some one — it proved afterwards to be Hagthorpe — had the wit to reply in the same fashion. The comedy was ended. Yet there was something else to follow as an epilogue, a thing that added a grim ironic flavour to the whole.

As they stepped into the waist of the *Cinco Llagas*, Hagthorpe advanced to receive them. Blood observed the set, almost scared expression on his face.

"I see that you've found it," he said quietly.

Hagthorpe's eyes looked a question. But his mind dismissed whatever thought it held.

"Don Diego . . ." he was beginning, and then stopped, and looked curiously at Blood.

Noting the pause and the look, Esteban bounded forward, his face livid.

"Have you broken faith, you curs? Has he come to harm?" he cried — and the six Spaniards behind him grew clamorous with furious questionings.

"We do not break faith," said Hagthorpe firmly, so firmly that he quieted them. "And in this case there was not the need. Don Diego died in his bonds before ever you reached the *Encarnacion.*"

Peter Blood said nothing.

"Died?" screamed Esteban. "You killed him, you mean. Of what did he die?"

Hagthorpe looked at the boy. "If I am a judge," he said, "Don Diego died of fear."

Don Esteban struck Hagthorpe across the face at that, and Hagthorpe would have struck back, but that Blood got between, whilst his followers seized the lad.

"Let be," said Blood. "You provoked the boy by your insult to his father."

"I was not concerned to insult," said Hagthorpe, nursing his cheek. "It is what has happened. Come and look."

"I have seen," said Blood. "He died before I left the *Cinco Llagas.* He was hanging dead in his bonds when I spoke to him before leaving."

"What are you saying?" cried Esteban.

Blood looked at him gravely. Yet for all his gravity he seemed almost to smile, though without mirth.

"If you had known that, eh?" he asked at last.

For a moment Don Esteban stared at him wide-eyed, incredulous. "I don't believe you," he said at last.

"Yet you may. I am a doctor, and I know death when I see it."

Again there came a pause, whilst conviction sank into the lad's mind. "If I had known that," he said at last in a thick voice, "you would be hanging from the yardarm of the *Encarnacion* at this moment."

"I know," said Blood. "I am considering it — the profit that a man may find in the ignorance of others."

"But you'll hang there yet," the boy raved.

Captain Blood shrugged, and turned on his heel. But he did not on that account disregard the words, nor did Hagthorpe, nor yet the others who overheard them, as they showed at a council held that night in the cabin.

This council was met to determine what should be done with the Spanish prisoners. Considering that Curaçao now lay beyond their reach, as they were running short of water and provisions, and also that Pitt was hardly yet in case to undertake the navigation of the vessel, it had been decided that, going east of Hispaniola, and then sailing along its northern coast, they should make for Tortuga, that haven of the buccaneers, in which lawless port they had at least no danger of recapture to apprehend. It was now a question whether they should convey the Spaniards thither with them, or turn them off in a boat to make the best of their way to the coast of Hispaniola, which was but ten miles off. This was the course urged by Blood himself.

"There's nothing else to be done," he insisted. "In Tortuga they would be flayed alive."

"Which is less than the swine deserve," growled Wolverstone.

"And you'll remember, Peter," put in Hagthorpe, "that boy's threat to you this morning. If he escapes, and carries word of all this to his uncle, the Admiral, the execution of that threat will become more than possible."

It says much for Peter Blood that the argument should have left him unmoved. It is a little thing, perhaps, but in a narrative in which there is so much that tells against him, I cannot — since my story is in the nature of a brief for the defence — afford to slur a circumstance that is so strongly in his favour, a circumstance revealing that the cynicism attributed to him proceeded from his reason and from a brooding over wrongs rather than from any natural instincts.

"I care nothing for his threats."

"You should," said Wolverstone. "The wise thing'd be to hang him, along o' all the rest."

"It is not human to be wise," said Blood. "It is much more human to err, though perhaps exceptional to err on the side of mercy. We'll be exceptional. Oh, faugh! I've no stomach for cold-blooded killing. At daybreak pack the Spaniards into a boat with a keg of water and a sack of dumplings, and let them go to the devil."

That was his last word on the subject, and it prevailed by virtue of the authority they had vested in him, and of which he had taken so firm a grip. At daybreak Don Esteban and his followers were put off in a boat.

Two days later, the *Cinco Llagas* sailed into the rock-bound bay of Cayona, which Nature seemed to have designed for the stronghold of those who had appropriated it.

CHAPTER XIII

TORTUGA

IT is time fully to disclose the fact that the survival of the story of Captain Blood's exploits is due entirely to the industry of Jeremy Pitt, the Somersetshire shipmaster. In addition to his ability as a navigator, this amiable young man appears to have wielded an indefatigable pen, and to have been inspired to indulge its fluency by the affection he very obviously bore to Peter Blood.

He kept the log of the forty-gun frigate *Arabella*, on which he served as master, or, as we should say to-day, navigating officer, as no log that I have seen was ever kept. It runs into some twenty-odd volumes of assorted sizes, some of which are missing altogether and others of which are so sadly depleted of leaves as to be of little use. But if at times in the laborious perusal of them — they are preserved in the library of Mr. James Speke of Comerton — I have inveighed against these lacunæ, at others I have been equally troubled by the excessive prolixity of what remains and the difficulty of disintegrating from the confused whole the really essential parts.

I have a suspicion that Esquemeling — though how or where I can make no surmise — must have obtained access to these records, and that he plucked from them the brilliant feathers of several exploits to stick them into the tail of his own hero, Captain Morgan. But that is by the way. I mention it chiefly as a

warning, for when presently I come to relate the affair of Maracaybo, those of you who have read Esquemeling may be in danger of supposing that Henry
Morgan really performed those things which here are
veraciously attributed to Peter Blood. I think, however, that when you come to weigh the motives actu-
ating both Blood and the Spanish Admiral, in that
affair, and when you consider how integrally the
event is a part of Blood's history — whilst merely a
detached incident in Morgan's — you will reach my
own conclusion as to which is the real plagiarist.

The first of these logs of Pitt's is taken up almost
entirely with a retrospective narrative of the events
up to the time of Blood's first coming to Tortuga.
This and the Tannatt Collection of State Trials are
the chief — though not the only — sources of my
history so far.

Pitt lays great stress upon the fact that it was the
circumstances upon which I have dwelt, and these
alone, that drove Peter Blood to seek an anchorage at
Tortuga. He insists at considerable length, and with
a vehemence which in itself makes it plain that an
opposite opinion was held in some quarters, that it
was no part of the design of Blood or of any of his
companions in misfortune to join hands with the
buccaneers who, under a semi-official French protection, made of Tortuga a lair whence they could
sally out to drive their merciless piratical trade chiefly
at the expense of Spain.

It was, Pitt tells us, Blood's original intention to
make his way to France or Holland. But in the long
weeks of waiting for a ship to convey him to one or
the other of these countries, his resources dwindled

and finally vanished. Also, his chronicler thinks that
he detected signs of some secret trouble in his friend,
and he attributes to this the abuses of the potent West
Indian spirit of which Blood became guilty in those
days of inaction, thereby sinking to the level of the
wild adventurers with whom ashore he associated.

I do not think that Pitt is guilty in this merely of
special pleading, that he is putting forward excuses
for his hero. I think that in those days there was a
good deal to oppress Peter Blood. There was the
thought of Arabella Bishop — and that this thought
loomed large in his mind we are not permitted to
doubt. He was maddened by the tormenting lure of
the unattainable. He desired Arabella, yet knew her
beyond his reach irrevocably and for all time. Also,
whilst he may have desired to go to France or Holland, he had no clear purpose to accomplish when he
reached one or the other of these countries. He was,
when all is said, an escaped slave, an outlaw in his
own land and a homeless outcast in any other. There
remained the sea, which is free to all, and particularly alluring to those who feel themselves at war
with humanity. And so, considering the adventurous
spirit that once already had sent him a-roving for the
sheer love of it, considering that this spirit was height-
ened now by a recklessness begotten of his outlawry,
that his training and skill in militant seamanship
clamorously supported the temptations that were
put before him, can you wonder, or dare you blame
him, that in the end he succumbed? And remember that these temptations proceeded not only from
adventurous buccaneering acquaintances in the taverns of that evil haven of Tortuga, but even from

M. d'Ogeron, the governor of the island, who levied as his harbour dues a percentage of one tenth of all spoils brought into the bay, and who profited further by commissions upon money which he was desired to convert into bills of exchange upon France.

A trade that might have worn a repellent aspect when urged by greasy, half-drunken adventurers, boucan-hunters, lumbermen, beach-combers, English, French, and Dutch, became a dignified, almost official form of privateering when advocated by the courtly, middle-aged gentleman who in representing the French West India Company seemed to represent France herself.

Moreover, to a man — not excluding Jeremy Pitt himself, in whose blood the call of the sea was insistent and imperative — those who had escaped with Peter Blood from the Barbados plantations, and who, consequently, like himself, knew not whither to turn, were all resolved upon joining the great Brotherhood of the Coast, as those rovers called themselves. And they united theirs to the other voices that were persuading Blood, demanding that he should continue now in the leadership which he had enjoyed since they had left Barbados, and swearing to follow him loyally whithersoever he should lead them.

And so, to condense all that Jeremy has recorded in the matter, Blood ended by yielding to external and internal pressure, abandoned himself to the stream of Destiny. "Fata viam invenerunt," is his own expression of it.

If he resisted so long, it was, I think, the thought of Arabella Bishop that restrained him. That they should be destined never to meet again did not weigh at first, or, indeed, ever. He conceived the scorn with which she would come to hear of his having turned pirate, and the scorn, though as yet no more than imagined, hurt him as if it were already a reality. And even when he conquered this, still the thought of her was ever present. He compromised with the conscience that her memory kept so disconcertingly active. He vowed that the thought of her should continue ever before him to help him keep his hands as clean as a man might in this desperate trade upon which he was embarking. And so, although he might entertain no delusive hope of ever winning her for his own, of ever even seeing her again, yet the memory of her was to abide in his soul as a bitter-sweet, purifying influence. The love that is never to be realized will often remain a man's guiding ideal.

The resolve being taken, he went actively to work. Ogeron, most accommodating of governors, advanced him money for the proper equipment of his ship the *Cinco Llagas*, which he renamed the *Arabella*. This after some little hesitation, fearful of thus setting his heart upon his sleeve. But his Barbados friends accounted it merely an expression of the ever-ready irony in which their leader dealt.

To the score of followers he already possessed, he added threescore more, picking his men with caution and discrimination — and he was an exceptional judge of men — from amongst the adventurers of Tortuga. With them all he entered into the articles usual among the Brethren of the Coast under which each man was to be paid by a share in the prizes captured. In other respects, however, the articles were different. Aboard the *Arabella* there was to be none of the ruffianly indiscipline that normally prevailed in buccaneering vessels. Those who shipped with him undertook obedience and submission in all things to himself and to the officers appointed by election. Any to whom this clause in the articles was distasteful might follow some other leader.

Towards the end of December, when the hurricane season had blown itself out, he put to sea in his well-found, well-manned ship, and before he returned in the following May from a protracted and adventurous cruise, the fame of Captain Peter Blood had run like ripples before the breeze across the face of the Caribbean Sea. There was a fight in the Windward Passage at the outset with a Spanish galleon, which had resulted in the gutting and finally the sinking of the Spaniard. There was a daring raid effected by means of several appropriated piraguas upon a Spanish pearl fleet in the Rio de la Hacha, from which they had taken a particularly rich haul of pearls. There was an overland expedition to the goldfields of Sancta Maria, on the Main, the full tale of which is hardly credible, and there were lesser adventures through all of which the crew of the *Arabella* came with credit and profit if not entirely unscathed.

And so it happened that before the *Arabella* came homing to Tortuga in the following May to refit and repair — for she was not without scars, as you conceive — the fame of her and of Peter Blood her captain had swept from the Bahamas to the Windward Isles, from New Providence to Trinidad.

An echo of it had reached Europe, and at the Court of St. James's angry representations were made by the Ambassador of Spain, to whom it was answered that it must not be supposed that this Captain Blood held any commission from the King of England; that he was, in fact, a proscribed rebel, an escaped slave, and that any measures against him by His Catholic Majesty would receive the cordial approbation of King James II.

Don Miguel de Espinosa, the Admiral of Spain in the West Indies, and his nephew Don Esteban who sailed with him, did not lack the will to bring the adventurer to the yardarm. With them this business of capturing Blood, which was now an international affair, was also a family matter.

Spain, through the mouth of Don Miguel, did not spare her threats. The report of them reached Tortuga, and with it the assurance that Don Miguel had behind him not only the authority of his own nation, but that of the English King as well.

It was a brutum fulmen that inspired no terrors in Captain Blood. Nor was he likely, on account of it, to allow himself to run to rust in the security of Tortuga. For what he had suffered at the hands of Man he had chosen to make Spain the scapegoat. Thus he accounted that he served a twofold purpose: he took compensation and at the same time served, not indeed the Stuart King, whom he despised, but England and, for that matter, all the rest of civilized mankind which cruel, treacherous, greedy, bigoted Castile sought to exclude from intercourse with the New World.

One day, as he sat with Hagthorpe and Wolverstone over a pipe and a bottle of rum in the stifling reek of tar and stale tobacco of a waterside tavern, he was accosted by a splendid ruffian in a gold-laced coat of dark-blue satin with a crimson sash, a foot wide, about the waist.

"C'est vous qu'on appelle Le Sang?" the fellow hailed him.

Captain Blood looked up to consider the questioner before replying. The man was tall and built on lines of agile strength, with a swarthy, aquiline face that was brutally handsome. A diamond of great price flamed on the indifferently clean hand resting on the pummel of his long rapier, and there were gold rings in his ears, half-concealed by long ringlets of oily chestnut hair.

Captain Blood took the pipe-stem from between his lips.

"My name," he said, "is Peter Blood. The Spaniards know me for Don Pedro Sangre, and a Frenchman may call me Le Sang if he pleases."

"Good," said the gaudy adventurer in English, and without further invitation he drew up a stool and sat down at that greasy table. "My name," he informed the three men, two of whom at least were eyeing him askance, "it is Levasseur. You may have heard of me."

They had, indeed. He commanded a privateer of twenty guns that had dropped anchor in the bay a week ago, manned by a crew mainly composed of French boucan-hunters from Northern Hispaniola, men who had good cause to hate the Spaniard with an intensity exceeding that of the English. Levasseur had brought them back to Tortuga from an indifferently successful cruise. It would need more, however, than lack of success to abate the fellow's monstrous vanity. A roaring, quarrelsome, hard-drinking, hard-gaming scoundrel, his reputation as a buccaneer stood high among the wild Brethren of the Coast. He enjoyed also a reputation of another sort. There was about his gaudy, swaggering raffishness something that the women found singularly alluring. That he should boast openly of his bonnes fortunes did not seem strange to Captain Blood; what he might have found strange was that there appeared to be some measure of justification for these boasts.

It was current gossip that even Mademoiselle d'Ogeron, the Governor's daughter, had been caught in the snare of his wild attractiveness, and that Levasseur had gone the length of audacity of asking her hand in marriage of her father. M. d'Ogeron had made him the only possible answer. He had shown him the door. Levasseur had departed in a rage, swearing that he would make mademoiselle his wife in the teeth of all the fathers in Christendom, and that M. d'Ogeron should bitterly rue the affront he had put upon him.

This was the man who now thrust himself upon Captain Blood with a proposal of association, offering him not only his sword, but his ship and the men who sailed in her.

A dozen years ago, as a lad of barely twenty, Levasseur had sailed with that monster of cruelty L'Ollonais, and his own subsequent exploits bore witness and did credit to the school in which he had been reared. I doubt if in his day there was a greater scoundrel among the Brethren of the Coast than this Levasseur. And yet, repulsive though he found him, Captain Blood could not deny that the fellow's proposals displayed boldness, imagination, and resource, and he was forced to admit that jointly they could undertake operations of a greater magnitude than was possible singly to either of them. The climax of Levasseur's project was to be a raid upon the wealthy mainland city of Maracaybo; but for this, he admitted, six hundred men at the very least would be required, and six hundred men were not to be conveyed in the two bottoms they now commanded. Preliminary cruises must take place, having for one of their objects the capture of further ships.

Because he disliked the man, Captain Blood would not commit himself at once. But because he liked the proposal he consented to consider it. Being afterwards pressed by both Hagthorpe and Wolverstone, who did not share his own personal dislike of the Frenchman, the end of the matter was that within a week articles were drawn up between Levasseur and Blood, and signed by them and — as was usual — by the chosen representatives of their followers.

These articles contained, inter alia, the common provisions that, should the two vessels separate, a strict account must afterwards be rendered of all prizes severally taken, whilst the vessel taking a prize should retain three fifths of its value, surrendering two fifths to its associate. These shares were subsequently to be subdivided among the crew of each vessel, in accordance with the articles already obtaining between each captain and his own men. For the rest, the articles contained all the clauses that were usual, among which was the clause that any man found guilty of abstracting or concealing any part of a prize, be it of the value of no more than a peso, should be summarily hanged from the yardarm.

All being now settled they made ready for sea, and on the very eve of sailing, Levasseur narrowly escaped being shot in a romantic attempt to scale the wall of the Governor's garden, with the object of taking passionate leave of the infatuated Mademoiselle d'Ogeron. He desisted after having been twice fired upon from a fragrant ambush of pimento trees where the Governor's guards were posted, and he departed vowing to take different and very definite measures on his return.

That night he slept on board his ship, which with characteristic flamboyance he had named *La Foudre*, and there on the following day he received a visit from Captain Blood, whom he greeted half-mockingly as his admiral. The Irishman came to settle certain final details of which all that need concern us is an understanding that, in the event of the two vessels becoming separated by accident or design, they should rejoin each other as soon as might be at Tortuga.

Thereafter Levasseur entertained his admiral to dinner, and jointly they drank success to the expedition, so copiously on the part of Levasseur that when the time came to separate he was as nearly drunk as it seemed possible for him to be and yet retain his understanding.

Finally, towards evening, Captain Blood went over the side and was rowed back to his great ship with her red bulwarks and gilded ports, touched into a lovely thing of flame by the setting sun.

He was a little heavy-hearted. I have said that he was a judge of men, and his judgment of Levasseur filled him with misgivings which were growing heavier in a measure as the hour of departure approached.

He expressed it to Wolverstone, who met him as he stepped aboard the *Arabella:*

"You overpersuaded me into those articles, you blackguard; and it'll surprise me if any good comes of this association."

The giant rolled his single bloodthirsty eye, and sneered, thrusting out his heavy jaw. "We'll wring the dog's neck if there's any treachery."

"So we will — if we are there to wring it by then." And on that, dismissing the matter: "We sail in the morning, on the first of the ebb," he announced, and went off to his cabin.

CHAPTER XIV

LEVASSEUR'S HEROICS

IT would be somewhere about ten o'clock on the following morning, a full hour before the time appointed for sailing, when a canoe brought up alongside *La Foudre*, and a half-caste Indian stepped out of her and went up the ladder. He was clad in drawers of hairy, untanned hide, and a red blanket served him for a cloak. He was the bearer of a folded scrap of paper for Captain Levasseur.

The Captain unfolded the letter, sadly soiled and crumpled by contact with the half-caste's person. Its contents may be roughly translated thus:

"*My well-beloved* — I am in the Dutch brig *Jongvrouw*, which is about to sail. Resolved to separate us for ever, my cruel father is sending me to Europe in my brother's charge. I implore you, come to my rescue. Deliver me, my well-beloved hero! — Your desolated Madeleine, who loves you."

The well-beloved hero was moved to the soul of him by that passionate appeal. His scowling glance swept the bay for the Dutch brig, which he knew had been due to sail for Amsterdam with a cargo of hides and tobacco.

She was nowhere to be seen among the shipping in that narrow, rock-bound harbour. He roared out the question in his mind.

In answer the half-caste pointed out beyond the frothing surf that marked the position of the reef constituting one of the stronghold's main defences. Away beyond it, a mile or so distant, a sail was standing out to sea.

"There she go," he said.

"There!" The Frenchman gazed and stared, his face growing white. The man's wicked temper awoke, and turned to vent itself upon the messenger. "And where have you been that you come here only now with this? Answer me!"

The half-caste shrank terrified before his fury. His explanation, if he had one, was paralyzed by fear. Levasseur took him by the throat, shook him twice, snarling the while, then hurled him into the scuppers. The man's head struck the gunwale as he fell, and he lay there, quite still, a trickle of blood issuing from his mouth.

Levasseur dashed one hand against the other, as if dusting them.

"Heave that muck overboard," he ordered some of those who stood idling in the waist. "Then up anchor, and let us after the Dutchman."

"Steady, Captain. What's that?" There was a restraining hand upon his shoulder, and the broad face of his lieutenant Cahusac, a burly, callous Breton scoundrel, was stolidly confronting him.

Levasseur made clear his purpose with a deal of unnecessary obscenity.

Cahusac shook his head. "A Dutch brig!" said he. "Impossible! We should never be allowed."

"And who the devil will deny us?" Levasseur was between amazement and fury.

"For one thing, there's your own crew will be none too willing. For another there's Captain Blood."

"I care nothing for Captain Blood . . ."

"But it is necessary that you should. He has the power, the weight of metal and of men, and if I know him at all he'll sink us before he'll suffer interference with the Dutch. He has his own views of privateering, this Captain Blood, as I warned you."

"Ah!" said Levasseur, showing his teeth. But his eyes, riveted upon that distant sail, were gloomily thoughtful. Not for long. The imagination and resource which Captain Blood had detected in the fellow soon suggested a course.

Cursing in his soul, and even before the anchor was weighed, the association into which he had entered, he was already studying ways of evasion. What Cahusac implied was true: Blood would never suffer violence to be done in his presence to a Dutchman; but it might be done in his absence; and, being done, Blood must perforce condone it, since it would then be too late to protest.

Within the hour the *Arabella* and *La Foudre* were beating out to sea together. Without understanding the change of plan involved, Captain Blood, nevertheless, accepted it, and weighed anchor before the appointed time upon perceiving his associate to do so.

All day the Dutch brig was in sight, though by evening she had dwindled to the merest speck on the northern horizon. The course prescribed for Blood and Levasseur lay eastward along the northern shores of Hispaniola. To that course the *Arabella* continued to hold steadily throughout the night. When day broke again, she was alone. *La Foudre* under cover of the darkness had struck away to the northeast with every rag of canvas on her yards

Cahusac had attempted yet again to protest against this.

"The devil take you!" Levasseur had answered him. "A ship's a ship, be she Dutch or Spanish, and ships are our present need. That will suffice for the men."

His lieutenant said no more. But from his glimpse of the letter, knowing that a girl and not a ship was his captain's real objective, he gloomily shook his head as he rolled away on his bowed legs to give the necessary orders.

Dawn found *La Foudre* close on the Dutchman's heels, not a mile astern, and the sight of her very evidently flustered the *Jongvrouw*. No doubt mademoiselle's brother recognizing Levasseur's ship would be responsible for the Dutch uneasiness. They saw the *Jongvrouw* crowding canvas in a futile endeavour to outsail them, whereupon they stood off to starboard and raced on until they were in a position whence they could send a warning shot across her bow. The *Jongvrouw* veered, showed them her rudder, and opened fire with her stern chasers. The small shot went whistling through *La Foudre's* shrouds with some slight damage to her canvas. Followed a brief running fight in the course of which the Dutchman let fly a broadside.

Five minutes after that they were board and board, the *Jongvrouw* held tight in the clutches of *La Foudre's* grapnels, and the buccaneers pouring noisily into her waist.

The Dutchman's master, purple in the face, stood forward to beard the pirate, followed closely by an elegant, pale-faced young gentleman in whom Levasseur recognized his brother-in-law elect.

"Captain Levasseur, this is an outrage for which you shall be made to answer. What do you seek aboard my ship?"

"At first I sought only that which belongs to me, something of which I am being robbed. But since you chose war and opened fire on me with some damage to my ship and loss of life to five of my men, why, war it is, and your ship a prize of war."

From the quarter rail Mademoiselle d'Ogeron looked down with glowing eyes in breathless wonder upon her well-beloved hero. Gloriously heroic he seemed as he stood towering there, masterful, audacious, beautiful. He saw her, and with a glad shout sprang towards her. The Dutch master got in his way with hands upheld to arrest his progress. Levasseur did not stay to argue with him: he was too impatient to reach his mistress. He swung the poleaxe that he carried, and the Dutchman went down in blood with a cloven skull. The eager lover stepped across the body and came on, his countenance joyously alight. But mademoiselle was shrinking now, in horror. She was a girl upon the threshold of glorious womanhood, of a fine height and nobly moulded, with heavy coils of glossy black hair above and about a face that was of the colour of old ivory. Her countenance was cast in lines of arrogance, stressed by the low lids of her full dark eyes.

In a bound her well-beloved was beside her. Flinging away his bloody poleaxe, he opened wide his arms to enfold her. But she still shrank even within his embrace, which would not be denied; a look of dread had come to temper the normal arrogance of her almost perfect face.

"Mine, mine at last, and in spite of all!" he cried exultantly, theatrically, truly heroic.

But she, endeavouring to thrust him back, her hands against his breast, could only falter: "Why, why did you kill him?"

He laughed, as a hero should; and answered her heroically, with the tolerance of a god for the mortal to whom he condescends: "He stood between us. Let his death be a symbol, a warning. Let all who would stand between us mark it and beware."

It was so splendidly terrific, the gesture of it was so broad and fine and his magnetism so compelling, that she cast her silly tremors and yielded herself freely, intoxicated, to his fond embrace. Thereafter he swung her to his shoulder, and stepping with ease beneath that burden, bore her in a sort of triumph, lustily cheered by his men, to the deck of his own ship. Her inconsiderate brother might have ruined that romantic scene but for the watchful Cahusac, who quietly tripped him up, and then trussed him like a fowl.

Thereafter, what time the Captain languished in his lady's smile within the cabin, Cahusac was dealing with the spoils of war. The Dutch crew was ordered into the longboat, and bidden go to the devil. Fortunately, as they numbered fewer than thirty, the longboat, though perilously overcrowded, could yet contain them. Next, Cahusac having inspected the cargo, put a quartermaster and a score of men aboard the *Jongvrouw*, and left her to follow *La Foudre*, which he now headed south for the Leeward Islands.

Cahusac was disposed to be ill-humoured. The risk they had run in taking the Dutch brig and doing vio-

lence to members of the family of the Governor of
Tortuga, was out of all proportion to the value of
their prize. He said so, sullenly, to Levasseur.

"You'll keep that opinion to yourself," the Captain
answered him. "Don't think I am the man to thrust
my neck into a noose, without knowing how I am going to take it out again. I shall send an offer of terms
to the Governor of Tortuga that he will be forced to
accept. Set a course for the Virgen Magra. We'll go
ashore, and settle things from there. And tell them to
fetch that milksop Ogeron to the cabin." Levasseur
went back to the adoring lady. Thither, too, the
lady's brother was presently conducted. The Captain rose to receive him, bending his stalwart height
to avoid striking the cabin roof with his head.

Mademoiselle rose too. "Why this?" she asked
Levasseur, pointing to her brother's pinioned wrists
— the remains of Cahusac's precautions.

"I deplore it," said he. "I desire it to end. Let
M. d'Ogeron give me his parole . . ."

"I give you nothing," flashed the white-faced
youth, who did not lack for spirit.

"You see." Levasseur shrugged his deep regret,
and mademoiselle turned protesting to her brother.

"Henri, this is foolish! You are not behaving as
my friend. You . . ."

"Little fool," her brother answered her — and the
"little" was out of place; she was the taller of the
twain. "Little fool, do you think I should be acting
as your friend to make terms with this blackguard
pirate?"

"Steady, my young cockerel!" Levasseur laughed.
But his laugh was not nice.

"Don't you perceive your wicked folly in the harm it has brought already? Lives have been lost — men have died — that this monster might overtake you. And don't you yet realize where you stand — in the power of this beast, of this cur born in a kennel and bred in thieving and murder?"

He might have said more but that Levasseur struck him across the mouth. Levasseur, you see, cared as little as another to hear the truth about himself.

Mademoiselle suppressed a scream, as the youth staggered back under the blow. He came to rest against a bulkhead, and leaned there with bleeding lips. But his spirit was unquenched, and there was a ghastly smile on his white face as his eyes sought his sister's.

"You see," he said simply. "He strikes a man whose hands are bound."

The simple words, and, more than the words, their tone of ineffable disdain, aroused the passion that never slumbered deeply in Levasseur.

"And what should you do, puppy, if your hands were unbound?" He took his prisoner by the breast of his doublet and shook him. "Answer me! What should you do? Tchah! You empty windbag! You . . ." And then came a torrent of words unknown to mademoiselle, yet of whose foulness her intuitions made her conscious.

With blenched cheeks she stood by the cabin table, and cried out to Levasseur to stop. To obey her, he opened the door, and flung her brother through it.

"Put that rubbish under hatches until I call for it again," he roared, and shut the door.

Composing himself, he turned to the girl again with

a deprecatory smile. But no smile answered him from
her set face. She had seen her beloved hero's nature
in curl-papers, as it were, and she found the spectacle disgusting and terrifying. It recalled the brutal
slaughter of the Dutch captain, and suddenly she
realized that what her brother had just said of this
man was no more than true. Fear growing to panic
was written on her face, as she stood there leaning for
support against the table.

"Why, sweetheart, what is this?" Levasseur moved
towards her. She recoiled before him. There was a
smile on his face, a glitter in his eyes that fetched her
heart into her throat.

He caught her, as she reached the uttermost limits
of the cabin, seized her in his long arms and pulled
her to him.

"No, no!" she panted.

"Yes, yes," he mocked her, and his mockery was
the most terrible thing of all. He crushed her to him
brutally, deliberately hurtful because she resisted, and
kissed her whilst she writhed in his embrace. Then,
his passion mounting, he grew angry and stripped off
the last rag of hero's mask that still may have hung
upon his face. "Little fool, did you not hear your
brother say that you are in my power? Remember it,
and remember that of your own free will you came. I
am not the man with whom a woman can play fast
and loose. So get sense, my girl, and accept what you
have invited." He kissed her again, almost contemptuously, and flung her off. "No more scowls," he said.
"You'll be sorry else."

Some one knocked. Cursing the interruption,
Levasseur strode off to open. Cahusac stood before

him. The Breton's face was grave. He came to report that they had sprung a leak between wind and water, the consequence of damage sustained from one of the Dutchman's shots. In alarm Levasseur went off with him. The leakage was not serious so long as the weather kept fine; but should a storm overtake them it might speedily become so. A man was slung overboard to make a partial stoppage with a sail-cloth, and the pumps were got to work.

Ahead of them a low cloud showed on the horizon, which Cahusac pronounced one of the northernmost of the Virgin Islands.

"We must run for shelter there, and careen her," said Levasseur. "I do not trust this oppressive heat. A storm may catch us before we make land."

"A storm or something else," said Cahusac grimly. "Have you noticed that?" He pointed away to starboard.

Levasseur looked, and caught his breath. Two ships that at the distance seemed of considerable burden were heading towards them some five miles away.

"If they follow us what is to happen?" demanded Cahusac.

"We'll fight whether we're in case to do so or not," swore Levasseur.

"Counsels of despair." Cahusac was contemptuous. To mark it he spat upon the deck. "This comes of going to sea with a lovesick madman. Now, keep your temper, Captain, for the hands will be at the end of theirs if we have trouble as a result of this Dutchman business."

For the remainder of that day Levasseur's thoughts

were of anything but love. He remained on deck, his eyes now upon the land, now upon those two slowly gaining ships. To run for the open could avail him nothing, and in his leaky condition would provide an additional danger. He must stand at bay and fight. And then, towards evening, when within three miles of shore and when he was about to give the order to strip for battle, he almost fainted from relief to hear a voice from the crow's-nest above announce that the larger of the two ships was the *Arabella*. Her companion was presumably a prize.

But the pessimism of Cahusac abated nothing.

"That is but the lesser evil," he growled. "What will Blood say about this Dutchman?"

"Let him say what he pleases." Levasseur laughed in the immensity of his relief.

"And what about the children of the Governor of Tortuga?"

"He must not know."

"He'll come to know in the end."

"Aye, but by then, morbleu, the matter will be settled. I shall have made my peace with the Governor. I tell you I know the way to compel Ogeron to come to terms."

Presently the four vessels lay to off the northern coast of La Virgen Magra, a narrow little island arid and treeless, some twelve miles by three, uninhabited save by birds and turtles and unproductive of anything but salt, of which there were considerable ponds to the south.

Levasseur put off in a boat accompanied by Cahusac and two other officers, and went to visit Captain Blood aboard the *Arabella*.

"Our brief separation has been mighty profitable," was Captain Blood's greeting. "It's a busy morning we've both had." He was in high good-humour as he led the way to the great cabin for a rendering of accounts.

The tall ship that accompanied the *Arabella* was a Spanish vessel of twenty-six guns, the *Santiago* from Puerto Rico with a hundred and twenty thousand weight of cacao, forty thousand pieces of eight, and the value of ten thousand more in jewels. A rich capture of which two fifths under the articles went to Levasseur and his crew. Of the money and jewels a division was made on the spot. The cacao it was agreed should be taken to Tortuga to be sold.

Then it was the turn of Levasseur, and black grew the brow of Captain Blood as the Frenchman's tale was unfolded.

At the end he roundly expressed his disapproval. The Dutch were a friendly people whom it was a folly to alienate, particularly for so paltry a matter as these hides and tobacco, which at most would fetch a bare twenty thousand pieces.

But Levasseur answered him, as he had answered Cahusac, that a ship was a ship, and it was ships they needed against their projected enterprise. Perhaps because things had gone well with him that day, Blood ended by shrugging the matter aside. Thereupon Levasseur proposed that the *Arabella* and her prize should return to Tortuga there to unload the cacao and enlist the further adventurers that could now be shipped. Levasseur meanwhile would effect certain necessary repairs, and then proceeding south, await his admiral at Saltatudos, an island conveniently situated — in the latitude of 11° 11′ N. — for their enterprise against Maracaybo.

To Levasseur's relief, Captain Blood not only agreed, but pronounced himself ready to set sail at once.

No sooner had the *Arabella* departed than Levasseur brought his ships into the lagoon, and set his crew to work upon the erection of temporary quarters ashore for himself, his men, and his enforced guests during the careening and repairing of *La Foudre*.

At sunset that evening the wind freshened; it grew to a gale, and from that to such a hurricane that Levasseur was thankful to find himself ashore and his ships in safe shelter. He wondered a little how it might be faring with Captain Blood out there at the mercy of that terrific storm; but he did not permit concern to trouble him unduly.

CHAPTER XV

THE RANSOM

IN the glory of the following morning, sparkling and clear after the storm, with an invigorating, briny tang in the air from the salt-ponds on the south of the island, a curious scene was played on the beach of the Virgen Magra, at the foot of a ridge of bleached dunes, beside the spread of sail from which Levasseur had improvised a tent.

Enthroned upon an empty cask sat the French fili-buster to transact important business: the business of making himself safe with the Governor of Tortuga.

A guard of honour of a half-dozen officers hung about him; five of them were rude boucan-hunters, in stained jerkins and leather breeches; the sixth was Cahusac. Before him, guarded by two half-naked negroes, stood young d'Ogeron, in frilled shirt and satin small-clothes and fine shoes of Cordovan leather. He was stripped of doublet, and his hands were tied behind him. The young gentleman's comely face was haggard. Near at hand, and also under guard, but unpinioned, mademoiselle his sister sat hunched upon a hillock of sand. She was very pale, and it was in vain that she sought to veil in a mask of arrogance the fears by which she was assailed.

Levasseur addressed himself to M. d'Ogeron. He spoke at long length. In the end —

"I trust, monsieur," said he, with mock suavity, "that I have made myself quite clear. So that there may be no misunderstandings, I will recapitulate. Your ransom is fixed at twenty thousand pieces of eight, and you shall have liberty on parole to go to Tortuga to collect it. In fact, I shall provide the means to convey you thither, and you shall have a month in which to come and go. Meanwhile, your sister remains with me as a hostage. Your father should not consider such a sum excessive as the price of his son's liberty and to provide a dowry for his daughter. Indeed, if anything, I am too modest, pardi! M. d'Ogeron is reputed a wealthy man."

M. d'Ogeron the younger raised his head and looked the Captain boldly in the face.

"I refuse — utterly and absolutely, do you understand? So do your worst, and be damned for a filthy pirate without decency and without honour."

"But what words!" laughed Levasseur. "What heat and what foolishness! You have not considered the alternative. When you do, you will not persist in your refusal. You will not do that in any case. We have spurs for the reluctant. And I warn you against giving me your parole under stress, and afterwards playing me false. I shall know how to find and punish you. Meanwhile, remember your sister's honour is in pawn to me. Should you forget to return with the dowry, you will not consider it unreasonable that I forget to marry her."

Levasseur's smiling eyes, intent upon the young man's face, saw the horror that crept into his glance. M. d'Ogeron cast a wild glance at mademoiselle, and observed the grey despair that had almost stamped the beauty from her face.

Disgust and fury swept across his countenance.

Then he braced himself and answered resolutely: "No, you dog! A thousand times, no!"

"You are foolish to persist." Levasseur spoke without anger, with a coldly mocking regret. His fingers had been busy tying knots in a length of whipcord. He held it up. "You know this? It is a rosary of pain that has wrought the conversion of many a stubborn heretic. It is capable of screwing the eyes out of a man's head by way of helping him to see reason. As you please."

He flung the length of knotted cord to one of the negroes, who in an instant made it fast about the prisoner's brows. Then between cord and cranium the black inserted a short length of metal, round and slender as a pipe-stem. That done he rolled his eyes towards Levasseur, awaiting the Captain's signal.

Levasseur considered his victim, and beheld him tense and braced, his haggard face of a leaden hue, beads of perspiration glinting on his pallid brow just beneath the whipcord.

Mademoiselle cried out, and would have risen: but her guards restrained her, and she sank down again, moaning.

"I beg that you will spare yourself and your sister," said the Captain, "by being reasonable. What, after all, is the sum I have named? To your wealthy father a bagatelle. I repeat, I have been too modest. But since I have said twenty thousand pieces of eight, twenty thousand pieces it shall be."

"And for what, if you please, have you said twenty thousand pieces of eight?"

In execrable French, but in a voice that was crisp and pleasant, seeming to echo some of the mockery that had invested Levasseur's, that question floated over their heads.

Startled, Levasseur and his officers looked up and round.

On the crest of the dunes behind them, in sharp silhouette against the deep cobalt of the sky, they beheld a tall, lean figure scrupulously dressed in black with silver lace, a crimson ostrich plume curled about the broad brim of his hat affording the only touch of colour. Under that hat was the tawny face of Captain Blood. Levasseur gathered himself up with an oath of amazement. He had conceived Captain Blood by now well below the horizon, on his way to Tortuga, assuming him to have been so fortunate as to have weathered last night's storm.

Launching himself upon the yielding sand, into which he sank to the level of the calves of his fine boots of Spanish leather, Captain Blood came sliding erect to the beach. He was followed by Wolverstone, and a dozen others. As he came to a standstill, he doffed his hat, with a flourish, to the lady. Then he turned to Levasseur.

"Good-morning, my Captain," said he, and proceeded to explain his presence. "It was last night's hurricane compelled our return. We had no choice but to ride before it with stripped poles, and it drove us back the way we had gone. Moreover — as the devil would have it! — the *Santiago* sprang her mainmast; and so I was glad to put into a cove on the west of the island a couple of miles away, and we've walked across to stretch our legs, and to give you good-day. But who are these?" And he designated the man and the woman.

Cahusac shrugged his shoulders, and tossed his long arms to heaven.

"Voilà!" said he, pregnantly, to the firmament.

Levasseur gnawed his lip, and changed colour. But he controlled himself to answer civilly:

"As you see, two prisoners."

"Ah! Washed ashore in last night's gale, eh?

"Not so." Levasseur contained himself with difficulty before that irony. "They were in the Dutch brig."

"I don't remember that you mentioned them before."

"I did not. They are prisoners of my own — a personal matter. They are French."

"French!" Captain Blood's light eyes stabbed at Levasseur, then at the prisoners.

M. d'Ogeron stood tense and braced as before, but the grey horror had left his face. Hope had leapt within him at this interruption, obviously as little expected by his tormentor as by himself. His sister, moved by a similar intuition, was leaning forward with parted lips and gaping eyes.

Captain Blood fingered his lip, and frowned thoughtfully upon Levasseur.

"Yesterday you surprised me by making war upon the friendly Dutch. But now it seems that not even your own countrymen are safe from you."

"Have I not said that these . . . that this is a matter personal to me?"

"Ah! And their names?"

Captain Blood's crisp, authoritative, faintly disdainful manner stirred Levasseur's quick anger. The blood crept slowly back into his blenched face, and his glance grew in insolence, almost in menace. Meanwhile the prisoner answered for him.

"I am Henri d'Ogeron, and this is my sister."

"D'Ogeron?" Captain Blood stared. "Are you related by chance to my good friend the Governor of Tortuga?"

"He is my father."

Levasseur swung aside with an imprecation. In Captain Blood, amazement for the moment quenched every other emotion.

"The saints preserve us now! Are you quite mad, Levasseur? First you molest the Dutch, who are our friends; next you take prisoners two persons that are French, your own countrymen; and now, faith, they're no less than the children of the Governor of Tortuga, which is the one safe place of shelter that we enjoy in these islands . . ."

Levasseur broke in angrily:

"Must I tell you again that it is a matter personal to me? I make myself alone responsible to the Governor of Tortuga."

"And the twenty thousand pieces of eight? Is that also a matter personal to you?"

"It is."

"Now I don't agree with you at all." Captain Blood sat down on the cask that Levasseur had lately occupied, and looked up blandly. "I may inform you, to save time, that I heard the entire proposal that you made to this lady and this gentleman, and I'll also remind you that we sail under articles that admit no ambiguities. You have fixed their ransom at twenty thousand pieces of eight. That sum then belongs to your crews and mine in the proportions by the articles established. You'll hardly wish to dispute it. But what is far more grave is that you have concealed from me this part of the prizes taken on your last cruise, and for such an offence as that the articles provide certain penalties that are something severe in character."

"Ho, ho!" laughed Levasseur unpleasantly. Then added: "If you dislike my conduct we can dissolve the association."

"That is my intention. But we'll dissolve it when and in the manner that I choose, and that will be as soon as you have satisfied the articles under which we sailed upon this cruise."

"What do you mean?"

"I'll be as short as I can," said Captain Blood. "I'll waive for the moment the unseemliness of making war upon the Dutch, of taking French prisoners, and of provoking the anger of the Governor of Tortuga. I'll accept the situation as I find it. Yourself you've fixed the ransom of this couple at twenty thousand pieces, and, as I gather, the lady is to be your perquisite. But why should she be your perquisite more than another's, seeing that she belongs by the articles to all of us, as a prize of war?"

Black as thunder grew the brow of Levasseur.

"However," added Captain Blood, "I'll not dispute her to you if you are prepared to buy her."

"Buy her?"

"At the price you have set upon her."

Levasseur contained his rage, that he might reason with the Irishman. "That is the ransom of the man. It is to be paid for him by the Governor of Tortuga."

"No, no. Ye've parcelled the twain together —

very oddly, I confess. Ye've set their value at twenty
thousand pieces, and for that sum you may have
them, since you desire it; but you'll pay for them the
twenty thousand pieces that are ultimately to come
to you as the ransom of one and the dowry of the
other; and that sum shall be divided among our
crews. So that you do that, it is conceivable that our
followers may take a lenient view of your breach of
the articles we jointly signed."

Levasseur laughed savagely. "Ah ça! Crédieu!
The good jest!"

"I quite agree with you," said Captain Blood.

To Levasseur the jest lay in that Captain Blood,
with no more than a dozen followers, should come
there attempting to hector him who had a hundred
men within easy call. But it seemed that he had left
out of his reckoning something which his opponent
had counted in. For as, laughing still, Levasseur
swung to his officers, he saw that which choked the
laughter in his throat. Captain Blood had shrewdly
played upon the cupidity that was the paramount inspiration of those adventurers. And Levasseur now
read clearly on their faces how completely they
adopted Captain Blood's suggestion that all must par-
ticipate in the ransom which their leader had thought
to appropriate to himself.

It gave the gaudy ruffian pause, and whilst in his
heart he cursed those followers of his, who could be
faithful only to their greed, he perceived — and only
just in time — that he had best tread warily.

"You misunderstand," he said, swallowing his
rage. "The ransom is for division, when it comes. The
girl, meanwhile, is mine on that understanding."

"Good!" grunted Cahusac. "On that understanding all arranges itself."

"You think so?" said Captain Blood. "But if M. d'Ogeron should refuse to pay the ransom? What then?" He laughed, and got lazily to his feet. "No, no. If Captain Levasseur is meanwhile to keep the girl, as he proposes, then let him pay this ransom, and be his the risk if it should afterwards not be forthcoming."

"That's it!" cried one of Levasseur's officers. And Cahusac added: "It's reasonable, that! Captain Blood is right. It is in the articles."

"What is in the articles, you fools?" Levasseur was in danger of losing his head. "Sacré Dieu! Where do you suppose that I have twenty thousand pieces? My whole share of the prizes of this cruise does not come to half that sum. I'll be your debtor until I've earned it. Will that content you?"

All things considered, there is not a doubt that it would have done so had not Captain Blood intended otherwise.

"And if you should die before you have earned it? Ours is a calling fraught with risks, my Captain."

"Damn you!" Levasseur flung upon him livid with fury. "Will nothing satisfy you?"

"Oh, but yes. Twenty thousand pieces of eight for immediate division."

"I haven't got it."

"Then let some one buy the prisoners who has."

"And who do you suppose has it if I have not?"

"I have," said Captain Blood.

"You have!" Levasseur's mouth fell open. "You ... you want the girl?"

"Why not? And I exceed you in gallantry in that I will make sacrifices to obtain her, and in honesty in that I am ready to pay for what I want."

Levasseur stared at him foolishly agape. Behind him pressed his officers, gaping also.

Captain Blood sat down again on the cask, and drew from an inner pocket of his doublet a little leather bag. "I am glad to be able to resolve a difficulty that at one moment seemed insoluble." And under the bulging eyes of Levasseur and his officers, he untied the mouth of the bag and rolled into his left palm four or five pearls each of the size of a sparrow's egg. There were twenty such in the bag, the very pick of those taken in that raid upon the pearl fleet. "You boast a knowledge of pearls, Cahusac. At what do you value this?"

The Breton took between coarse finger and thumb the proffered lustrous, delicately iridescent sphere, his shrewd eyes appraising it.

"A thousand pieces," he answered shortly.

"It will fetch rather more in Tortuga or Jamaica," said Captain Blood, "and twice as much in Europe. But I'll accept your valuation. They are almost of a size, as you can see. Here are twelve, representing twelve thousand pieces of eight, which is *La Foudre's* share of three fifths of the prize, as provided by the articles. For the eight thousand pieces that go to the *Arabella*, I make myself responsible to my own men. And now, Wolverstone, if you please, will you take my property aboard the *Arabella?*" He stood up again, indicating the prisoners.

"Ah, no!" Levasseur threw wide the floodgates of his fury. "Ah, that, no, by example! You shall not take her . . ." He would have sprung upon Captain Blood, who stood aloof, alert, tight-lipped, and watchful.

But it was one of Levasseur's own officers who hindered him.

"Nom de Dieu, my Captain! What will you do? It is settled; honourably settled with satisfaction to all."

"To all?" blazed Levasseur. "Ah ça! To all of you, you animals! But what of me?"

Cahusac, with the pearls clutched in his capacious hand, stepped up to him on the other side. "Don't be a fool, Captain. Do you want to provoke trouble between the crews? His men outnumber us by nearly two to one. What's a girl more or less? In Heaven's name, let her go. He's paid handsomely for her, and dealt fairly with us."

"Dealt fairly?" roared the infuriated Captain. "You . . ." In all his foul vocabulary he could find no epithet to describe his lieutenant. He caught him a blow that almost sent him sprawling. The pearls were scattered in the sand.

Cahusac dived after them, his fellows with him. Vengeance must wait. For some moments they groped there on hands and knees, oblivious of all else. And yet in those moments vital things were happening.

Levasseur, his hand on his sword, his face a white mask of rage, was confronting Captain Blood to hinder his departure.

"You do not take her while I live!" he cried.

"Then I'll take her when you're dead," said Captain Blood, and his own blade flashed in the sunlight.

"The articles provide that any man of whatever rank concealing any part of a prize, be it of the value of no more than a peso, shall be hanged at the yardarm. It's what I intended for you in the end. But since ye prefer it this way, ye muckrake, faith, I'll be humouring you."

He waved away the men who would have interfered, and the blades rang together.

M. d'Ogeron looked on, a man bemused, unable to surmise what the issue either way could mean for him. Meanwhile, two of Blood's men who had taken the place of the Frenchman's negro guards, had removed the crown of whipcord from his brow. As for mademoiselle, she had risen, and was leaning forward, a hand pressed tightly to her heaving breast, her face deathly pale, a wild terror in her eyes.

It was soon over. The brute strength, upon which Levasseur so confidently counted, could avail nothing against the Irishman's practised skill. When, with both lungs transfixed, he lay prone on the white sand, coughing out his rascally life, Captain Blood looked calmly at Cahusac across the body.

"I think that cancels the articles between us," he said.

With soulless, cynical eyes Cahusac considered the twitching body of his recent leader. Had Levasseur been a man of different temper, the affair might have ended in a very different manner. But, then, it is certain that Captain Blood would have adopted in dealing with him different tactics. As it was, Levasseur commanded neither love nor loyalty. The men who followed him were the very dregs of that vile trade, and cupidity was their only inspiration. Upon that cupidity Captain Blood had deftly played, until he had brought them to find Levasseur guilty of the one offence they deemed unpardonable, the crime of appropriating to himself something which might be converted into gold and shared amongst them all.

Thus now the threatening mob of buccaneers that came hastening to the theatre of that swift tragi-comedy were appeased by a dozen words of Cahusac's.

Whilst still they hesitated, Blood added something to quicken their decision.

"If you will come to our anchorage, you shall receive at once your share of the booty of the *Santiago*, that you may dispose of it as you please."

They crossed the island, the two prisoners accompanying them, and later that day, the division made, they would have parted company but that Cahusac, at the instances of the men who had elected him Levasseur's successor, offered Captain Blood anew the services of that French contingent.

"If you will sail with me again," the Captain answered him, "you may do so on the condition that you make your peace with the Dutch, and restore the brig and her cargo."

The condition was accepted, and Captain Blood went off to find his guests, the children of the Governor of Tortuga.

Mademoiselle d'Ogeron and her brother — the latter now relieved of his bonds — sat in the great cabin of the *Arabella*, whither they had been conducted.

Wine and food had been placed upon the table by Benjamin, Captain Blood's negro steward and cook, who had intimated to them that it was for their entertainment. But it had remained untouched.

Brother and sister sat there in agonized bewilderment, conceiving that their escape was but from frying-pan to fire. At length, overwrought by the suspense, mademoiselle flung herself upon her knees before her brother to implore his pardon for all the evil brought upon them by her wicked folly.

M. d'Ogeron was not in a forgiving mood.

"I am glad that at least you realize what you have done. And now this other filibuster has bought you, and you belong to him. You realize that, too, I hope."

He might have said more, but he checked upon perceiving that the door was opening. Captain Blood, coming from settling matters with the followers of Levasseur, stood on the threshold. M. d'Ogeron had not troubled to restrain his high-pitched voice, and the Captain had overheard the Frenchman's last two sentences. Therefore he perfectly understood why mademoiselle should bound up at sight of him, and shrink back in fear.

He doffed his feathered hat, and came forward to the table.

"Mademoiselle," said he in his vile but fluent French, "I beg you to dismiss your fears. Aboard this ship you shall be treated with all honour. So soon as we are in case to put to sea again, we steer a course for Tortuga to take you home to your father. And pray do not consider that I have bought you, as your brother has just said. All that I have done has been to provide the ransom necessary to bribe a gang of scoundrels to depart from obedience to the arch-scoundrel who commanded them, and so deliver you from all peril. Count it, if you please, a friendly loan to be repaid entirely at your convenience."

Mademoiselle stared at him in unbelief. M. d'Ogeron rose to his feet.

"Monsieur, is it possible that you are serious?"

"I am. It may not happen often nowadays. I may be a pirate. But my ways are not the ways of Levasseur, who should have stayed in Europe, and practised purse-cutting. I have a sort of honour — shall we say, some rags of honour? — remaining me from better days." Then on a brisker note he added: "We dine in an hour, and I trust that you will honour my table with your company. Meanwhile, Benjamin will see, monsieur, that you are more suitably provided in the matter of wardrobe."

He bowed to them, and turned to depart again, but mademoiselle detained him.

"Monsieur!" she cried sharply.

He checked and turned, whilst slowly she approached him, regarding him between dread and wonder.

"Oh, you are noble!"

"I shouldn't put it as high as that myself," said he.

"You are, you are! And it is but right that you should know all."

"Madelon!" her brother cried out, to restrain her.

But she would not be restrained. Her surcharged heart must overflow in confidence.

"Monsieur, for what befell I am greatly at fault. This man — this Levasseur . . ."

He stared, incredulous in his turn. "My God! Is it possible? That animal!"

Abruptly she fell on her knees, caught his hand and kissed it before he could wrench it from her.

"What do you do?" he cried.

"An amende. In my mind I dishonoured you by deeming you his like, by conceiving your fight with Levasseur a combat between jackals. On my knees, monsieur, I implore you to forgive me."

Captain Blood looked down upon her, and a smile broke on his lips, irradiating the blue eyes that looked so oddly light in that tawny face.

"Why, child," said he, "I might find it hard to forgive you the stupidity of having thought otherwise."

As he handed her to her feet again, he assured himself that he had behaved rather well in the affair. Then he sighed. That dubious fame of his that had spread so quickly across the Caribbean would by now have reached the ears of Arabella Bishop. That she would despise him, he could not doubt, deeming him no better than all the other scoundrels who drove this villainous buccaneering trade. Therefore he hoped that some echo of this deed might reach her also, and be set by her against some of that contempt. For the whole truth, which he withheld from Mademoiselle d'Ogeron, was that in venturing his life to save her, he had been driven by the thought that the deed must be pleasing in the eyes of Miss Bishop could she but witness it.

CHAPTER XVI

THE TRAP

THAT affair of Mademoiselle d'Ogeron bore as its natural fruit an improvement in the already cordial relations between Captain Blood and the Governor of Tortuga. At the fine stone house, with its green-jalousied windows, which M. d'Ogeron had built himself in a spacious and luxuriant garden to the east of Cayona, the Captain became a very welcome guest. M. d'Ogeron was in the Captain's debt for more than the twenty thousand pieces of eight which he had provided for mademoiselle's ransom; and shrewd, hard bargain-driver though he might be, the Frenchman could be generous and understood the sentiment of gratitude. This he now proved in every possible way, and under his powerful protection the credit of Captain Blood among the buccaneers very rapidly reached its zenith.

So when it came to fitting out his fleet for that enterprise against Maracaybo, which had originally been Levasseur's project, he did not want for either ships or men to follow him. He recruited five hundred adventurers in all, and he might have had as many thousands if he could have offered them accommodation. Similarly without difficulty he might have increased his fleet to twice its strength of ships but that he preferred to keep it what it was. The three vessels to which he confined it were the *Arabella*, the *La Foudre*, which Cahusac now commanded with a contingent of some sixscore Frenchmen, and the *Santiago*, which had been refitted and rechristened the *Elizabeth*, after that Queen of England whose seamen had humbled Spain as Captain Blood now hoped to humble it again. Hagthorpe, in virtue of his service in the navy, was appointed by Blood to command her, and the appointment was confirmed by the men.

It was some months after the rescue of Mademoiselle d'Ogeron — in August of that year 1687 — that this little fleet, after some minor adventures which I pass over in silence, sailed into the great lake of Maracaybo and effected its raid upon that opulent city of the Main.

The affair did not proceed exactly as was hoped, and Blood's force came to find itself in a precarious position. This is best explained in the words employed by Cahusac — which Pitt has carefully recorded — in the course of an altercation that broke out on the steps of the Church of Nuestra Señora del Carmen, which Captain Blood had impiously appropriated for the purpose of a corps-de-garde. I have said already that he was a papist only when it suited him.

The dispute was being conducted by Hagthorpe, Wolverstone, and Pitt on the one side, and Cahusac, out of whose uneasiness it all arose, on the other. Behind them in the sun-scorched, dusty square, sparsely fringed by palms, whose fronds drooped listlessly in the quivering heat, surged a couple of hundred wild fellows belonging to both parties, their own excitement momentarily quelled so that they might listen to what passed among their leaders.

Cahusac appeared to be having it all his own way, and he raised his harsh, querulous voice so that all might hear his truculent denunciation. He spoke, Pitt tells us, a dreadful kind of English, which the ship-master, however, makes little attempt to reproduce. His dress was as discordant as his speech. It was of a kind to advertise his trade, and ludicrously in contrast with the sober garb of Hagthorpe and the almost foppish daintiness of Jeremy Pitt. His soiled and blood-stained shirt of blue cotton was open in front, to cool his hairy breast, and the girdle about the waist of his leather breeches carried an arsenal of pistols and a knife, whilst a cutlass hung from a leather baldrick loosely slung about his body; above his countenance, broad and flat as a Mongolian's, a red scarf was swathed, turbanwise, about his head.

"Is it that I have not warned you from the beginning that all was too easy?" he demanded between plaintiveness and fury. "I am no fool, my friends. I have eyes, me. And I see. I see an abandoned fort at the entrance of the lake, and nobody there to fire a gun at us when we came in. Then I suspect the trap. Who would not that had eyes and brain? Bah! we come on. What do we find? A city, abandoned like the fort; a city out of which the people have taken all things of value. Again I warn Captain Blood. It is a trap, I say. We are to come on; always to come on, without opposition, until we find that it is too late to go to sea again, that we cannot go back at all. But no one will listen to me. You all know so much more. Name of God! Captain Blood, he will go on, and we go on. We go to Gibraltar. True that at last, after long time, we catch the Deputy-Governor; true, we make him pay big ransom for Gibraltar; true between that ransom and the loot we return here with some two thousand pieces of eight. But what is it, in reality, will you tell me? Or shall I tell you? It is a piece of cheese — a piece of cheese in a mousetrap, and we are the little mice. Goddam! And the cats — oh, the cats they wait for us! The cats are those four Spanish ships of war that have come meantime. And they wait for us outside the bottle-neck of this lagoon. Mort de Dieu! That is what comes of the damned obstinacy of your fine Captain Blood."

Wolverstone laughed. Cahusac exploded in fury.

"Ah, sangdieu! Tu ris, animal? You laugh! Tell me this: How do we get out again unless we accept the terms of Monsieur the Admiral of Spain?"

From the buccaneers at the foot of the steps came an angry rumble of approval. The single eye of the gigantic Wolverstone rolled terribly and he clenched his great fists as if to strike the Frenchman, who was exposing them to mutiny. But Cahusac was not daunted. The mood of the men enheartened him.

"You think, perhaps, this your Captain Blood is the good God. That he can make miracles, eh? He is ridiculous, you know, this Captain Blood; with his grand air and his . . ."

He checked. Out of the church at that moment, grand air and all, sauntered Peter Blood. With him came a tough, long-legged French sea-wolf named Yberville, who, though still young, had already won fame as a privateer commander before the loss of his own ship had driven him to take service under Blood. The Captain advanced towards that disputing group, leaning lightly upon his long ebony cane, his face shaded by a broad-plumed hat. There was in his appearance nothing of the buccaneer. He had much more the air of a lounger in the Mall or the Almeda, — the latter rather, since his elegant suit of violet taffetas with gold-embroidered button-holes was in the Spanish fashion. But the long, stout, serviceable rapier, thrust up behind by the left hand resting lightly on the pummel, corrected the impression. That and those steely eyes of his announced the adventurer.

"You find me ridiculous, eh, Cahusac?" said he, as he came to a halt before the Breton, whose anger seemed already to have gone out of him. "What, then, must I find you?" He spoke quietly, almost wearily. "You will be telling them that we have delayed, and that it is the delay that has brought about our danger. But whose is the fault of that delay? We have been a month in doing what should have been done, and what but for your blundering would have been done, inside of a week."

"Ah ça! Nom de Dieu! Was it my fault that . . ."

"Was it any one else's fault that you ran your ship *La Foudre* aground on the shoal in the middle of the lake? You would not be piloted. You knew your way. You took no soundings even. The result was that we lost three precious days in getting canoes to bring off your men and your gear. Those three days gave the folk at Gibraltar not only time to hear of our coming, but time in which to get away. After that, and because of it, we had to follow the Governor to his infernal island fortress, and a fortnight and best part of a hundred lives were lost in reducing it. That's how we come to have delayed until this Spanish fleet is fetched round from La Guayra by a guarda-costa; and if ye hadn't lost *La Foudre*, and so reduced our fleet from three ships to two, we should even now be able to fight our way through with a reasonable hope of succeeding. Yet you think it is for you to come hectoring here, upbraiding us for a situation that is just the result of your own ineptitude."

He spoke with a restraint which I trust you will agree was admirable when I tell you that the Spanish fleet guarding the bottle-neck exit of the great Lake of Maracaybo, and awaiting there the coming forth of Captain Blood with a calm confidence based upon its overwhelming strength, was commanded by his implacable enemy, Don Miguel de Espinosa y Valdez, the Admiral of Spain. In addition to his duty to his country, the Admiral had, as you know, a further personal incentive arising out of that business aboard the *Encarnacion* a year ago, and the death of his brother Don Diego; and with him sailed his nephew Esteban, whose vindictive zeal exceeded the Admiral's own.

Yet, knowing all this, Captain Blood could preserve his calm in reproving the cowardly frenzy of one for whom the situation had not half the peril with which it was fraught for himself. He turned from Cahusac to address the mob of buccaneers, who had surged nearer to hear him, for he had not troubled to raise his voice. "I hope that will correct some of the misapprehension that appears to have been disturbing you," said he.

"There's no good can come of talking of what's past and done," cried Cahusac, more sullen now than truculent. Whereupon Wolverstone laughed, a laugh that was like the neighing of a horse. "The question is: what are we to do now?"

"Sure, now, there's no question at all," said Captain Blood.

"Indeed, but there is," Cahusac insisted. "Don Miguel, the Spanish Admiral, have offer' us safe passage to sea if we will depart at once, do no damage to the town, release our prisoners, and surrender all that we took at Gibraltar."

Captain Blood smiled quietly, knowing precisely how much Don Miguel's word was worth. It was Yberville who replied, in manifest scorn of his compatriot:

"Which argues that, even at this disadvantage as he has us, the Spanish Admiral is still afraid of us."

"That can be only because he not know our real weakness," was the fierce retort. "And, anyway, we must accept these terms. We have no choice. That is my opinion."

"Well, it's not mine, now," said Captain Blood. "So, I've refused them."

"Refuse'!" Cahusac's broad face grew purple. A muttering from the men behind enheartened him. "You have refuse'? You have refuse' already — and without consulting me?"

"Your disagreement could have altered nothing. You'd have been outvoted, for Hagthorpe here was entirely of my own mind. Still," he went on, "if you and your own French followers wish to avail yourselves of the Spaniard's terms, we shall not hinder you. Send one of your prisoners to announce it to the Admiral. Don Miguel will welcome your decision, you may be sure."

Cahusac glowered at him in silence for a moment.

Then, having controlled himself, he asked in a concentrated voice:

"Precisely what answer have you make to the Admiral?"

A smile irradiated the face and eyes of Captain Blood.

"I have answered him that unless within four-and-twenty hours we have his parole to stand out to sea, ceasing to dispute our passage or hinder our departure, and a ransom of fifty thousand pieces of eight for Maracaybo, we shall reduce this beautiful city to ashes, and thereafter go out and destroy his fleet."

The impudence of it left Cahusac speechless. But among the English buccaneers in the square there were many who savoured the audacious humour of the trapped dictating terms to the trappers. Laughter broke from them. It spread into a roar of acclamation; for bluff is a weapon dear to every adventurer. Presently, when they understood it, even Cahusac's French followers were carried off their feet by that wave of jocular enthusiasm, until in his truculent obstinacy Cahusac remained the only dissentient. He withdrew in mortification. Nor was he to be mollified until the following day brought him his revenge. This came in the shape of a messenger from Don Miguel with a letter in which the Spanish Admiral solemnly vowed to God that, since the pirates had refused his magnanimous offer to permit them to surrender with the honours of war, he would now await them at the mouth of the lake there to destroy them on their coming forth. He added that should they delay their departure, he would so soon as he was reënforced by a fifth ship, the *Santo Niño*, on its way to join him from La Guayra, himself come inside to seek them at Maracaybo.

This time Captain Blood was put out of temper.

"Trouble me no more," he snapped at Cahusac, who came growling to him again. "Send word to Don Miguel that you have seceded from me. He'll give you safe conduct, devil a doubt. Then take one of the sloops, order your men aboard and put to sea, and the devil go with you."

Cahusac would certainly have adopted that course if only his men had been unanimous in the matter. They, however, were torn between greed and apprehension. If they went they must abandon their share of the plunder, which was considerable, as well as the slaves and other prisoners they had taken. If they did this, and Captain Blood should afterwards contrive to get away unscathed — and from their knowledge of his resourcefulness, the thing, however unlikely, need not be impossible — he must profit by that which they now relinquished. This was a contingency too bitter for contemplation. And so, in the end, despite all that Cahusac could say, the surrender was not to Don Miguel, but to Peter Blood. They had come into the venture with him, they asserted, and they would go out of it with him or not at all. That was the message he received from them that same evening by the sullen mouth of Cahusac himself.

He welcomed it, and invited the Breton to sit down and join the council which was even then deliberating upon the means to be employed. This council occupied the spacious patio of the Governor's house — which Captain Blood had appropriated to his own uses — a cloistered stone quadrangle in the middle of which a fountain played coolly under a trellis of vine. Orange-trees grew on two sides of it, and the still, evening air was heavy with the scent of them. It was one of those pleasant exterior-interiors which Moorish architects had introduced to Spain and the Spaniards had carried with them to the New World.

Here that council of war, composed of six men in all, deliberated until late that night upon the plan of action which Captain Blood put forward.

The great freshwater lake of Maracaybo, nourished by a score of rivers from the snow-capped ranges that surround it on two sides, is some hundred and twenty miles in length and almost the same distance across at its widest. It is — as has been indicated — in the shape of a great bottle having its neck towards the sea at Maracaybo.

Beyond this neck it widens again, and then the two long, narrow strips of land known as the islands of Vigilias and Palomas block the channel, standing lengthwise across it. The only passage out to sea for vessels of any draught lies in the narrow strait between these islands. Palomas, which is some ten miles in length, is unapproachable for half a mile on either side by any but the shallowest craft save at its eastern end, where, completely commanding the narrow passage out to sea, stands the massive fort which the buccaneers had found deserted upon their coming. In the broader water between this passage and the bar, the four Spanish ships were at anchor in mid-channel. The Admiral's *Encarnacion*, which we already know, was a mighty galleon of forty-eight great guns and eight small. Next in importance was the *Salvador* with thirty-six guns; the other two, the *In-*

fanta and the *San Felipe*, though smaller vessels, were still formidable enough with their twenty guns and a hundred and fifty men apiece.

Such was the fleet of which the gauntlet was to be run by Captain Blood with his own *Arabella* of forty guns, the *Elizabeth* of twenty-six, and two sloops captured at Gibraltar, which they had indifferently armed with four culverins each. In men they had a bare four hundred survivors of the five hundred-odd that had left Tortuga, to oppose to fully a thousand Spaniards manning the galleons.

The plan of action submitted by Captain Blood to that council was a desperate one, as Cahusac uncompromisingly pronounced it.

"Why, so it is," said the Captain. "But I've done things more desperate." Complacently he pulled at a pipe that was loaded with that fragrant Sacerdotes tobacco for which Gibraltar was famous, and of which they had brought away some hogsheads. "And what is more, they've succeeded. Audaces fortuna juvat. Bedad, they knew their world, the old Romans."

He breathed into his companions and even into Cahusac some of his own spirit of confidence, and in confidence all went busily to work. For three days from sunrise to sunset, the buccaneers laboured and sweated to complete the preparations for the action that was to procure them their deliverance. Time pressed. They must strike before Don Miguel de Espinosa received the reënforcement of that fifth galleon, the *Santo Niño*, which was coming to join him from La Guayra.

Their principal operations were on the larger of the two sloops captured at Gibraltar; to which vessel

was assigned the leading part in Captain Blood's
scheme. They began by tearing down all bulkheads,
until they had reduced her to the merest shell, and in
her sides they broke open so many ports that her gunwale was converted into the semblance of a grating.
Next they increased by a half-dozen the scuttles in
her deck, whilst into her hull they packed all the tar
and pitch and brimstone that they could find in the
town, to which they added six barrels of gunpowder,
placed on end like guns at the open ports on her larboard side.

On the evening of the fourth day, everything being
now in readiness, all were got aboard, and the empty,
pleasant city of Maracaybo was at last abandoned.
But they did not weigh anchor until some two hours
after midnight. Then, at last, on the first of the ebb,
they drifted silently down towards the bar with all
canvas furled save only their spritsails, which, so as
to give them steering way, were spread to the faint
breeze that stirred through the purple darkness of the
tropical night.

The order of their going was as follows: Ahead went
the improvised fire-ship in charge of Wolverstone, with
a crew of six volunteers, each of whom was to have a
hundred pieces of eight over and above his share of
plunder as a special reward. Next came the *Arabella*.
She was followed at a distance by the *Elizabeth*, commanded by Hagthorpe, with whom was the now ship-
less Cahusac and the bulk of his French followers.
The rear was brought up by the second sloop and
some eight canoes aboard of which had been shipped
the prisoners, the slaves, and most of the captured
merchandise. The prisoners were all pinioned, and

guarded by four buccaneers with musketoons who manned these boats in addition to the two fellows who were to sail them. Their place was to be in the rear and they were to take no part whatever in the coming fight.

As the first glimmerings of opalescent dawn dissolved the darkness, the straining eyes of the buccaneers were able to make out the tall rigging of the Spanish vessels, riding at anchor less than a quarter of a mile ahead. Entirely without suspicion as the Spaniards were, and rendered confident by their own overwhelming strength, it is unlikely that they used a vigilance keener than their careless habit. Certain it is that they did not sight Blood's fleet in that dim light until some time after Blood's fleet had sighted them. By the time that they had actively roused themselves, Wolverstone's sloop was almost upon them, speeding under canvas which had been crowded to her yards the moment the galleons had loomed into view.

Straight for the Admiral's great ship, the *Encarnacion*, did Wolverstone head the sloop; then, lashing down the helm, he kindled from a match that hung ready lighted beside him a great torch of thickly plaited straw that had been steeped in bitumen. First it glowed, then as he swung it round his head, it burst into flame, just as the slight vessel went crashing and bumping and scraping against the side of the flagship, whilst rigging became tangled with rigging, to the straining of yards and snapping of spars overhead. His six men stood at their posts on the larboard side, stark naked, each armed with a grapnel, four of them on the gunwale, two of them aloft. At the moment of impact these grapnels were slung to bind the Span-

iard to them, those aloft being intended to complete
and preserve the entanglement of the rigging.

Aboard the rudely awakened galleon all was confused hurrying, scurrying, trumpeting, and shouting.
At first there had been a desperately hurried attempt
to get up the anchor; but this was abandoned as being
already too late; and conceiving themselves on the
point of being boarded, the Spaniards stood to arms
to ward off the onslaught. Its slowness in coming intrigued them, being so different from the usual tactics
of the buccaneers. Further intrigued were they by the
sight of the gigantic Wolverstone speeding naked
along his deck with a great flaming torch held high.
Not until he had completed his work did they begin
to suspect the truth — that he was lighting slow-
matches — and then one of their officers rendered
reckless by panic ordered a boarding-party on to the
sloop.

The order came too late. Wolverstone had seen his
six fellows drop overboard after the grapnels were
fixed, and then had sped, himself, to the starboard
gunwale. Thence he flung his flaming torch down the
nearest gaping scuttle into the hold, and thereupon
dived overboard in his turn, to be picked up presently
by the longboat from the *Arabella*. But before that
happened the sloop was a thing of fire, from which
explosions were hurling blazing combustibles aboard
the *Encarnacion*, and long tongues of flame were lick-
ing out to consume the galleon, beating back those
daring Spaniards who, too late, strove desperately to
cut her adrift.

And whilst the most formidable vessel of the Spanish fleet was thus being put out of action at the outset

Blood had sailed in to open fire upon the *Salvador*. First athwart her hawse he had loosed a broadside that had swept her decks with terrific effect, then going on and about, he had put a second broadside into her hull at short range. Leaving her thus half-crippled, temporarily, at least, and keeping to his course, he had bewildered the crew of the *Infanta* by a couple of shots from the chasers on his beak-head, then crashed alongside to grapple and board her, whilst Hagthorpe was doing the like by the *San Felipe*.

And in all this time not a single shot had the Spaniards contrived to fire, so completely had they been taken by surprise, and so swift and paralyzing had been Blood's stroke.

Boarded now and faced by the cold steel of the buccaneers, neither the *San Felipe* nor the *Infanta* offered much resistance. The sight of their admiral in flames, and the *Salvador* drifting crippled from the action, had so utterly disheartened them that they accounted themselves vanquished, and laid down their arms.

If by a resolute stand the *Salvador* had encouraged the other two undamaged vessels to resistance, the Spaniards might well have retrieved the fortunes of the day. But it happened that the *Salvador* was handicapped in true Spanish fashion by being the treasure-ship of the fleet, with plate on board to the value of some fifty thousand pieces. Intent above all upon saving this from falling into the hands of the pirates, Don Miguel, who, with a remnant of his crew, had meanwhile transferred himself aboard her, headed her down towards Palomas and the fort that guarded the passage. This fort the Admiral, in those days of wait-

ing, had taken the precaution secretly to garrison and
rearm. For the purpose he had stripped the fort of
Cojero, farther out on the gulf, of its entire armament,
which included some cannon-royal of more than ordinary range and power.

With no suspicion of this, Captain Blood gave
chase, accompanied by the *Infanta*, which was manned
now by a prize-crew under the command of Yberville. The stern chasers of the *Salvador* desultorily
returned the punishing fire of the pursuers; but such
was the damage she, herself, sustained, that presently, coming under the guns of the fort, she began to
sink, and finally settled down in the shallows with
part of her hull above water. Thence, some in boats
and some by swimming, the Admiral got his crew
ashore on Palomas as best he could.

And then, just as Captain Blood accounted the victory won, and that his way out of that trap to the
open sea beyond lay clear, the fort suddenly revealed
its formidable and utterly unsuspected strength. With
a roar the cannons-royal proclaimed themselves, and
the *Arabella* staggered under a blow that smashed her
bulwarks at the waist and scattered death and confusion among the seamen gathered there.

Had not Pitt, her master, himself seized the whipstaff and put the helm hard over to swing her sharply
off to starboard, she must have suffered still worse
from the second volley that followed fast upon the
first.

Meanwhile it had fared even worse with the frailer
Infanta. Although hit by one shot only, this had
crushed her larboard timbers on the waterline, starting a leak that must presently have filled her, but for

the prompt action of the experienced Yberville in ordering her larboard guns to be flung overboard. Thus lightened, and listing now to starboard, he fetched her about, and went staggering after the retreating *Arabella*, followed by the fire of the fort, which did them, however, little further damage.

Out of range, at last, they lay to, joined by the *Elizabeth* and the *San Felipe*, to consider their position.

CHAPTER XVII

THE DUPES

IT was a crestfallen Captain Blood who presided over that hastily summoned council held on the poop-deck of the *Arabella* in the brilliant morning sunshine. It was, he declared afterwards, one of the bitterest moments in his career. He was compelled to digest the fact that having conducted the engagement with a skill of which he might justly be proud, having destroyed a force so superior in ships and guns and men that Don Miguel de Espinosa had justifiably deemed it overwhelming, his victory was rendered barren by three lucky shots from an unsuspected battery by which they had been surprised. And barren must their victory remain until they could reduce the fort that still remained to defend the passage.

At first Captain Blood was for putting his ships in order and making the attempt there and then. But the others dissuaded him from betraying an impetuosity usually foreign to him, and born entirely of chagrin and mortification, emotions which will render unreasonable the most reasonable of men. With returning calm, he surveyed the situation. The *Arabella* was no longer in case to put to sea; the *Infanta* was merely kept afloat by artifice, and the *San Felipe* was almost as sorely damaged by the fire she had sustained from the buccaneers before surrendering.

Clearly, then, he was compelled to admit in the end that nothing remained but to return to Maracaybo, there to refit the ships before attempting to force the passage.

And so, back to Maracaybo came those defeated victors of that short, terrible fight. And if anything had been wanting further to exasperate their leader, he had it in the pessimism of which Cahusac did not economize expressions. Transported at first to heights of dizzy satisfaction by the swift and easy victory of their inferior force that morning, the Frenchman was now plunged back and more deeply than ever into the abyss of hopelessness. And his mood infected at least the main body of his own followers.

"It is the end," he told Captain Blood. "This time we are checkmated."

"I'll take the liberty of reminding you that you said the same before," Captain Blood answered him as patiently as he could. "Yet you've seen what you've seen, and you'll not deny that in ships and guns we are returning stronger than we went. Look at our present fleet, man."

"I am looking at it," said Cahusac.

"Pish! Ye're a white-livered cur when all is said."

"You call me a coward?"

"I'll take that liberty."

The Breton glared at him, breathing hard. But he had no mind to ask satisfaction for the insult. He knew too well the kind of satisfaction that Captain Blood was likely to afford him. He remembered the fate of Levasseur. So he confined himself to words.

"It is too much! You go too far!" he complained bitterly.

"Look you, Cahusac: it's sick and tired I am of

your perpetual whining and complaining when things
are not as smooth as a convent dining-table. If ye
wanted things smooth and easy, ye shouldn't have
taken to the sea, and ye should never ha' sailed with
me, for with me things are never smooth and easy.
And that, I think, is all I have to say to you this
morning."

Cahusac flung away cursing, and went to take the
feeling of his men.

. Captain Blood went off to give his surgeon's skill
to the wounded, among whom he remained engaged
until late afternoon. Then, at last, he went ashore, his
mind made up, and returned to the house of the Governor, to indite a truculent but very scholarly letter in
purest Castilian to Don Miguel.

"I have shown your excellency this morning of
what I am capable," he wrote. "Although outnum-
bered by more than two to one in men, in ships, and
in guns, I have sunk or captured the vessels of the
great fleet with which you were to come to Maracaybo to destroy us. So that you are no longer in
case to carry out your boast, even when your reën-
forcements on the *Santo Niño* reach you from La
Guayra. From what has occurred, you may judge of
what must occur. I should not trouble your excellency with this letter but that I am a humane man,
abhorring bloodshed. Therefore before proceeding to
deal with your fort, which you may deem invincible,
as I have dealt already with your fleet, which you
deemed invincible, I make you, purely out of humanitarian considerations, this last offer of terms. I will
spare this city of Maracaybo and forthwith evacuate
it, leaving behind me the forty prisoners I have taken,

in consideration of your paying me the sum of fifty thousand pieces of eight and one hundred head of cattle as a ransom, thereafter granting me unmolested passage of the bar. My prisoners, most of whom are persons of consideration, I will retain as hostages until after my departure, sending them back in the canoes which we shall take with us for that purpose. If your excellency should be so ill-advised as to refuse these terms, and thereby impose upon me the necessity of reducing your fort at the cost of some lives, I warn you that you may expect no quarter from us, and that I shall begin by leaving a heap of ashes where this pleasant city of Maracaybo now stands."

The letter written, he bade them bring him from among the prisoners the Deputy-Governor of Maracaybo, who had been taken at Gibraltar. Disclosing its contents to him, he despatched him with it to Don Miguel.

His choice of a messenger was shrewd. The Deputy-Governor was of all men the most anxious for the deliverance of his city, the one man who on his own account would plead most fervently for its preservation at all costs from the fate with which Captain Blood was threatening it.

And as he reckoned so it befell. The Deputy-Governor added his own passionate pleading to the proposals of the letter.

But Don Miguel was of stouter heart. True, his fleet had been partly destroyed and partly captured. But then, he argued, he had been taken utterly by surprise. That should not happen again. There should be no surprising the fort. Let Captain Blood do his worst at Maracaybo, there should be a bitter reckoning for him when eventually he decided — as, sooner or later, decide he must — to come forth.

The Deputy-Governor was flung into panic. He lost his temper, and said some hard things to the Admiral. But they were not as hard as the thing the Admiral said to him in answer.

"Had you been as loyal to your King in hindering the entrance of these cursed pirates as I shall be in hindering their going forth again, we should not now find ourselves in our present straits. So weary me no more with your coward counsels. I make no terms with Captain Blood. I know my duty to my King, and I intend to perform it. I also know my duty to myself. I have a private score with this rascal, and I intend to settle it. Take you that message back."

So back to Maracaybo, back to his own handsome house in which Captain Blood had established his quarters, came the Deputy-Governor with the Admiral's answer. And because he had been shamed into a show of spirit by the Admiral's own stout courage in adversity, he delivered it as truculently as the Admiral could have desired.

"And is it like that?" said Captain Blood with a quiet smile, though the heart of him sank at this failure of his bluster. "Well, well, it's a pity now that the Admiral's so headstrong. It was that way he lost his fleet, which was his own to lose. This pleasant city of Maracaybo isn't. So no doubt he'll lose it with fewer misgivings. I am sorry. Waste, like bloodshed, is a thing abhorrent to me. But there ye are! I'll have the faggots to the place in the morning, and maybe when he sees the blaze to-morrow night he'll begin to believe that Peter Blood is a man of his word. Ye may go, Don Francisco."

The Deputy-Governor went out with dragging feet, followed by guards, his momentary truculence utterly spent.

But no sooner had he departed than up leapt Cahusac, who had been of the council assembled to receive the Admiral's answer. His face was white and his hands shook as he held them out in protest.

"Death of my life, what have you to say now?" he cried, his voice husky. And without waiting to hear what it might be, he raved on: "I knew you not frighten the Admiral so easy. He hold us entrap', and he knows it; yet you dream that he will yield himself to your impudent message. Your fool letter it have seal' the doom of us all."

"Have ye done?" quoth Blood quietly, as the Frenchman paused for breath.

"No, I have not."

"Then spare me the rest. It'll be of the same quality, devil a doubt, and it doesn't help us to solve the riddle that's before us."

"But what are you going to do? Is it that you will tell me?" It was not a question, it was a demand.

"How the devil do I know? I was hoping you'd have some ideas yourself. But since ye're so desperately concerned to save your skin, you and those that think like you are welcome to leave us. I've no doubt at all the Spanish Admiral will welcome the abatement of our numbers even at this late date. Ye shall have the sloop as a parting gift from us, and ye can join Don Miguel in the fort for all I care, or for all the good ye're likely to be to us in this present pass."

"It is to my men to decide," Cahusac retorted, swallowing his fury, and on that stalked out to talk to them, leaving the others to deliberate in peace.

Next morning early he sought Captain Blood again. He found him alone in the patio, pacing to and fro, his head sunk on his breast. Cahusac mistook consideration for dejection. Each of us carries in himself a standard by which to measure his neighbour.

"We have take' you at your word, Captain," he announced, between sullenness and defiance. Captain Blood paused, shoulders hunched, hands behind his back, and mildly regarded the buccaneer in silence. Cahusac explained himself. "Last night I send one of my men to the Spanish Admiral with a letter. I make him offer to capitulate if he will accord us passage with the honours of war. This morning I receive his answer. He accord us this on the understanding that we carry nothing away with us. My men they are embarking them on the sloop. We sail at once."

"Bon voyage," said Captain Blood, and with a nod he turned on his heel again to resume his interrupted meditation.

"Is that all that you have to say to me?" cried Cahusac.

"There are other things," said Blood over his shoulder. "But I know ye wouldn't like them."

"Ha! Then it's adieu, my Captain." Venomously he added: "It is my belief that we shall not meet again."

"Your belief is my hope," said Captain Blood.

Cahusac flung away, obscenely vituperative. Before noon he was under way with his followers, some sixty dejected men who had allowed themselves to be persuaded by him into that empty-handed departure — in spite even of all that Yberville could do to prevent it. The Admiral kept faith with him, and allowed him free passage out to sea, which, from his knowledge of Spaniards, was more than Captain Blood had expected.

Meanwhile, no sooner had the deserters weighed anchor than Captain Blood received word that the Deputy-Governor begged to be allowed to see him again. Admitted, Don Francisco at once displayed the fact that a night's reflection had quickened his apprehensions for the city of Maracaybo and his condemnation of the Admiral's intransigence.

Captain Blood received him pleasantly.

"Good-morning to you, Don Francisco. I have postponed the bonfire until nightfall. It will make a better show in the dark."

Don Francisco, a slight, nervous, elderly man of high lineage and low vitality, came straight to business.

"I am here to tell you, Don Pedro, that if you will hold your hand for three days, I will undertake to raise the ransom you demand, which Don Miguel de Espinosa refuses."

Captain Blood confronted him, a frown contracting the dark brows above his light eyes:

"And where will you be raising it?" quoth he, faintly betraying his surprise.

Don Francisco shook his head. "That must remain my affair," he answered. "I know where it is to be found, and my compatriots must contribute. Give me leave for three days on parole, and I will see you fully satisfied. Meanwhile my son remains in your hands as a hostage for my return." And upon that he fell to pleading. But in this he was crisply interrupted.

"By the Saints! Ye're a bold man, Don Francisco, to come to me with such a tale — to tell me that ye know where the ransom's to be raised, and yet to refuse to say. D'ye think now that with a match between your fingers ye'd grow more communicative?"

If Don Francisco grew a shade paler, yet again he shook his head.

"That was the way of Morgan and L'Ollonais and other pirates. But it is not the way of Captain Blood. If I had doubted that I should not have disclosed so much."

The Captain laughed. "You old rogue," said he. "Ye play upon my vanity, do you?"

"Upon your honour, Captain."

"The honour of a pirate? Ye're surely crazed!"

"The honour of Captain Blood," Don Francisco insisted. "You have the repute of making war like a gentleman."

Captain Blood laughed again, on a bitter, sneering note that made Don Francisco fear the worst. He was not to guess that it was himself the Captain mocked.

"That's merely because it's more remunerative in the end. And that is why you are accorded the three days you ask for. So about it, Don Francisco. You shall have what mules you need. I'll see to it."

Away went Don Francisco on his errand, leaving Captain Blood to reflect, between bitterness and satisfaction, that a reputation for as much chivalry as is consistent with piracy is not without its uses.

Punctually on the third day the Deputy-Governor was back in Maracaybo with his mules laden with plate and money to the value demanded and a herd of a hundred head of cattle driven in by negro slaves.

These bullocks were handed over to those of the company who ordinarily were boucan-hunters, and therefore skilled in the curing of meats, and for best part of a week thereafter they were busy at the water-side with the quartering and salting of carcases.

While this was doing on the one hand and the ships were being refitted for sea on the other, Captain Blood was pondering the riddle on the solution of which his own fate depended. Indian spies whom he employed brought him word that the Spaniards, working at low tide, had salved the thirty guns of the *Salvador*, and thus had added yet another battery to their already overwhelming strength. In the end, and hoping for inspiration on the spot, Captain Blood made a reconnaissance in person. At the risk of his life, accompanied by two friendly Indians, he crossed to the island in a canoe under cover of dark. They concealed themselves and the canoe in the short thick scrub with which that side of the island was densely covered, and lay there until daybreak. Then Blood went forward alone, and with infinite precaution, to make his survey. He went to verify a suspicion that he had formed, and approached the fort as nearly as he dared and a deal nearer than was safe.

On all fours he crawled to the summit of an emi-nence a mile or so away, whence he found himself commanding a view of the interior dispositions of the stronghold. By the aid of a telescope with which he had equipped himself he was able to verify that, as he had suspected and hoped, the fort's artillery was all mounted on the seaward side.

Satisfied, he returned to Maracaybo, and laid before the six who composed his council — Pitt, Hagthorpe, Yberville, Wolverstone, Dyke, and Ogle — a proposal to storm the fort from the landward side. Crossing to the island under cover of night, they would take the Spaniards by surprise and attempt to overpower them before they could shift their guns to meet the onslaught.

With the exception of Wolverstone, who was by temperament the kind of man who favours desperate chances, those officers received the proposal coldly. Hagthorpe incontinently opposed it.

"It's a harebrained scheme, Peter," he said gravely, shaking his handsome head. "Consider now that we cannot depend upon approaching unperceived to a distance whence we might storm the fort before the cannon could be moved. But even if we could, we can take no cannon ourselves; we must depend entirely upon our small arms, and how shall we, a bare three hundred" (for this was the number to which Cahusac's defection had reduced them), "cross the open to attack more than twice that number under cover?"

The others — Dyke, Ogle, Yberville, and even Pitt, whom loyalty to Blood may have made reluctant — loudly approved him. When they had done, "I have considered all," said Captain Blood. "I have weighed the risks and studied how to lessen them. In these desperate straits ..."

He broke off abruptly. A moment he frowned, deep in thought; then his face was suddenly alight with inspiration. Slowly he drooped his head, and sat there considering, weighing, chin on breast. Then he nodded, muttering, "Yes," and again, "Yes." He looked up, to face them. "Listen," he cried. "You may be right. The risks may be too heavy. Whether or not, I have thought of a better way. That which should have been the real attack shall be no more than a feint. Here, then, is the plan I now propose."

He talked swiftly and clearly, and as he talked one by one his officers' faces became alight with eagerness. When he had done, they cried as with one voice that he had saved them.

"That is yet to be proved in action," said he.

Since for the last twenty-four hours all had been in readiness for departure, there was nothing now to delay them, and it was decided to move next morning.

Such was Captain Blood's assurance of success that he immediately freed the prisoners held as hostages, and even the negro slaves, who were regarded by the others as legitimate plunder. His only precaution against those released prisoners was to order them into the church and there lock them up, to await deliverance at the hands of those who should presently be coming into the city.

Then, all being aboard the three ships, with the treasure safely stowed in their holds and the slaves under hatches, the buccaneers weighed anchor and stood out for the bar, each vessel towing three piraguas astern.

The Admiral, beholding their stately advance in the full light of noon, their sails gleaming white in the glare of the sunlight, rubbed his long, lean hands in satisfaction, and laughed through his teeth.

"At last!" he cried. "God delivers him into my hands!" He turned to the group of staring officers behind him. "Sooner or later it had to be," he said. "Say now, gentlemen, whether I am justified of my patience. Here end to-day the troubles caused to the subjects of the Catholic King by this infamous Don Pedro Sangre, as he once called himself to me."

He turned to issue orders, and the fort became lively as a hive. The guns were manned, the gunners already kindling fuses, when the buccaneer fleet, whilst still heading for Palomas, was observed to bear away to the west. The Spaniards watched them, intrigued.

Within a mile and a half to westward of the fort, and within a half-mile of the shore — that is to say, on the very edge of the shoal water that makes Palomas unapproachable on either side by any but vessels of the shallowest draught — the four ships cast anchor well within the Spaniards' view, but just out of range of their heaviest cannon.

Sneeringly the Admiral laughed.

"Aha! They hesitate, these English dogs! Por Dios, and well they may."

"They will be waiting for night," suggested his nephew, who stood at his elbow quivering with excitement.

Don Miguel looked at him, smiling. "And what shall the night avail them in this narrow passage, under the very muzzles of my guns? Be sure, Esteban, that to-night your father will be paid for."

He raised his telescope to continue his observation of the buccaneers. He saw that the piraguas towed by each vessel were being warped alongside, and he wondered a little what this manœuvre might portend.

Awhile those piraguas were hidden from view behind
the hulls. Then one by one they reappeared, rowing
round and away from the ships, and each boat, he observed, was crowded with armed men. Thus laden,
they were headed for the shore, at a point where it
was densely wooded to the water's edge. The eyes of
the wondering Admiral followed them until the foli-
age screened them from his view.

Then he lowered his telescope and looked at his
officers.

"What the devil does it mean?" he asked.

None answered him, all being as puzzled as he was
himself.

After a little while, Esteban, who kept his eyes on
the water, plucked at his uncle's sleeve. "There they
go!" he cried, and pointed.

And there, indeed, went the piraguas on their way
back to the ships. But now it was observed that they
were empty, save for the men who rowed them. Their
armed cargo had been left ashore.

Back to the ships they pulled, to return again presently with a fresh load of armed men, which similarly
they conveyed to Palomas. And at last one of the
Spanish officers ventured an explanation:

"They are going to attack us by land — to attempt
to storm the fort."

"Of course." The Admiral smiled. "I had guessed
it. Whom the gods would destroy they first make
mad."

"Shall we make a sally?" urged Esteban, in his
excitement.

"A sally? Through that scrub? That would be to
play into their hands. No, no, we will wait here to re-

ceive this attack. Whenever it comes, it is themselves will be destroyed, and utterly. Have no doubt of that."

But by evening the Admiral's equanimity was not quite so perfect. By then the piraguas had made a half-dozen journeys with their loads of men, and they had landed also — as Don Miguel had clearly observed through his telescope — at least a dozen guns.

His countenance no longer smiled; it was a little wrathful and a little troubled now as he turned again to his officers.

"Who was the fool who told me that they number but three hundred men in all? They have put at least twice that number ashore already."

Amazed as he was, his amazement would have been deeper had he been told the truth: that there was not a single buccaneer or a single gun ashore on Palomas. The deception had been complete. Don Miguel could not guess that the men he had beheld in those piraguas were always the same; that on the journeys to the shore they sat and stood upright in full view; and that on the journeys back to the ships, they lay invisible at the bottom of the boats, which were thus made to appear empty.

The growing fears of the Spanish soldiery at the prospect of a night attack from the landward side by the entire buccaneer force — and a force twice as strong as they had suspected the pestilent Blood to command — began to be communicated to the Admiral.

In the last hours of fading daylight, the Spaniards did precisely what Captain Blood so confidently counted that they would do — precisely what they must do to meet the attack, preparations for which had been so thoroughly simulated. They set themselves to labour like the damned at those ponderous guns emplaced to command the narrow passage out to sea.

Groaning and sweating, urged on by the curses and even the whips of their officers, they toiled in a frenzy of panic-stricken haste to shift the greater number and the more powerful of their guns across to the landward side, there to emplace them anew, so that they might be ready to receive the attack which at any moment now might burst upon them from the woods not half a mile away.

Thus, when night fell, although in mortal anxiety of the onslaught of those wild devils whose reckless courage was a byword on the seas of the Main, at least the Spaniards were tolerably prepared for it. Waiting, they stood to their guns.

And whilst they waited thus, under cover of the darkness and as the tide began to ebb, Captain Blood's fleet weighed anchor quietly; and, as once before, with no more canvas spread than that which their sprits could carry, so as to give them steering way — and even these having been painted black — the four vessels, without a light showing, groped their way by soundings to the channel which led to that narrow passage out to sea.

The *Elizabeth* and the *Infanta*, leading side by side, were almost abreast of the fort before their shadowy bulks and the soft gurgle of water at their prows were detected by the Spaniards, whose attention until that moment had been all on the other side. And now there arose on the night air such a sound of human baffled fury as may have resounded about Babel at

the confusion of tongues. To heighten that confusion, and to scatter disorder among the Spanish
soldiery, the *Elizabeth* emptied her larboard guns into
the fort as she was swept past on the swift ebb.

At once realizing — though not yet how — he had
been duped, and that his prey was in the very act of
escaping after all, the Admiral frantically ordered
the guns that had been so laboriously moved to be
dragged back to their former emplacements, and commanded his gunners meanwhile to the slender batter-
ies that of all his powerful, but now unavailable, armament still remained trained upon the channel.
With these, after the loss of some precious moments,
the fort at last made fire.

It was answered by a terrific broadside from the
Arabella, which had now drawn abreast, and was
crowding canvas to her yards. The enraged and gibbering Spaniards had a brief vision of her as the line
of flame spurted from her red flank, and the thunder
of her broadside drowned the noise of the creaking
halyards. After that they saw her no more. Assimi-
lated by the friendly darkness which the lesser Spanish guns were speculatively stabbing, the escaping
ships fired never another shot that might assist their
baffled and bewildered enemies to locate them.

Some slight damage was sustained by Blood's fleet.
But by the time the Spaniards had resolved their confusion into some order of dangerous offence, that fleet,
well served by a southerly breeze, was through the
narrows and standing out to sea.

Thus was Don Miguel de Espinosa left to chew the
bitter cud of a lost opportunity, and to consider in
what terms he would acquaint the Supreme Council

of the Catholic King that Peter Blood had got away from Maracaybo, taking with him two twenty-gun frigates that were lately the property of Spain, to say nothing of two hundred and fifty thousand pieces of eight and other plunder. And all this in spite of Don Miguel's four galleons and his heavily armed fort that at one time had held the pirates so securely trapped.

Heavy, indeed, grew the account of Peter Blood, which Don Miguel swore passionately to Heaven should at all costs to himself be paid in full.

Nor were the losses already detailed the full total of those suffered on this occasion by the King of Spain. For on the following evening, off the coast of Oruba, at the mouth of the Gulf of Venezuela, Captain Blood's fleet came upon the belated *Santo Niño*, speeding under full sail to reënforce Don Miguel at Maracaybo.

At first the Spaniard had conceived that she was meeting the victorious fleet of Don Miguel, returning from the destruction of the pirates. When at comparatively close quarters the pennon of St. George soared to the *Arabella's* masthead to disillusion her, the *Santo Niño* chose the better part of valour, and struck her flag.

Captain Blood ordered her crew to take to the boats, and land themselves at Oruba or wherever else they pleased. So considerate was he that to assist them he presented them with several of the piraguas which he still had in tow.

"You will find," said he to her captain, "that Don Miguel is in an extremely bad temper. Commend me to him, and say that I venture to remind him that he must blame himself for all the ills that have befallen him. The evil has recoiled upon him which he loosed when he sent his brother unofficially to make a raid upon the island of Barbados. Bid him think twice before he lets his devils loose upon an English settlement again."

With that he dismissed the Captain, who went over the side of the *Santo Niño*, and Captain Blood proceeded to investigate the value of this further prize. When her hatches were removed, a human cargo was disclosed in her hold.

"Slaves," said Wolverstone, and persisted in that belief, cursing Spanish devilry until Cahusac crawled up out of the dark bowels of the ship, and stood blinking in the sunlight.

There was more than sunlight to make the Breton pirate blink. And those that crawled out after him — the remnants of his crew — cursed him horribly for the pusillanimity which had brought them into the ignominy of owing their deliverance to those whom they had deserted as lost beyond hope.

Their sloop had encountered and had been sunk three days ago by the *Santo Niño*, and Cahusac had narrowly escaped hanging merely that for some time he might be a mock among the Brethren of the Coast.

For many a month thereafter he was to hear in Tortuga the jeering taunt:

"Where do you spend the gold that you brought back from Maracaybo?"

CHAPTER XVIII

THE *MILAGROSA*

THE affair at Maracaybo is to be considered as Captain Blood's buccaneering masterpiece. Although there is scarcely one of the many actions that he fought — recorded in such particular detail by Jeremy Pitt — which does not afford some instance of his genius for naval tactics, yet in none is this more shiningly displayed than in those two engagements by which he won out of the trap which Don Miguel de Espinosa had sprung upon him.

The fame which he had enjoyed before this, great as it already was, is dwarfed into insignificance by the fame that followed. It was a fame such as no buccaneer — not even Morgan — has ever boasted, before or since.

In Tortuga, during the months he spent there refitting the three ships he had captured from the fleet that had gone out to destroy him, he found himself almost an object of worship in the eyes of the wild Brethren of the Coast, all of whom now clamoured for the honour of serving under him. It placed him in the rare position of being able to pick and choose the crews for his augmented fleet, and he chose fastidiously. When next he sailed away it was with a fleet of five fine ships in which went something over a thousand men. Thus you behold him not merely famous, but really formidable. The three captured Spanish vessels he had renamed with a certain scholarly hu-

mour the *Clotho*, *Lachesis*, and *Atropos*, a grimly jocular manner of conveying to the world that he made
them the arbiters of the fate of any Spaniards he
should henceforth encounter upon the seas.

In Europe the news of this fleet, following upon the
news of the Spanish Admiral's defeat at Maracaybo,
produced something of a sensation. Spain and England were variously and unpleasantly exercised, and
if you care to turn up the diplomatic correspondence
exchanged on the subject, you will find that it is considerable and not always amiable.

And meanwhile in the Caribbean, the Spanish Admiral Don Miguel de Espinosa might be said — to
use a term not yet invented in his day — to have run
amok. The disgrace into which he had fallen as a result of the disasters suffered at the hands of Captain
Blood had driven the Admiral all but mad. It is impossible, if we dispose our minds impartially, to withhold a certain sympathy from Don Miguel. Hate was
now this unfortunate man's daily bread, and the hope
of vengeance an obsession to his mind. As a madman
he went raging up and down the Caribbean seeking
his enemy, and in the meantime, as an hors-d'œuvre
to his vindictive appetite, he fell upon any ship of
England or of France that loomed above his horizon.

I need say no more to convey the fact that this illustrious sea-captain and great gentleman of Castile
had lost his head, and was become a pirate in his turn.
The Supreme Council of Castile might anon condemn
him for his practices. But how should that matter to
one who already was condemned beyond redemption?
On the contrary, if he should live to lay the audacious
and ineffable Blood by the heels, it was possible that

Spain might view his present irregularities and earlier losses with a more lenient eye.

And so, reckless of the fact that Captain Blood was now in vastly superior strength, the Spaniard sought him up and down the trackless seas. But for a whole year he sought him vainly. The circumstances in which eventually they met are very curious.

An intelligent observation of the facts of human existence will reveal to shallow-minded folk who sneer at the use of coincidence in the arts of fiction and drama that life itself is little more than a series of coincidences. Open the history of the past at whatsoever page you will, and there you shall find coincidence at work bringing about events that the merest chance might have averted. Indeed, coincidence may be defined as the very tool used by Fate to shape the destinies of men and nations.

Observe it now at work in the affairs of Captain Blood and of some others.

On the 15th September of the year 1688 — a memorable year in the annals of England — three ships were afloat upon the Caribbean, which in their coming conjunctions were to work out the fortunes of several persons.

The first of these was Captain Blood's flagship the *Arabella*, which had been separated from the buccaneer fleet in a hurricane off the Lesser Antilles. In somewhere about 17° N. Lat., and 74° Long., she was beating up for the Windward Passage, before the intermittent southeasterly breezes of that stifling season, homing for Tortuga, the natural rendezvous of the dispersed vessels.

The second ship was the great Spanish galleon, the

Milagrosa, which, accompanied by the smaller frigate *Hidalga*, lurked off the Caymites, to the north of the long peninsula that thrusts out from the southwest corner of Hispaniola. Aboard the *Milagrosa* sailed the vindictive Don Miguel.

The third and last of these ships with which we are at present concerned was an English man-of-war, which on the date I have given was at anchor in the French port of St. Nicholas on the northwest coast of Hispaniola. She was on her way from Plymouth to Jamaica, and carried on board a very distinguished passenger in the person of Lord Julian Wade, who came charged by his kinsman, my Lord Sunderland, with a mission of some consequence and delicacy, directly arising out of that vexatious correspondence between England and Spain.

The French Government, like the English, excessively annoyed by the depredations of the buccaneers, and the constant straining of relations with Spain that ensued, had sought in vain to put them down by enjoining the utmost severity against them upon her various overseas governors. But these, either — like the Governor of Tortuga — throve out of a scarcely tacit partnership with the filibusters, or — like the Governor of French Hispaniola — felt that they were to be encouraged as a check upon the power and greed of Spain, which might otherwise be exerted to the disadvantage of the colonies of other nations. They looked, indeed, with apprehension upon recourse to any vigorous measures which must result in driving many of the buccaneers to seek new hunting-grounds in the South Sea.

To satisfy King James's anxiety to conciliate Spain,

and in response to the Spanish Ambassador's constant and grievous expostulations, my Lord Sunderland, the Secretary of State, had appointed a strong man to the deputy-governorship of Jamaica. This strong man was that Colonel Bishop who for some years now had been the most influential planter in Barbados.

Colonel Bishop had accepted the post, and departed from the plantations in which his great wealth was being amassed with an eagerness that had its roots in a desire to pay off a score of his own with Peter Blood.

From his first coming to Jamaica, Colonel Bishop had made himself felt by the buccaneers. But do what he might, the one buccaneer whom he made his particular quarry — that Peter Blood who once had been his slave — eluded him ever, and continued undeterred and in great force to harass the Spaniards upon sea and land, and to keep the relations between England and Spain in a state of perpetual ferment, particularly dangerous in those days when the peace of Europe was precariously maintained.

Exasperated not only by his own accumulated chagrin, but also by the reproaches for his failure which reached him from London, Colonel Bishop actually went so far as to consider hunting his quarry in Tortuga itself and making an attempt to clear the island of the buccaneers it sheltered. Fortunately for himself, he abandoned the notion of so insane an enterprise, deterred not only by the enormous natural strength of the place, but also by the reflection that a raid upon what was, nominally at least, a French settlement, must be attended by grave offence to France.

Yet short of some such measure, it appeared to Colonel Bishop that he was baffled. He confessed as much in a letter to the Secretary of State.

This letter and the state of things which it disclosed made my Lord Sunderland despair of solving this vexatious problem by ordinary means. He turned to the consideration of extraordinary ones, and bethought him of the plan adopted with Morgan, who had been enlisted into the King's service under Charles II. It occurred to him that a similar course might be similarly effective with Captain Blood. His lordship did not omit the consideration that Blood's present outlawry might well have been undertaken not from inclination, but under stress of sheer necessity; that he had been forced into it by the circumstances of his transportation, and that he would welcome the opportunity of emerging from it.

Acting upon this conclusion, Sunderland sent out his kinsman, Lord Julian Wade, with some commissions made out in blank, and full directions as to the course which the Secretary considered it desirable to pursue and yet full discretion in the matter of pursuing them. The crafty Sunderland, master of all labyrinths of intrigue, advised his kinsman that in the event of his finding Blood intractable, or judging for other reasons that it was not desirable to enlist him in the King's service, he should turn his attention to the officers serving under him, and by seducing them away from him leave him so weakened that he must fall an easy victim to Colonel Bishop's fleet.

The *Royal Mary* — the vessel bearing that ingenious, tolerably accomplished, mildly dissolute, entirely elegant envoy of my Lord Sunderland's —

made a good passage to St. Nicholas, her last port of call before Jamaica. It was understood that as a preliminary Lord Julian should report himself to the Deputy-Governor at Port Royal, whence at need he might have himself conveyed to Tortuga. Now it happened that the Deputy-Governor's niece had come to St. Nicholas some months earlier on a visit to some relatives, and so that she might escape the insufferable heat of Jamaica in that season. The time for her return being now at hand, a passage was sought for her aboard the *Royal Mary,* and in view of her uncle's rank and position promptly accorded.

Lord Julian hailed her advent with satisfaction. It gave a voyage that had been full of interest for him just the spice that it required to achieve perfection as an experience. His lordship was one of your gallants to whom existence that is not graced by womankind is more or less of a stagnation.

Miss Arabella Bishop — this straight up and down slip of a girl with her rather boyish voice and her almost boyish ease of movement — was not perhaps a lady who in England would have commanded much notice in my lord's discerning eyes. His very sophisticated, carefully educated tastes in such matters inclined him towards the plump, the languishing, and the quite helplessly feminine. Miss Bishop's charms were undeniable. But they were such that it would take a delicate-minded man to appreciate them; and my Lord Julian, whilst of a mind that was very far from gross, did not possess the necessary degree of delicacy. I must not by this be understood to imply anything against him.

It remained, however, that Miss Bishop was a

young woman and a lady; and in the latitude into which Lord Julian had strayed this was a phenomenon sufficiently rare to command attention. On his side, with his title and position, his personal grace and the charm of a practised courtier, he bore about him the atmosphere of the great world in which normally he had his being — a world that was little more than a name to her, who had spent most of her life in the Antilles. It is not therefore wonderful that they should have been attracted to each other before the *Royal Mary* was warped out of St. Nicholas. Each could tell the other much upon which the other desired information. He could regale her imagination with stories of St. James's — in many of which he assigned himself a heroic, or at least a distinguished part — and she could enrich his mind with information concerning this new world to which he had come.

Before they were out of sight of St. Nicholas they were good friends, and his lordship was beginning to correct his first impressions of her and to discover the charm of that frank, straightforward attitude of comradeship which made her treat every man as a brother. Considering how his mind was obsessed with the business of his mission, it is not wonderful that he should have come to talk to her of Captain Blood. Indeed, there was a circumstance that directly led to it.

"I wonder now," he said, as they were sauntering on the poop, "if you ever saw this fellow Blood, who was at one time on your uncle's plantations as a slave."

Miss Bishop halted. She leaned upon the taffrail, looking out towards the receding land, and it was a moment before she answered in a steady, level voice: "I saw him often. I knew him very well."

"Ye don't say!" His lordship was slightly moved out of an imperturbability that he had studiously cultivated. He was a young man of perhaps eight-and-twenty, well above the middle height in stature and appearing taller by virtue of his exceeding leanness. He had a thin, pale, rather pleasing hatchet-face, framed in the curls of a golden periwig, a sensitive mouth and pale blue eyes that lent his countenance a dreamy expression, a rather melancholy pensiveness. But they were alert, observant eyes notwithstanding, although they failed on this occasion to observe the slight change of colour which his question had brought to Miss Bishop's cheeks or the suspiciously excessive composure of her answer.

"Ye don't say!" he repeated, and came to lean beside her. "And what manner of man did you find him?"

"In those days I esteemed him for an unfortunate gentleman."

"You were acquainted with his story?"

"He told it me. That is why I esteemed him — for the calm fortitude with which he bore adversity. Since then, considering what he has done, I have almost come to doubt if what he told me of himself was true."

"If you mean of the wrongs he suffered at the hands of the Royal Commission that tried the Monmouth rebels, there's little doubt that it would be true enough. He was never out with Monmouth; that is certain. He was convicted on a point of law of which he may well have been ignorant when he committed what was construed into treason. But, faith, he's had his revenge, after a fashion."

"That," she said in a small voice, "is the unforgivable thing. It has destroyed him — deservedly."

"Destroyed him?" His lordship laughed a little. "Be none so sure of that. He has grown rich, I hear. He has translated, so it is said, his Spanish spoils into French gold, which is being treasured up for him in France. His future father-in-law, M. d'Ogeron, has seen to that."

"His future father-in-law?" said she, and stared at him round-eyed, with parted lips. Then added: "M. d'Ogeron? The Governor of Tortuga?"

"The same. You see the fellow's well protected. It's a piece of news I gathered in St. Nicholas. I am not sure that I welcome it, for I am not sure that it makes any easier a task upon which my kinsman, Lord Sunderland, has sent me hither. But there it is. You didn't know?"

She shook her head without replying. She had averted her face, and her eyes were staring down at the gently heaving water. After a moment she spoke, her voice steady and perfectly controlled. "But surely, if this were true, there would have been an end to his piracy by now. If he . . . if he loved a woman and was betrothed, and was also rich as you say, surely he would have abandoned this desperate life, and . . ."

"Why, so I thought," his lordship interrupted, "until I had the explanation. D'Ogeron is avaricious for himself and for his child. And as for the girl, I'm told she's a wild piece, fit mate for such a man as Blood. Almost I marvel that he doesn't marry her and take her a-roving with him. It would be no new experience for her. And I marvel, too, at Blood's patience. He killed a man to win her."

"He killed a man for her, do you say?" There was horror now in her voice.

"Yes — a French buccaneer named Levasseur. He was the girl's lover and Blood's associate on a venture. Blood coveted the girl, and killed Levasseur to win her. Pah! It's an unsavoury tale, I own. But men live by different codes out in these parts . . ."

She had turned to face him. She was pale to the lips, and her hazel eyes were blazing, as she cut into his apologies for Blood.

"They must, indeed, if his other associates allowed him to live after that."

"Oh, the thing was done in fair fight, I am told."

"Who told you?"

"A man who sailed with them, a Frenchman named Cahusac, whom I found in a waterside tavern in St. Nicholas. He was Levasseur's lieutenant, and he was present on the island where the thing happened, and when Levasseur was killed."

"And the girl? Did he say the girl was present, too?"

"Yes. She was a witness of the encounter. Blood carried her off when he had disposed of his brother-buccaneer."

"And the dead man's followers allowed it?" He caught the note of incredulity in her voice, but missed the note of relief with which it was blent. "Oh, I don't believe the tale. I won't believe it!"

"I honour you for that, Miss Bishop. It strained my own belief that men should be so callous, until this Cahusac afforded me the explanation."

"What?" She checked her unbelief, an unbelief that had uplifted her from an inexplicable dismay. Clutching the rail, she swung round to face his lordship with that question. Later he was to remember and perceive in her present behaviour a certain oddness which went disregarded now.

"Blood purchased their consent, and his right to carry the girl off. He paid them in pearls that were worth more than twenty thousand pieces of eight." His lordship laughed again with a touch of contempt. "A handsome price! Faith, they're scoundrels all — just thieving, venal curs. And faith, it's a pretty tale this for a lady's ear."

She looked away from him again, and found that her sight was blurred. After a moment in a voice less steady than before she asked him:

"Why should this Frenchman have told you such a tale? Did he hate this Captain Blood?"

"I did not gather that," said his lordship slowly. "He related it . . . oh, just as a commonplace, an instance of buccaneering ways."

"A commonplace!" said she. "My God! A commonplace!"

"I dare say that we are all savages under the cloak that civilization fashions for us," said his lordship. "But this Blood, now, was a man of considerable parts, from what else this Cahusac told me. He was a bachelor of medicine . . ."

"That is true, to my own knowledge."

"And he has seen much foreign service on sea and land. Cahusac said — though this I hardly credit — that he had fought under de Ruyter."

"That also is true," said she. She sighed heavily.

"Your Cahusac seems to have been accurate enough. Alas!"

"You are sorry, then?"

She looked at him. She was very pale, he noticed.

"As we are sorry to hear of the death of one we have esteemed. Once I held him in regard for an unfortunate but worthy gentleman. Now . . ."

She checked, and smiled a little crooked smile. "Such a man is best forgotten." And upon that she passed at once to speak of other things.

The friendship, which it was her great gift to command in all she met, grew steadily between those two in the little time remaining, until the event befell that marred what was promising to be the pleasantest stage of his lordship's voyage.

The marplot was the mad-dog Spanish Admiral, whom they encountered on the second day out, when halfway across the Gulf of Gonaves. The Captain of the *Royal Mary* was not disposed to be intimidated even when Don Miguel opened fire on him. Observing the Spaniard's plentiful seaboard towering high above the water and offering him so splendid a mark, the Englishman was moved to scorn. If this Don who flew the banner of Castile wanted a fight, the *Royal Mary* was just the ship to oblige him. It may be that he was justified of his gallant confidence, and that he would that day have put an end to the wild career of Don Miguel de Espinosa, but that a lucky shot from the *Milagrosa* got among some powder stored in his forecastle, and blew up half his ship almost before the fight had started. How the powder came there will never now be known, and the gallant Captain himself did not survive to enquire into it.

Before the men of the *Royal Mary* had recovered from their consternation, their captain killed and a third of their number destroyed with him, the ship yawing and rocking helplessly in a crippled state, the Spaniards boarded her.

In the Captain's cabin under the poop, to which Miss Bishop had been conducted for safety, Lord Julian was seeking to comfort and encourage her, with assurances that all would yet be well, at the very moment when Don Miguel was stepping aboard. Lord Julian himself was none so steady, and his face was undoubtedly pale. Not that he was by any means a coward. But this cooped-up fighting on an unknown element in a thing of wood that might at any moment founder under his feet into the depths of ocean was disturbing to one who could be brave enough ashore. Fortunately Miss Bishop did not appear to be in desperate need of the poor comfort he was in case to offer. Certainly she, too, was pale, and her hazel eyes may have looked a little larger than usual. But she had herself well in hand. Half sitting, half leaning on the Captain's table, she preserved her courage sufficiently to seek to calm the octoroon waiting-woman who was grovelling at her feet in a state of terror.

And then the cabin-door flew open, and Don Miguel himself, tall, sunburned, and aquiline of face, strode in. Lord Julian span round, to face him, and clapped a hand to his sword.

The Spaniard was brisk and to the point.

"Don't be a fool," he said in his own tongue, "or you'll come by a fool's end. Your ship is sinking."

There were three or four men in morions behind Don Miguel, and Lord Julian realized the position.

He released his hilt, and a couple of feet or so of steel slid softly back into the scabbard. But Don Miguel smiled, with a flash of white teeth behind his grizzled beard, and held out his hand.

"If you please," he said.

Lord Julian hesitated. His eyes strayed to Miss Bishop's.

"I think you had better," said that composed young lady, whereupon with a shrug his lordship made the required surrender.

"Come you — all of you — aboard my ship," Don Miguel invited them, and strode out.

They went, of course. For one thing the Spaniard had force to compel them; for another a ship which he announced to be sinking offered them little inducement to remain. They stayed no longer than was necessary to enable Miss Bishop to collect some spare articles of dress and my lord to snatch up his valise.

As for the survivors in that ghastly shambles that had been the *Royal Mary*, they were abandoned by the Spaniards to their own resources. Let them take to the boats, and if those did not suffice them, let them swim or drown. If Lord Julian and Miss Bishop were retained, it was because Don Miguel perceived their obvious value. He received them in his cabin with great urbanity. Urbanely he desired to have the honour of being acquainted with their names.

Lord Julian, sick with horror of the spectacle he had just witnessed, commanded himself with difficulty to supply them. Then haughtily he demanded to know in his turn the name of their aggressor. He was in an exceedingly ill-temper. He realized that if he had done nothing positively discreditable in the

unusual and difficult position into which Fate had
thrust him, at least he had done nothing creditable.
This might have mattered less but that the spectator
of his indifferent performance was a lady. He was
determined if possible to do better now.

"I am Don Miguel de Espinosa," he was answered.
"Admiral of the Navies of the Catholic King."

Lord Julian gasped. If Spain made such a hubbub
about the depredations of a runagate adventurer like
Captain Blood, what could not England answer now?

"Will you tell me, then, why you behave like a
damned pirate?" he asked. And added: "I hope you
realize what will be the consequences, and the strict
account to which you shall be brought for this day's
work, for the blood you have murderously shed, and
for your violence to this lady and to myself."

"I offer you no violence," said the Admiral, smiling, as only the man who holds the trumps can smile.
"On the contrary, I have saved your lives . . ."

"Saved our lives!" Lord Julian was momentarily
speechless before such callous impudence. "And
what of the lives you have destroyed in wanton
butchery? By God, man, they shall cost you dear."

Don Miguel's smile persisted. "It is possible. All
things are possible. Meantime it is your own lives
that will cost you dear. Colonel Bishop is a rich man;
and you, milord, are no doubt also rich. I will consider and fix your ransom."

"So that you're just the damned murderous pirate
I was supposing you," stormed his lordship. "And
you have the impudence to call yourself the Admiral
of the Navies of the Catholic King? We shall see
what your Catholic King will have to say to it."

The Admiral ceased to smile. He revealed something of the rage that had eaten into his brain. "You do not understand," he said. "It is that I treat you English heretic dogs just as you English heretic dogs have treated Spaniards upon the seas — you robbers and thieves out of hell! I have the honesty to do it in my own name — but you, you perfidious beasts, you send your Captain Bloods, your Hagthorpes, and your Morgans against us and disclaim responsibility for what they do. Like Pilate, you wash your hands." He laughed savagely. "Let Spain play the part of Pilate. Let her disclaim responsibility for me, when your ambassador at the Escurial shall go whining to the Supreme Council of this act of piracy by Don Miguel de Espinosa."

"Captain Blood and the rest are not admirals of England!" cried Lord Julian.

"Are they not? How do I know? How does Spain know? Are you not liars all, you English heretics?"

"Sir!" Lord Julian's voice was harsh as a rasp, his eyes flashed. Instinctively he swung a hand to the place where his sword habitually hung. Then he shrugged and sneered: "Of course," said he, "it sorts with all I have heard of Spanish honour and all that I have seen of yours that you should insult a man who is unarmed and your prisoner."

The Admiral's face flamed scarlet. He half raised his hand to strike. And then, restrained, perhaps, by the very words that had cloaked the retorting insult, he turned on his heel abruptly and went out without answering.

CHAPTER XIX

THE MEETING

AS the door slammed after the departing Admiral, Lord Julian turned to Arabella, and actually smiled. He felt that he was doing better, and gathered from it an almost childish satisfaction — childish in all the circumstances. "Decidedly I think I had the last word there," he said, with a toss of his golden ringlets.

Miss Bishop, seated at the cabin-table, looked at him steadily, without returning his smile. "Does it matter, then, so much, having the last word? I am thinking of those poor fellows on the *Royal Mary*. Many of them have had their last word, indeed. And for what? A fine ship sunk, a score of lives lost, thrice that number now in jeopardy, and all for what?"

"You are overwrought, ma'am. I . . ."

"Overwrought!" She uttered a single sharp note of laughter. "I assure you I am calm. I am asking you a question, Lord Julian. Why has this Spaniard done all this? To what purpose?"

"You heard him." Lord Julian shrugged angrily. "Blood-lust," he explained shortly.

"Blood-lust?" she asked. She was amazed. "Does such a thing exist, then? It is insane, monstrous."

"Fiendish," his lordship agreed. "Devil's work."

"I don't understand. At Bridgetown three years ago there was a Spanish raid, and things were done that should have been impossible to men, horrible, revolting things which strain belief, which seem, when I think of them now, like the illusions of some evil dream. Are men just beasts?"

"Men?" said Lord Julian, staring. "Say Spaniards, and I'll agree." He was an Englishman speaking of hereditary foes. And yet there was a measure of truth in what he said. "This is the Spanish way in the New World. Faith, almost it justifies such men as Blood of what they do."

She shivered, as if cold, and setting her elbows on the table, she took her chin in her hands, and sat staring before her.

Observing her, his lordship noticed how drawn and white her face had grown. There was reason enough for that, and for worse. Not any other woman of his acquaintance would have preserved her self-control in such an ordeal; and of fear, at least, at no time had Miss Bishop shown any sign. It is impossible that he did not find her admirable.

A Spanish steward entered bearing a silver chocolate service and a box of Peruvian candies, which he placed on the table before the lady.

"With the Admiral's homage," he said, then bowed, and withdrew.

Miss Bishop took no heed of him or his offering, but continued to stare before her, lost in thought. Lord Julian took a turn in the long low cabin, which was lighted by a skylight above and great square windows astern. It was luxuriously appointed: there were rich Eastern rugs on the floor, well-filled bookcases stood against the bulkheads, and there was a carved walnut sideboard laden with silverware. On a long, low chest standing under the middle stern port lay a guitar that was gay with ribbons. Lord Julian picked it up, twanged the strings once as if moved by nervous irritation, and put it down.

He turned again to face Miss Bishop.

"I came out here," he said, "to put down piracy. But — blister me! — I begin to think that the French are right in desiring piracy to continue as a curb upon these Spanish scoundrels."

He was to be strongly confirmed in that opinion before many hours were past. Meanwhile their treatment at the hands of Don Miguel was considerate and courteous. It confirmed the opinion, contemptuously expressed to his lordship by Miss Bishop, that since they were to be held to ransom they need not fear any violence or hurt. A cabin was placed at the disposal of the lady and her terrified woman, and another at Lord Julian's. They were given the freedom of the ship, and bidden to dine at the Admiral's table; nor were his further intentions regarding them mentioned, nor yet his immediate destination.

The *Milagrosa*, with her consort the *Hidalga* rolling after her, steered a south by westerly course, then veered to the southeast round Cape Tiburon, and thereafter, standing well out to sea, with the land no more than a cloudy outline to larboard, she headed directly east, and so ran straight into the arms of Captain Blood, who was making for the Windward Passage, as we know. That happened early on the following morning. After having systematically hunted his enemy in vain for a year, Don Miguel chanced upon him in this unexpected and entirely fortuitous fashion. But that is the ironic way of

Fortune. It was also the way of Fortune that Don Miguel should thus come upon the *Arabella* at a time when, separated from the rest of the fleet, she was alone and at a disadvantage. It looked to Don Miguel as if the luck which so long had been on Blood's side had at last veered in his own favour.

Miss Bishop, newly risen, had come out to take the air on the quarter-deck with his lordship in attendance — as you would expect of so gallant a gentleman — when she beheld the big red ship that had once been the *Cinco Llagas* out of Cadiz. The vessel was bearing down upon them, her mountains of snowy canvas bellying forward, the long pennon with the cross of St. George fluttering from her main truck in the morning breeze, the gilded portholes in her red hull, and the gilded beak-head aflash in the morning sun.

Miss Bishop was not to recognize this for that same *Cinco Llagas* which she had seen once before — on a tragic day in Barbados three years ago. To her it was just a great ship that was heading resolutely, majestically, towards them, and an Englishman to judge by the pennon she was flying. The sight thrilled her curiously; it awoke in her an uplifting sense of pride that took no account of the danger to herself in the encounter that must now be inevitable.

Beside her on the poop, whither they had climbed to obtain a better view, and equally arrested and at gaze, stood Lord Julian. But he shared none of her exultation. He had been in his first sea-fight yesterday, and he felt that the experience would suffice him for a very considerable time. This, I insist, is no reflection upon his courage.

"Look," said Miss Bishop, pointing; and to his
infinite amazement he observed that her eyes were
sparkling. Did she realize, he wondered, what was
afoot? Her next sentence resolved his doubt. "She is
English, and she comes resolutely on. She means to
fight."

"God help her, then," said his lordship gloomily.
"Her captain must be mad. What can he hope to do
against two such heavy hulks as these? If they could
so easily blow the *Royal Mary* out of the water, what
will they do to this vessel? Look at that devil Don
Miguel. He's utterly disgusting in his glee."

From the quarter-deck, where he moved amid the
frenzy of preparation, the Admiral had turned to
flash a backward glance at his prisoners. His eyes
were alight, his face transfigured. He flung out an
arm to point to the advancing ship, and bawled something in Spanish that was lost to them in the noise of
the labouring crew.

They advanced to the poop-rail, and watched the
bustle. Telescope in hand on the quarter-deck, Don
Miguel was issuing his orders. Already the gunners
were kindling their matches; sailors were aloft, taking
in sail; others were spreading a stout rope net above
the waist, as a protection against falling spars. And
meanwhile Don Miguel had been signalling to his
consort, in response to which the *Hidalga* had drawn
steadily forward until she was now abeam of the
Milagrosa, half a cable's length to starboard, and
from the height of the tall poop my lord and Miss
Bishop could see her own bustle of preparation. And
they could discern signs of it now aboard the advancing English ship as well. She was furling tops and

mainsail, stripping in fact to mizzen and sprit for the coming action. Thus, almost silently without challenge or exchange of signals, had action been mutually determined.

Of necessity now, under diminished sail, the advance of the *Arabella* was slower; but it was none the less steady. She was already within saker shot, and they could make out the figures stirring on her forecastle and the brass guns gleaming on her prow. The gunners of the *Milagrosa* raised their linstocks and blew upon their smouldering matches, looking up impatiently at the Admiral.

But the Admiral solemnly shook his head.

"Patience," he exhorted them. "Save your fire until we have him. He is coming straight to his doom — straight to the yardarm and the rope that have been so long waiting for him."

"Stab me!" said his lordship. "This Englishman may be gallant enough to accept battle against such odds. But there are times when discretion is a better quality than gallantry in a commander."

"Gallantry will often win through, even against overwhelming strength," said Miss Bishop. He looked at her, and noted in her bearing only excitement. Of fear he could still discern no trace. His lordship was past amazement. She was not by any means the kind of woman to which life had accustomed him.

"Presently," he said, "you will suffer me to place you under cover."

"I can see best from here," she answered him. And added quietly: "I am praying for this Englishman. He must be very brave."

Under his breath Lord Julian damned the fellow's bravery.

The *Arabella* was advancing now along a course which, if continued, must carry her straight between the two Spanish ships. My lord pointed it out. "He's crazy surely!" he cried. "He's driving straight into a death-trap. He'll be crushed to splinters between the two. No wonder that black-faced Don is holding his fire. In his place, I should do the same."

But even at that moment the Admiral raised his hand; in the waist, below him, a trumpet blared, and immediately the gunner on the prow touched off his guns. As the thunder of them rolled out, his lordship saw ahead beyond the English ship and to larboard of her two heavy splashes. Almost at once two successive spurts of flame leapt from the brass cannon on the *Arabella's* beak-head, and scarcely had the watchers on the poop seen the shower of spray, where one of the shots struck the water near them, than with a rending crash and a shiver that shook the *Milagrosa* from stem to stern, the other came to lodge in her forecastle. To avenge that blow, the *Hidalga* blazed at the Englishman with both her forward guns. But even at that short range — between two and three hundred yards — neither shot took effect.

At a hundred yards the *Arabella's* forward guns, which had meanwhile been reloaded, fired again at the *Milagrosa*, and this time smashed her bowsprit into splinters; so that for a moment she yawed wildly to port. Don Miguel swore profanely, and then, as the helm was put over to swing her back to her course, his own prow replied. But the aim was too high, and whilst one of the shots tore through the *Arabella's*

shrouds and scarred her mainmast, the other again
went wide. And when the smoke of that discharge had
lifted, the English ship was found almost between the
Spaniards, her bows in line with theirs and coming
steadily on into what his lordship deemed a death-
trap.

Lord Julian held his breath, and Miss Bishop
gasped, clutching the rail before her. She had a
glimpse of the wickedly grinning face of Don Miguel,
and the grinning faces of the men at the guns in the
waist.

At last the *Arabella* was right between the Spanish
ships prow to poop and poop to prow. Don Miguel
spoke to the trumpeter, who had mounted the
quarter-deck and stood now at the Admiral's elbow.
The man raised the silver bugle that was to give the
signal for the broadsides of both ships. But even as
he placed it to his lips, the Admiral seized his arm, to
arrest him. Only then had he perceived what was so
obvious — or should have been to an experienced sea-
fighter: he had delayed too long and Captain Blood
had outmanœuvred him. In attempting to fire now
upon the Englishman, the *Milagrosa* and her consort
would also be firing into each other. Too late he
ordered his helmsman to put the tiller hard over and
swing the ship to larboard, as a preliminary to ma-
nœuvring for a less impossible position of attack. At
that very moment the *Arabella* seemed to explode as
she swept by. Eighteen guns from each of her flanks
emptied themselves at that point-blank range into
the hulls of the two Spanish vessels.

Half stunned by that reverberating thunder, and
thrown off her balance by the sudden lurch of the

ship under her feet, Miss Bishop hurtled violently
against Lord Julian, who kept his feet only by clutching the rail on which he had been leaning. Billowing
clouds of smoke to starboard blotted out everything,
and its acrid odour, taking them presently in the
throat, set them gasping and coughing.

From the grim confusion and turmoil in the waist
below arose a clamour of fierce Spanish blasphemies
and the screams of maimed men. The *Milagrosa*
staggered slowly ahead, a gaping rent in her bulwarks;
her foremast was shattered, fragments of the yards
hanging in the netting spread below. Her beak-head
was in splinters, and a shot had smashed through into
the great cabin, reducing it to wreckage.

Don Miguel was bawling orders wildly, and peering
ever and anon through the curtain of smoke that was
drifting slowly astern, in his anxiety to ascertain how
it might have fared with the *Hidalga*.

Suddenly, and ghostly at first through that lifting
haze, loomed the outline of a ship; gradually the lines
of her red hull became more and more sharply defined
as she swept nearer with poles all bare save for the
spread of canvas on her sprit.

Instead of holding to her course as Don Miguel had
fully expected she would, the *Arabella* had gone about
under cover of the smoke, and sailing now in the
same direction as the *Milagrosa*, was converging
sharply upon her across the wind, so sharply that
almost before the frenzied Don Miguel had realized
the situation, his vessel staggered under the rending
impact with which the other came hurtling alongside.
There was a rattle and clank of metal as a dozen
grapnels fell, and tore and caught in the timbers of

the *Milagrosa*, and the Spaniard was firmly gripped in the tentacles of the English ship.

Beyond her and now well astern the veil of smoke was rent at last and the *Hidalga* was revealed in desperate case. She was bilging fast, with an ominous list to larboard, and it could be no more than a question of moments before she settled down. The attention of her hands was being entirely given to a desperate endeavour to launch the boats in time.

Of this Don Miguel's anguished eyes had no more than a fleeting but comprehensive glimpse before his own decks were invaded by a wild, yelling swarm of boarders from the grappling ship. Never was confidence so quickly changed into despair, never was hunter more swiftly converted into helpless prey. For helpless the Spaniards were. The swiftly executed boarding manoeuvre had caught them almost unawares in the moment of confusion following the punishing broadside they had sustained at such short range. For a moment there was a valiant effort by some of Don Miguel's officers to rally the men for a stand against these invaders. But the Spaniards, never at their best in close-quarter fighting, were here demoralized by knowledge of the enemies with whom they had to deal. Their hastily formed ranks were smashed before they could be steadied; driven across the waist to the break of the poop on the one side, and up to the forecastle bulkheads on the other, the fighting resolved itself into a series of skirmishes between groups. And whilst this was doing above, another horde of buccaneers swarmed through the hatch to the main deck below to overpower the gun-crews at their stations there.

On the quarter-deck, towards which an overwhelming wave of buccaneers was sweeping, led by a one-eyed giant, who was naked to the waist, stood Don Miguel, numbed by despair and rage. Above and behind him on the poop, Lord Julian and Miss Bishop looked on, his lordship aghast at the fury of this cooped-up fighting, the lady's brave calm conquered at last by horror so that she reeled there sick and faint.

Soon, however, the rage of that brief fight was spent. They saw the banner of Castile come fluttering down from the masthead. A buccaneer had slashed the halyard with his cutlass. The boarders were in possession, and on the upper deck groups of disarmed Spaniards stood huddled now like herded sheep.

Suddenly Miss Bishop recovered from her nausea, to lean forward staring wild-eyed, whilst if possible her cheeks turned yet a deadlier hue than they had been already.

Picking his way daintily through that shambles in the waist came a tall man with a deeply tanned face that was shaded by a Spanish headpiece. He was armed in back-and-breast of black steel beautifully damascened with golden arabesques. Over this, like a stole, he wore a sling of scarlet silk, from each end of which hung a silver-mounted pistol. Up the broad companion to the quarter-deck he came, moving with easy assurance, until he stood before the Spanish Admiral. Then he bowed stiff and formally. A crisp, metallic voice, speaking perfect Spanish, reached those two spectators on the poop, and increased the admiring wonder in which Lord Julian had observed the man's approach.

"We meet again at last, Don Miguel," it said. "I hope you are satisfied. Although the meeting may not be exactly as you pictured it, at least it has been very ardently sought and desired by you."

Speechless, livid of face, his mouth distorted and his breathing laboured, Don Miguel de Espinosa received the irony of that man to whom he attributed his ruin and more beside. Then he uttered an inarticulate cry of rage, and his hand swept to his sword. But even as his fingers closed upon the hilt, the other's closed upon his wrist to arrest the action.

"Calm, Don Miguel!" he was quietly but firmly enjoined. "Do not recklessly invite the ugly extremes such as you would, yourself, have practised had the situation been reversed."

A moment they stood looking into each other's eyes.

"What do you intend by me?" the Spaniard enquired at last, his voice hoarse.

Captain Blood shrugged. The firm lips smiled a little. "All that I intend has been already accomplished. And lest it increase your rancour, I beg you to observe that you have brought it entirely upon yourself. You would have it so." He turned and pointed to the boats, which his men were heaving from the boom amidships. "Your boats are being launched. You are at liberty to embark in them with your men before we scuttle this ship. Yonder are the shores of Hispaniola. You should make them safely. And if you'll take my advice, sir, you'll not hunt me again. I think I am unlucky to you. Get you home, to Spain, Don Miguel, and to concerns that you understand better than this trade of the sea."

For a long moment the defeated Admiral continued to stare his hatred in silence, then, still without speaking, he went down the companion, staggering like a drunken man, his useless rapier clattering behind him. His conqueror, who had not even troubled to disarm him, watched him go, then turned and faced those two immediately above him on the poop. Lord Julian might have observed, had he been less taken up with other things, that the fellow seemed suddenly to stiffen, and that he turned pale under his deep tan. A moment he stood at gaze; then suddenly and swiftly he came up the steps. Lord Julian stood forward to meet him.

"Ye don't mean, sir, that you'll let that Spanish scoundrel go free?" he cried.

The gentleman in the black corselet appeared to become aware of his lordship for the first time.

"And who the devil may you be?" he asked, with a marked Irish accent. "And what business may it be of yours, at all?"

His lordship conceived that the fellow's truculence and utter lack of proper deference must be corrected. "I am Lord Julian Wade," he announced, with that object.

Apparently the announcement made no impression.

"Are you, indeed! Then perhaps ye'll explain what the plague you're doing aboard this ship?"

Lord Julian controlled himself to afford the desired explanation. He did so shortly and impatiently.

"He took you prisoner, did he — along with Miss Bishop there?"

"You are acquainted with Miss Bishop?" cried his lordship, passing from surprise to surprise,

But this mannerless fellow had stepped past him, and was making a leg to the lady, who on her side remained unresponsive and forbidding to the point of scorn. Observing this, he turned to answer Lord Julian's question.

"I had that honour once," said he. "But it seems that Miss Bishop has a shorter memory."

His lips were twisted into a wry smile, and there was pain in the blue eyes that gleamed so vividly under his black brows, pain blending with the mockery of his voice. But of all this it was the mockery alone that was perceived by Miss Bishop; she resented it.

"I do not number thieves and pirates among my acquaintance, Captain Blood," said she; whereupon his lordship exploded in excitement.

"Captain Blood!" he cried. "Are you Captain Blood?"

"What else were ye supposing?"

Blood asked the question wearily, his mind on other things. "I do not number thieves and pirates among my acquaintance." The cruel phrase filled his brain, reëchoing and reverberating there.

But Lord Julian would not be denied. He caught him by the sleeve with one hand, whilst with the other he pointed after the retreating, dejected figure of Don Miguel.

"Do I understand that ye're not going to hang that Spanish scoundrel?"

"What for should I be hanging him?"

"Because he's just a damned pirate, as I can prove, as I have proved already."

"Ah!" said Blood, and Lord Julian marvelled at

the sudden haggardness of a countenance that had been so devil-may-care but a few moments since. "I am a damned pirate, myself; and so I am merciful with my kind. Don Miguel goes free."

Lord Julian gasped. "After what I've told you that he has done? After his sinking of the *Royal Mary?* After his treatment of me — of us?" Lord Julian protested indignantly.

"I am not in the service of England, or of any nation, sir. And I am not concerned with any wrongs her flag may suffer."

His lordship recoiled before the furious glance that blazed at him out of Blood's haggard face. But the passion faded as swiftly as it had arisen. It was in a level voice that the Captain added:

"If you'll escort Miss Bishop aboard my ship, I shall be obliged to you. I beg that you'll make haste. We are about to scuttle this hulk."

He turned slowly to depart. But again Lord Julian interposed. Containing his indignant amazement, his lordship delivered himself coldly. "Captain Blood, you disappoint me. I had hopes of great things for you."

"Go to the devil," said Captain Blood, turning on his heel, and so departed.

CHAPTER XX

THIEF AND PIRATE

CAPTAIN BLOOD paced the poop of his ship alone in the tepid dusk, and the growing golden radiance of the great poop lantern in which a seaman had just lighted the three lamps. About him all was peace. The signs of the day's battle had been effaced, the decks had been swabbed, and order was restored above and below. A group of men squatting about the main hatch were drowsily chanting, their hardened natures softened, perhaps, by the calm and beauty of the night. They were the men of the larboard watch, waiting for eight bells which was imminent.

Captain Blood did not hear them; he did not hear anything save the echo of those cruel words which had dubbed him thief and pirate.

Thief and pirate!

It is an odd fact of human nature that a man may for years possess the knowledge that a certain thing must be of a certain fashion, and yet be shocked to discover through his own senses that the fact is in perfect harmony with his beliefs. When first, three years ago, at Tortuga he had been urged upon the adventurer's course which he had followed ever since, he had known in what opinion Arabella Bishop must hold him if he succumbed. Only the conviction that already she was for ever lost to him, by introducing a certain desperate recklessness into his soul had supplied the final impulse to drive him upon his rover's course.

That he should ever meet her again had not entered his calculations, had found no place in his dreams. They were, he conceived, irrevocably and for ever parted. Yet, in spite of this, in spite even of the persuasion that to her this reflection that was his torment could bring no regrets, he had kept the thought of her ever before him in all those wild years of filibustering. He had used it as a curb not only upon himself, but also upon those who followed him. Never had buccaneers been so rigidly held in hand, never had they been so firmly restrained, never so debarred from the excesses of rapine and lust that were usual in their kind as those who sailed with Captain Blood. It was, you will remember, stipulated in their articles that in these as in other matters they must submit to the commands of their leader. And because of the singular good fortune which had attended his leadership, he had been able to impose that stern condition of a discipline unknown before among buccaneers. How would not these men laugh at him now if he were to tell them that this he had done out of respect for a slip of a girl of whom he had fallen romantically enamoured? How would not that laughter swell if he added that this girl had that day informed him that she did not number thieves and pirates among her acquaintance.

Thief and pirate!

How the words clung, how they stung and burnt his brain!

It did not occur to him, being no psychologist, nor learned in the tortuous workings of the feminine

mind, that the fact that she should bestow upon him
those epithets in the very moment and circumstances of their meeting was in itself curious. He did
not perceive the problem thus presented; therefore he
could not probe it. Else he might have concluded
that if in a moment in which by delivering her from
captivity he deserved her gratitude, yet she expressed
herself in bitterness, it must be because that bitterness was anterior to the gratitude and deep-seated.
She had been moved to it by hearing of the course he
had taken. Why? It was what he did not ask himself, or some ray of light might have come to brighten
his dark, his utterly evil despondency. Surely she
would never have been so moved had she not cared —
had she not felt that in what he did there was a
personal wrong to herself. Surely, he might have
reasoned, nothing short of this could have moved her
to such a degree of bitterness and scorn as that which
she had displayed.

That is how you will reason. Not so, however,
reasoned Captain Blood. Indeed, that night he reasoned not at all. His soul was given up to conflict
between the almost sacred love he had borne her in
all these years and the evil passion which she had
now awakened in him. Extremes touch, and in
touching may for a space become confused, indis-
tinguishable. And the extremes of love and hate were
to-night so confused in the soul of Captain Blood that
in their fusion they made up a monstrous passion.

Thief and pirate!

That was what she deemed him, without qualifica-
tion, oblivious of the deep wrongs he had suffered, the
desperate case in which he found himself after his

escape from Barbados, and all the rest that had gone
to make him what he was. That he should have conducted his filibustering with hands as clean as were
possible to a man engaged in such undertakings had
also not occurred to her as a charitable thought with
which to mitigate her judgment of a man she had
once esteemed. She had no charity for him, no
mercy. She had summed him up, convicted him and
sentenced him in that one phrase. He was thief and
pirate in her eyes; nothing more, nothing less. What,
then, was she? What are those who have no charity?
he asked the stars.

Well, as she had shaped him hitherto, so let her
shape him now. Thief and pirate she had branded
him. She should be justified. Thief and pirate
should he prove henceforth; no more nor less; as
bowelless, as remorseless, as all those others who had
deserved those names. He would cast out the maudlin ideals by which he had sought to steer a course;
put an end to this idiotic struggle to make the best of
two worlds. She had shown him clearly to which
world he belonged. Let him now justify her. She
was aboard his ship, in his power, and he desired her.

He laughed softly, jeeringly, as he leaned on the
taffrail, looking down at the phosphorescent gleam in
the ship's wake, and his own laughter startled him by
its evil note. He checked suddenly, and shivered. A
sob broke from him to end that ribald burst of mirth.
He took his face in his hands and found a chill moisture on his brow.

Meanwhile, Lord Julian, who knew the feminine
part of humanity rather better than Captain Blood,
was engaged in solving the curious problem that had

so completely escaped the buccaneer. He was spurred
to it, I suspect, by certain vague stirrings of jealousy.
Miss Bishop's conduct in the perils through which
they had come had brought him at last to perceive
that a woman may lack the simpering graces of
cultured femininity and yet because of that lack be
the more admirable. He wondered what precisely
might have been her earlier relations with Captain
Blood, and was conscious of a certain uneasiness
which urged him now to probe the matter.

His lordship's pale, dreamy eyes had, as I have
said, a habit of observing things, and his wits were
tolerably acute.

He was blaming himself now for not having observed certain things before, or, at least, for not having studied them more closely, and he was busily
connecting them with more recent observations made
that very day.

He had observed, for instance, that Blood's ship
was named the *Arabella*, and he knew that Arabella
was Miss Bishop's name. And he had observed all
the odd particulars of the meeting of Captain Blood
and Miss Bishop, and the curious change that meeting had wrought in each.

The lady had been monstrously uncivil to the
Captain. It was a very foolish attitude for a lady in
her circumstances to adopt towards a man in Blood's;
and his lordship could not imagine Miss Bishop as
normally foolish. Yet, in spite of her rudeness, in
spite of the fact that she was the niece of a man whom
Blood must regard as his enemy, Miss Bishop and
his lordship had been shown the utmost consideration
aboard the Captain's ship. A cabin had been placed

`at the disposal of each, to which their scanty remaining belongings and Miss Bishop's woman had been duly transferred. They were given the freedom of the great cabin, and they had sat down to table with Pitt, the master, and Wolverstone, who was Blood's lieutenant, both of whom had shown them the utmost courtesy. Also there was the fact that Blood, himself, had kept almost studiously from intruding upon them.

His lordship's mind went swiftly but carefully down these avenues of thought, observing and connecting. Having exhausted them, he decided to seek additional information from Miss Bishop. For this he must wait until Pitt and Wolverstone should have withdrawn. He was hardly made to wait so long, for as Pitt rose from table to follow Wolverstone, who had already departed, Miss Bishop detained him with a question:

"Mr. Pitt," she asked, "were you not one of those who escaped from Barbados with Captain Blood?"

"I was. I, too, was one of your uncle's slaves."

"And you have been with Captain Blood ever since?"

"His shipmaster always, ma'am."

She nodded. She was very calm and self-contained; but his lordship observed that she was unusually pale, though considering what she had that day undergone this afforded no matter for wonder.

"Did you ever sail with a Frenchman named Cahusac?"

"Cahusac?" Pitt laughed. The name evoked a ridiculous memory. "Aye. He was with us at Maracaybo."

"And another Frenchman named Levasseur?"

His lordship marvelled at her memory of these names.

"Aye. Cahusac was Levasseur's lieutenant, until he died."

"Until who died?"

"Levasseur. He was killed on one of the Virgin Islands two years ago."

There was a pause. Then, in an even quieter voice than before, Miss Bishop asked: "Who killed him?"

Pitt answered readily. There was no reason why he should not, though he began to find the catechism intriguing.

"Captain Blood killed him."

"Why?"

Pitt hesitated. It was not a tale for a maid's ears.

"They quarrelled," he said shortly.

"Was it about a . . . a lady?" Miss Bishop relentlessly pursued him.

"You might put it that way."

"What was the lady's name?"

Pitt's eyebrows went up; still he answered.

"Miss d'Ogeron. She was the daughter of the Governor of Tortuga. She had gone off with this fellow Levasseur, and . . . and Peter delivered her out of his dirty clutches. He was a black-hearted scoundrel, and deserved what Peter gave him."

"I see. And . . . and yet Captain Blood has not married her?"

"Not yet," laughed Pitt, who knew the utter groundlessness of the common gossip in Tortuga which pronounced Mdlle. d'Ogeron the Captain's future wife.

Miss Bishop nodded in silence, and Jeremy Pitt turned to depart, relieved that the catechism was ended. He paused in the doorway to impart a piece of information.

"Maybe it'll comfort you to know that the Captain has altered our course for your benefit. It's his intention to put you both ashore on the coast of Jamaica, as near Port Royal as we dare venture. We've gone about, and if this wind holds ye'll soon be home again, mistress."

"Vastly obliging of him," drawled his lordship, seeing that Miss Bishop made no shift to answer. Sombre-eyed she sat, staring into vacancy.

"Indeed, ye may say so," Pitt agreed. "He's taking risks that few would take in his place. But that's always been his way."

He went out, leaving his lordship pensive, those dreamy blue eyes of his intently studying Miss Bishop's face for all their dreaminess; his mind increasingly uneasy. At length Miss Bishop looked at him, and spoke.

"Your Cahusac told you no more than the truth, it seems."

"I perceived that you were testing it," said his lordship. "I am wondering precisely why."

Receiving no answer, he continued to observe her silently, his long, tapering fingers toying with a ringlet of the golden periwig in which his long face was set.

Miss Bishop sat bemused, her brows knit, her brooding glance seeming to study the fine Spanish point that edged the tablecloth. At last his lordship broke the silence.

"He amazes me, this man," said he, in his slow, languid voice that never seemed to change its level. "That he should alter his course for us is in itself matter for wonder; but that he should take a risk on our behalf — that he should venture into Jamaica waters . . . It amazes me, as I have said."

Miss Bishop raised her eyes, and looked at him. She appeared to be very thoughtful. Then her lip flickered curiously, almost scornfully, it seemed to him. Her slender fingers drummed the table.

"What is still more amazing is that he does not hold us to ransom," said she at last.

"It's what you deserve."

"Oh, and why, if you please?"

"For speaking to him as you did."

"I usually call things by their names."

"Do you? Stab me! I shouldn't boast of it. It argues either extreme youth or extreme foolishness." His lordship, you see, belonged to my Lord Sunderland's school of philosophy. He added after a moment: "So does the display of ingratitude."

A faint colour stirred in her cheeks. "Your lordship is evidently aggrieved with me. I am disconsolate. I hope your lordship's grievance is sounder than your views of life. It is news to me that ingratitude is a fault only to be found in the young and the foolish."

"I didn't say so, ma'am." There was a tartness in his tone evoked by the tartness she had used. "If you would do me the honour to listen, you would not misapprehend me. For if unlike you I do not always say precisely what I think, at least I say precisely what I wish to convey. To be ungrateful may be human; but to display it is childish."

"I ... I don't think I understand." Her brows were knit. "How have I been ungrateful and to whom?"

"To whom? To Captain Blood. Didn't he come to our rescue?"

"Did he?" Her manner was frigid. "I wasn't aware that he knew of our presence aboard the *Milagrosa*."

His lordship permitted himself the slightest gesture of impatience.

"You are probably aware that he delivered us," said he. "And living as you have done in these savage places of the world, you can hardly fail to be aware of what is known even in England: that this fellow Blood strictly confines himself to making war upon the Spaniards. So that to call him thief and pirate as you did was to overstate the case against him at a time when it would have been more prudent to have understated it."

"Prudence?" Her voice was scornful. "What have I to do with prudence?"

"Nothing — as I perceive. But, at least, study generosity. I tell you frankly, ma'am, that in Blood's place I should never have been so nice. Sink me! When you consider what he has suffered at the hands of his fellow-countrymen, you may marvel with me that he should trouble to discriminate between Spanish and English. To be sold into slavery! Ugh!" His lordship shuddered. "And to a damned colonial planter!" He checked abruptly. "I beg your pardon, Miss Bishop. For the moment ..."

"You were carried away by your heat in defence of this ... sea-robber." Miss Bishop's scorn was almost fierce.

His lordship stared at her again. Then he half-closed his large, pale eyes, and tilted his head a little. "I wonder why you hate him so," he said softly.

He saw the sudden scarlet flame upon her cheeks, the heavy frown that descended upon her brow. He had made her very angry, he judged. But there was no explosion. She recovered.

"Hate him? Lord! What a thought! I don't regard the fellow at all."

"Then ye should, ma'am." His lordship spoke his thought frankly. "He's worth regarding. He'd be an acquisition to the King's navy — a man that can do the things he did this morning. His service under de Ruyter wasn't wasted on him. That was a great seaman, and — blister me! — the pupil's worthy the master if I am a judge of anything. I doubt if the Royal Navy can show his equal. To thrust himself deliberately between those two, at point-blank range, and so turn the tables on them! It asks courage, resource, and invention. And we land-lubbers were not the only ones he tricked by his manœuvre. That Spanish Admiral never guessed the intent until it was too late and Blood held him in check. A great man, Miss Bishop. A man worth regarding."

Miss Bishop was moved to sarcasm.

"You should use your influence with my Lord Sunderland to have the King offer him a commission."

His lordship laughed softly. "Faith, it's done already. I have his commission in my pocket." And he increased her amazement by a brief exposition of the circumstances. In that amazement he left her, and went in quest of Blood. But he was still intrigued. If she were a little less uncompromising in her attitude towards Blood, his lordship would have been happier.

He found the Captain pacing the quarter-deck, a man mentally exhausted from wrestling with the Devil, although of this particular occupation his lordship could have no possible suspicion. With the amiable familiarity he used, Lord Julian slipped an arm through one of the Captain's, and fell into step beside him.

"What's this?" snapped Blood, whose mood was fierce and raw. His lordship was not disturbed.

"I desire, sir, that we be friends," said he suavely.

"That's mighty condescending of you!"

Lord Julian ignored the obvious sarcasm.

"It's an odd coincidence that we should have been brought together in this fashion, considering that I came out to the Indies especially to seek you."

"Ye're not by any means the first to do that," the other scoffed. "But they've mainly been Spaniards, and they hadn't your luck."

"You misapprehend me completely," said Lord Julian. And on that he proceeded to explain himself and his mission.

When he had done, Captain Blood, who until that moment had stood still under the spell of his astonishment, disengaged his arm from his lordship's, and stood squarely before him.

"Ye're my guest aboard this ship," said he, "and I still have some notion of decent behaviour left me from other days, thief and pirate though I may be. So I'll not be telling you what I think of you for daring to bring me this offer, or of my Lord Sunderland

— since he's your kinsman — for having the impudence to send it. But it does not surprise me at all that one who is a minister of James Stuart's should conceive that every man is to be seduced by bribes into betraying those who trust him." He flung out an arm in the direction of the waist, whence came the half-melancholy chant of the lounging buccaneers.

"Again you misapprehend me," cried Lord Julian, between concern and indignation. "That is not intended. Your followers will be included in your commission."

"And d'ye think they'll go with me to hunt their brethren — the Brethren of the Coast? On my soul, Lord Julian, it is yourself does the misapprehending. Are there not even notions of honour left in England? Oh, and there's more to it than that, even. D'ye think I could take a commission of King James's? I tell you I wouldn't be soiling my hands with it — thief and pirate's hands though they be. Thief and pirate is what you heard Miss Bishop call me to-day — a thing of scorn, an outcast. And who made me that? Who made me thief and pirate?"

"If you were a rebel . . . ?" his lordship was beginning.

"Ye must know that I was no such thing — no rebel at all. It wasn't even pretended. If it were, I could forgive them. But not even that cloak could they cast upon their foulness. Oh, no; there was no mistake. I was convicted for what I did, neither more nor less. That bloody vampire Jeffreys — bad cess to him! — sentenced me to death, and his worthy master James Stuart afterwards sent me into slavery, because I had performed an act of mercy; because compassionately and without thought for creed or politics I had sought to relieve the sufferings of a fellow-creature; because I had dressed the wounds of a man who was convicted of treason. That was all my offence. You'll find it in the records. And for that I was sold into slavery: because by the law of England, as administered by James Stuart in violation of the laws of God, who harbours or comforts a rebel is himself adjudged guilty of rebellion. D'ye dream, man, what it is to be a slave?"

He checked suddenly at the very height of his passion. A moment he paused, then cast it from him as if it had been a cloak. His voice sank again. He uttered a little laugh of weariness and contempt.

"But there! I grow hot for nothing at all. I explain myself, I think, and God knows, it is not my custom. I am grateful to you, Lord Julian, for your kindly intentions. I am so. But ye'll understand, perhaps. Ye look as if ye might."

Lord Julian stood still. He was deeply stricken by the other's words, the passionate, eloquent outburst that in a few sharp, clear-cut strokes had so convincingly presented the man's bitter case against humanity, his complete apologia and justification for all that could be laid to his charge. His lordship looked at that keen, intrepid face gleaming lividly in the light of the great poop lantern, and his own eyes were troubled. He was abashed.

He fetched a heavy sigh. "A pity," he said slowly. "Oh, blister me — a cursed pity!" He held out his hand, moved to it on a sudden generous impulse. "But no offence between us, Captain Blood."

"Oh, no offence. But ... I'm a thief and a pirate."

He laughed without mirth, and, disregarding the proffered hand, swung on his heel.

Lord Julian stood a moment, watching the tall figure as it moved away towards the taffrail. Then letting his arms fall helplessly to his sides in dejection, he departed.

Just within the doorway of the alley leading to the cabin, he ran into Miss Bishop. Yet she had not been coming out, for her back was towards him, and she was moving in the same direction. He followed her, his mind too full of Captain Blood to be concerned just then with her movements.

In the cabin he flung into a chair, and exploded, with a violence altogether foreign to his nature.

"Damme if ever I met a man I liked better, or even a man I liked as well. Yet there's nothing to be done with him."

"So I heard," she admitted in a small voice. She was very white, and she kept her eyes upon her folded hands.

He looked up in surprise, and then sat conning her with brooding glance. "I wonder, now," he said presently, "if the mischief is of your working. Your words have rankled with him. He threw them at me again and again. He wouldn't take the King's commission; he wouldn't take my hand even. What's to be done with a fellow like that? He'll end on a yard-arm for all his luck. And the quixotic fool is running into danger at the present moment on our behalf."

"How?" she asked him with a sudden startled interest.

"How? Have you forgotten that he's sailing to Jamaica, and that Jamaica is the headquarters of the

English fleet? True, your uncle commands it . . ."

She leaned across the table to interrupt him, and he observed that her breathing had grown laboured, that her eyes were dilating in alarm.

"But there is no hope for him in that!" she cried. "Oh, don't imagine it! He has no bitterer enemy in the world! My uncle is a hard, unforgiving man. I believe that it was nothing but the hope of taking and hanging Captain Blood that made my uncle leave his Barbados plantations to accept the deputy-governorship of Jamaica. Captain Blood doesn't know that, of course . . ." She paused with a little gesture of helplessness.

"I can't think that it would make the least difference if he did," said his lordship gravely. "A man who can forgive such an enemy as Don Miguel and take up this uncompromising attitude with me isn't to be judged by ordinary rules. He's chivalrous to the point of idiocy."

"And yet he has been what he has been and done what he has done in these last three years," said she, but she said it sorrowfully now, without any of her earlier scorn.

Lord Julian was sententious, as I gather that he often was. "Life can be infernally complex," he sighed.

CHAPTER XXI

THE SERVICE OF KING JAMES

MISS ARABELLA BISHOP was aroused very early on the following morning by the brazen voice of a bugle and the insistent clanging of a bell in the ship's belfry. As she lay awake, idly watching the rippled green water that appeared to be streaming past the heavily glazed porthole, she became gradually aware of the sounds of swift, laboured bustle — the clatter of many feet, the shouts of hoarse voices, and the persistent trundlings of heavy bodies in the ward-room immediately below the deck of the cabin. Conceiving these sounds to portend a more than normal activity, she sat up, pervaded by a vague alarm, and roused her still slumbering woman.

In his cabin on the starboard side Lord Julian, disturbed by the same sounds, was already astir and hurriedly dressing. When presently he emerged under the break of the poop, he found himself staring up into a mountain of canvas. Every foot of sail that she could carry had been crowded to the *Arabella's* yards, to catch the morning breeze. Ahead and on either side stretched the limitless expanse of ocean, sparkling golden in the sun, as yet no more than a half-disc of flame upon the horizon straight ahead.

About him in the waist, where all last night had been so peaceful, there was a frenziedly active bustle of some threescore men. By the rail, immediately above and behind Lord Julian, stood Captain Blood in altercation with a one-eyed giant, whose head was swathed in a red cotton kerchief, whose blue shirt hung open at the waist. As his lordship, moving forward, revealed himself, their voices ceased, and Blood turned to greet him.

"Good-morning to you," he said, and added: "I've blundered badly, so I have. I should have known better than to come so close to Jamaica by night. But I was in haste to land you. Come up here. I have something to show you."

Wondering, Lord Julian mounted the companion as he was bidden. Standing beside Captain Blood, he looked astern, following the indication of the Captain's hand, and cried out in his amazement. There, not more than three miles away, was land — an uneven wall of vivid green that filled the western horizon. And a couple of miles this side of it, bearing after them, came speeding three great white ships.

"They fly no colours, but they're part of the Jamaica fleet." Blood spoke without excitement, almost with a certain listlessness. "When dawn broke we found ourselves running to meet them. We went about, and it's been a race ever since. But the *Arabella's* been at sea these four months, and her bottom's too foul for the speed we're needing."

Wolverstone hooked his thumbs into his broad leather belt, and from his great height looked down sardonically upon Lord Julian, tall man though his lordship was. "So that you're like to be in yet another sea-fight afore ye've done wi' ships, my lord."

"That's a point we were just arguing," said Blood. "For I hold that we're in no case to fight against such odds."

"The odds be damned!" Wolverstone thrust out his heavy jowl. "We're used to odds. The odds was heavier at Maracaybo; yet we won out, and took three ships. They was heavier yesterday when we engaged Don Miguel."

"Aye — but those were Spaniards."

"And what better are these? — Are ye afeard of a lubberly Barbados planter? Whatever ails you, Peter? I've never known ye scared afore."

A gun boomed out behind them.

"That'll be the signal to lie to," said Blood, in the same listless voice; and he fetched a sigh.

Wolverstone squared himself defiantly before his captain.

"I'll see Colonel Bishop in hell or ever I lies to for him." And he spat, presumably for purposes of emphasis.

His lordship intervened. "Oh, but — by your leave — surely there is nothing to be apprehended from Colonel Bishop. Considering the service you have rendered to his niece and to me. . ."

Wolverstone's horse-laugh interrupted him. "Hark to the gentleman!" he mocked. "Ye don't know Colonel Bishop, that's clear. Not for his niece, not for his daughter, not for his own mother, would he forgo the blood what he thinks due to him. A drinker of blood, he is. A nasty beast. We knows, the Cap'n and me. We been his slaves."

"But there is myself," said Lord Julian, with great dignity.

Wolverstone laughed again, whereat his lordship flushed. He was moved to raise his voice above its usual languid level.

"I assure you that my word counts for something in England."

"Oh, aye — in England. But this ain't England, damme."

Came the roar of a second gun, and a round shot splashed the water less than half a cable's-length astern. Blood leaned over the rail to speak to the fair young man immediately below him by the helmsman at the whipstaff.

"Bid them take in sail, Jeremy," he said quietly. "We lie to."

But Wolverstone interposed again.

"Hold there a moment, Jeremy!" he roared. "Wait!" He swung back to face the Captain, who had placed a hand on his shoulder and was smiling, a trifle wistfully.

"Steady, Old Wolf! Steady!" Captain Blood admonished him.

"Steady, yourself, Peter. Ye've gone mad! Will ye doom us all to hell out of tenderness for that cold slip of a girl?"

"Stop!" cried Blood in sudden fury.

But Wolverstone would not stop. "It's the truth, you fool. It's that cursed petticoat's making a coward of you. It's for her that ye're afeard — and she, Colonel Bishop's niece! My God, man, ye'll have a mutiny aboard, and I'll lead it myself sooner than surrender to be hanged in Port Royal."

Their glances met, sullen defiance braving dull anger, surprise, and pain.

"There is no question," said Blood, "of surrender for any man aboard save only myself. If Bishop can report to England that I am taken and hanged, he will magnify himself and at the same time gratify his personal rancour against me. That should satisfy him. I'll send him a message offering to surrender aboard his ship, taking Miss Bishop and Lord Julian with me, but only on condition that the *Arabella* is allowed to proceed unharmed. It's a bargain that he'll accept, if I know him at all."

"It's a bargain he'll never be offered," retorted Wolverstone, and his earlier vehemence was as nothing to his vehemence now. "Ye're surely daft even to think of it, Peter!"

"Not so daft as you when you talk of fighting that." He flung out an arm as he spoke to indicate the pursuing ships, which were slowly but surely creeping nearer. "Before we've run another half-mile we shall be within range."

Wolverstone swore elaborately, then suddenly checked. Out of the tail of his single eye he had espied a trim figure in grey silk that was ascending the companion. So engrossed had they been that they had not seen Miss Bishop come from the door of the passage leading to the cabin. And there was something else that those three men on the poop, and Pitt immediately below them, had failed to observe. Some moments ago Ogle, followed by the main body of his gun-deck crew, had emerged from the booby hatch, to fall into muttered, angrily vehement talk with those who, abandoning the gun-tackles upon which they were labouring, had come to crowd about him.

Even now Blood had no eyes for that. He turned to look at Miss Bishop, marvelling a little, after the manner in which yesterday she had avoided him, that she should now venture upon the quarter-deck. Her presence at this moment, and considering the nature of his altercation with Wolverstone, was embarrassing.

Very sweet and dainty she stood before him in her gown of shimmering grey, a faint excitement tinting her fair cheeks and sparkling in her clear, hazel eyes, that looked so frank and honest. She wore no hat, and the ringlets of her gold-brown hair fluttered distractingly in the morning breeze.

Captain Blood bared his head and bowed silently in a greeting which she returned composedly and formally.

"What is happening, Lord Julian?" she enquired.

As if to answer her a third gun spoke from the ships towards which she was looking intent and wonderingly. A frown rumpled her brow. She looked from one to the other of the men who stood there so glum and obviously ill at ease.

"They are ships of the Jamaica fleet," his lordship answered her.

It should in any case have been a sufficient explanation. But before more could be added, their attention was drawn at last to Ogle, who came bounding up the broad ladder, and to the men lounging aft in his wake, in all of which, instinctively, they apprehended a vague menace.

At the head of the companion, Ogle found his progress barred by Blood, who confronted him, a sudden sternness in his face and in every line of him.

"What's this?" the Captain demanded sharply. "Your station is on the gun-deck. Why have you left it?"

Thus challenged, the obvious truculence faded out of Ogle's bearing, quenched by the old habit of obedience and the natural dominance that was the secret of the Captain's rule over his wild followers. But it gave no pause to the gunner's intention. If anything it increased his excitement.

"Captain," he said, and as he spoke he pointed to the pursuing ships, "Colonel Bishop holds us. We're in no case either to run or fight."

Blood's height seemed to increase, as did his sternness.

"Ogle," said he, in a voice cold and sharp as steel, "your station is on the gun-deck. You'll return to it at once, and take your crew with you, or else . . ."

But Ogle, violent of mien and gesture, interrupted him.

"Threats will not serve, Captain."

"Will they not?"

It was the first time in his buccaneering career that an order of his had been disregarded, or that a man had failed in the obedience to which he pledged all those who joined him. That this insubordination should proceed from one of those whom he most trusted, one of his old Barbados associates, was in itself a bitterness, and made him reluctant to that which instinct told him must be done. His hand closed over the butt of one of the pistols slung before him.

"Nor will that serve you," Ogle warned him, still more fiercely. "The men are of my thinking, and they'll have their way."

"And what way may that be?"

"The way to make us safe. We'll neither sink nor hang whiles we can help it."

From the three or four score men massed below in the waist came a rumble of approval. Captain Blood's glance raked the ranks of those resolute, fierce-eyed fellows, then it came to rest again on Ogle. There was here quite plainly a vague threat, a mutinous spirit he could not understand.

"You come to give advice, then, do you?" quoth he, relenting nothing of his sternness.

"That's it, Captain; advice. That girl, there." He flung out a bare arm to point to her. "Bishop's girl; the Governor of Jamaica's niece ... We want her as a hostage for our safety."

"Aye!" roared in chorus the buccaneers below, and one or two of them elaborated that affirmation.

In a flash Captain Blood saw what was in their minds. And for all that he lost nothing of his outward stern composure, fear invaded his heart.

"And how," he asked, "do you imagine that Miss Bishop will prove such a hostage?"

"It's a providence having her aboard; a providence. Heave to, Captain, and signal them to send a boat, and assure themselves that Miss is here. Then let them know that if they attempt to hinder our sailing hence, we'll hang the doxy first and fight for it after. That'll cool Colonel Bishop's heat, maybe."

"And maybe it won't." Slow and mocking came Wolverstone's voice to answer the other's confident excitement, and as he spoke he advanced to Blood's side, an unexpected ally. "Some o' them dawcocks may believe that tale." He jerked a contemptuous thumb towards the men in the waist, whose ranks were steadily being increased by the advent of others from the forecastle. "Although even some o' they

should know better, for there's still a few was on
Barbados with us, and are acquainted like me and
you with Colonel Bishop. If ye're counting on pulling
Bishop's heartstrings, ye're a bigger fool, Ogle, than
I've always thought you was with anything but guns.
There's no heaving to for such a matter as that unless
you wants to make quite sure of our being sunk.
Though we had a cargo of Bishop's nieces it wouldn't
make him hold his hand. Why, as I was just telling
his lordship here, who thought like you that having
Miss Bishop aboard would make us safe, not for his
mother would that filthy slaver forgo what's due to
him. And if ye weren't a fool, Ogle, you wouldn't
need me to tell you this. We've got to fight, my
lads . . ."

"How can we fight, man?" Ogle stormed at him,
furiously battling the conviction which Wolverstone's argument was imposing upon his listeners.
"You may be right, and you may be wrong. We've
got to chance it. It's our only chance . . ."

The rest of his words were drowned in the shouts of
the hands insisting that the girl be given up to be held
as a hostage. And then louder than before roared a
gun away to leeward, and away on their starboard
beam they saw the spray flung up by the shot, which
had gone wide.

"They are within range," cried Ogle. And leaning
from the rail, "Put down the helm," he commanded.

Pitt, at his post beside the helmsman, turned
intrepidly to face the excited gunner.

"Since when have you commanded on the main
deck, Ogle? I take my orders from the Captain."

"You'll take this order from me, or, by God,
you'll . . ."

"Wait!" Blood bade him, interrupting, and he set a restraining hand upon the gunner's arm. "There is, I think, a better way."

He looked over his shoulder, aft, at the advancing ships, the foremost of which was now a bare quarter of a mile away. His glance swept in passing over Miss Bishop and Lord Julian standing side by side some paces behind him. He observed her pale and tense, with parted lips and startled eyes that were fixed upon him, an anxious witness of this deciding of her fate. He was thinking swiftly, reckoning the chances if by pistolling Ogle he were to provoke a mutiny. That some of the men would rally to him, he was sure. But he was no less sure that the main body would oppose him, and prevail in spite of all that he could do, taking the chance that holding Miss Bishop to ransom seemed to afford them. And if they did that, one way or the other, Miss Bishop would be lost. For even if Bishop yielded to their demand, they would retain her as a hostage.

Meanwhile Ogle was growing impatient. His arm still gripped by Blood, he thrust his face into the Captain's.

"What better way?" he demanded. "There is none better. I'll not be bubbled by what Wolverstone has said. He may be right, and he may be wrong. We'll test it. It's our only chance, I've said, and we must take it."

The better way that was in Captain Blood's mind was the way that already he had proposed to Wolverstone. Whether the men in the panic Ogle had aroused among them would take a different view from Wolverstone's he did not know. But he saw quite clearly now that if they consented, they would not on that account depart from their intention in the matter of Miss Bishop; they would make of Blood's own surrender merely an additional card in this game against the Governor of Jamaica.

"It's through her that we're in this trap," Ogle stormed on. "Through her and through you. It was to bring her to Jamaica that you risked all our lives, and we're not going to lose our lives as long as there's a chance to make ourselves safe through her."

He was turning again to the helmsman below, when Blood's grip tightened on his arm. Ogle wrenched it free, with an oath. But Blood's mind was now made up. He had found the only way, and repellent though it might be to him, he must take it.

"That is a desperate chance," he cried. "Mine is the safe and easy way. Wait!" He leaned over the rail. "Put the helm down," he bade Pitt. "Heave her to, and signal to them to send a boat."

A silence of astonishment fell upon the ship — of astonishment and suspicion at this sudden yielding. But Pitt, although he shared it, was prompt to obey. His voice rang out, giving the necessary orders, and after an instant's pause, a score of hands sprang to execute them. Came the creak of blocks and the rattle of slatting sails as they swung aweather, and Captain Blood turned and beckoned Lord Julian forward. His lordship, after a moment's hesitation, advanced in surprise and mistrust — a mistrust shared by Miss Bishop, who, like his lordship and all else aboard, though in a different way, had been taken aback by Blood's sudden submission to the demand to lie to.

Standing now at the rail, with Lord Julian beside him, Captain Blood explained himself.

Briefly and clearly he announced to all the object of Lord Julian's voyage to the Caribbean, and he informed them of the offer which yesterday Lord Julian had made to him.

"That offer I rejected, as his lordship will tell you, deeming myself affronted by it. Those of you who have suffered under the rule of King James will understand me. But now in the desperate case in which we find ourselves — outsailed, and likely to be outfought, as Ogle has said — I am ready to take the way of Morgan: to accept the King's commission and shelter us all behind it."

It was a thunderbolt that for a moment left them all dazed. Then Babel was reënacted. The main body of them welcomed the announcement as only men who have been preparing to die can welcome a new lease of life. But many could not resolve one way or the other until they were satisfied upon several questions, and chiefly upon one which was voiced by Ogle.

"Will Bishop respect the commission when you hold it?"

It was Lord Julian who answered:

"It will go very hard with him if he attempts to flout the King's authority. And though he should dare attempt it, be sure that his own officers will not dare to do other than oppose him."

"Aye," said Ogle, "that is true."

But there were some who were still in open and frank revolt against the course. Of these was Wolverstone, who at once proclaimed his hostility.

"I'll rot in hell or ever I serves the King," he bawled in a great rage.

But Blood quieted him and those who thought as he did.

"No man need follow me into the King's service who is reluctant. That is not in the bargain. What is in the bargain is that I accept this service with such of you as may choose to follow me. Don't think I accept it willingly. For myself, I am entirely of Wolverstone's opinion. I accept it as the only way to save us all from the certain destruction into which my own act may have brought us. And even those of you who do not choose to follow me shall share the immunity of all, and shall afterwards be free to depart. Those are the terms upon which I sell myself to the King. Let Lord Julian, the representative of the Secretary of State, say whether he agrees to them."

Prompt, eager, and clear came his lordship's agreement. And that was practically the end of the matter. Lord Julian, the butt now of good-humouredly ribald jests and half-derisive acclamations, plunged away to his cabin for the commission, secretly rejoicing at a turn of events which enabled him so creditably to discharge the business on which he had been sent.

Meanwhile the bo'sun signalled to the Jamaica ships to send a boat, and the men in the waist broke their ranks and went noisily flocking to line the bulwarks and view the great stately vessels that were racing down towards them.

As Ogle left the quarter-deck, Blood turned, and came face to face with Miss Bishop. She had been observing him with shining eyes, but at sight of his dejected countenance, and the deep frown that scarred his brow, her own expression changed. She approached him with a hesitation entirely unusual to her. She set a hand lightly upon his arm.

"You have chosen wisely, sir," she commended him, "however much against your inclinations."

He looked with gloomy eyes upon her for whom he had made this sacrifice.

"I owed it to you — or thought I did," he said.

She did not understand. "Your resolve delivered me from a horrible danger," she admitted. And she shivered at the memory of it. "But I do not understand why you should have hesitated when first it was proposed to you. It is an honourable service."

"King James's?" he sneered.

"England's," she corrected him in reproof. "The country is all, sir; the sovereign naught. King James will pass; others will come and pass; England remains, to be honourably served by her sons, whatever rancour they may hold against the man who rules her in their time."

He showed some surprise. Then he smiled a little. "Shrewd advocacy," he approved it. "You should have spoken to the crew."

And then, the note of irony deepening in his voice: "Do you suppose now that this honourable service might redeem one who was a pirate and a thief?"

Her glance fell away. Her voice faltered a little in replying. "If he ... needs redeeming. Perhaps ... perhaps he has been judged too harshly."

The blue eyes flashed, and the firm lips relaxed their grim set.

"Why ... if ye think that," he said, considering

her, an odd hunger in his glance, "life might have its uses, after all, and even the service of King James might become tolerable."

Looking beyond her, across the water, he observed a boat putting off from one of the great ships, which, hove to now, were rocking gently some three hundred yards away. Abruptly his manner changed. He was like one recovering, taking himself in hand again. "If you will go below, and get your gear and your woman, you shall presently be sent aboard one of the ships of the fleet." He pointed to the boat as he spoke.

She left him, and thereafter with Wolverstone, leaning upon the rail, he watched the approach of that boat, manned by a dozen sailors, and commanded by a scarlet figure seated stiffly in the stern sheets. He levelled his telescope upon that figure.

"It'll not be Bishop himself," said Wolverstone, between question and assertion.

"No." Blood closed his telescope. "I don't know who it is."

"Ha!" Wolverstone vented an ejaculation of sneering mirth. "For all his eagerness, Bishop'd be none so willing to come, hisself. He's been aboard this hulk afore, and we made him swim for it that time. He'll have his memories. So he sends a deputy."

This deputy proved to be an officer named Calverley, a vigorous, self-sufficient fellow, comparatively fresh from England, whose manner made it clear that he came fully instructed by Colonel Bishop upon the matter of how to handle the pirates.

His air, as he stepped into the waist of the *Arabella*, was haughty, truculent, and disdainful.

Blood, the King's commission now in his pocket,

and Lord Julian standing beside him, waited to receive him, and Captain Calverley was a little taken aback at finding himself confronted by two men so very different outwardly from anything that he had expected. But he lost none of his haughty poise, and scarcely deigned a glance at the swarm of fierce, half-naked fellows lounging in a semicircle to form a background.

"Good-day to you, sir," Blood hailed him pleasantly. "I have the honour to give you welcome aboard the *Arabella*. My name is Blood — Captain Blood, at your service. You may have heard of me."

Captain Calverley stared hard. The airy manner of this redoubtable buccaneer was hardly what he had looked for in a desperate fellow, compelled to ignominious surrender. A thin, sour smile broke on the officer's haughty lips.

"You'll ruffle it to the gallows, no doubt," he said contemptuously. "I suppose that is after the fashion of your kind. Meanwhile it's your surrender I require, my man, not your impudence."

Captain Blood appeared surprised, pained. He turned in appeal to Lord Julian.

"D'ye hear that now? And did ye ever hear the like? But what did I tell ye? Ye see, the young gentleman's under a misapprehension entirely. Perhaps it'll save broken bones if your lordship explains just who and what I am."

Lord Julian advanced a step and bowed perfunctorily and rather disdainfully to that very disdainful but now dumbfounded officer. Pitt, who watched the scene from the quarter-deck rail, tells us that his lordship was as grave as a parson at a hanging. But I suspect this gravity for a mask under which Lord Julian was secretly amused.

"I have the honour to inform you, sir," he said stiffly, "that Captain Blood holds a commission in the King's service under the seal of my Lord Sunderland, His Majesty's Secretary of State."

Captain Calverley's face empurpled; his eyes bulged. The buccaneers in the background chuckled and crowed and swore among themselves in their relish of this comedy. For a long moment Calverley stared in silence at his lordship, observing the costly elegance of his dress, his air of calm assurance, and his cold, fastidious speech, all of which savoured distinctly of the great world to which he belonged.

"And who the devil may you be?" he exploded at last.

Colder still and more distant than ever grew his lordship's voice.

"You're not very civil, sir, as I have already noticed. My name is Wade — Lord Julian Wade. I am His Majesty's envoy to these barbarous parts, and my Lord Sunderland's near kinsman. Colonel Bishop has been notified of my coming."

The sudden change in Calverley's manner at Lord Julian's mention of his name showed that the notification had been received, and that he had knowledge of it.

"I ... I believe that he has," said Calverley, between doubt and suspicion. "That is: that he has been notified of the coming of Lord Julian Wade. But ... but ... aboard this ship ...?" The officer made a gesture of helplessness, and, surrendering to his bewilderment, fell abruptly silent.

"I was coming out on the *Royal Mary* . . ."

"That is what we were advised."

"But the *Royal Mary* fell a victim to a Spanish privateer, and I might never have arrived at all but for the gallantry of Captain Blood, who rescued me."

Light broke upon the darkness of Calverley's mind. "I see. I understand."

"I will take leave to doubt it." His lordship's tone abated nothing of its asperity. "But that can wait. If Captain Blood will show you his commission, perhaps that will set all doubts at rest, and we may proceed. I shall be glad to reach Port Royal."

Captain Blood thrust a parchment under Calverley's bulging eyes. The officer scanned it, particularly the seals and signature. He stepped back, a baffled, impotent man. He bowed helplessly.

"I must return to Colonel Bishop for my orders," he informed them.

At that moment a lane was opened in the ranks of the men, and through this came Miss Bishop followed by her octoroon woman. Over his shoulder Captain Blood observed her approach.   .

"Perhaps, since Colonel Bishop is with you, you will convey his niece to him. Miss Bishop was aboard the *Royal Mary* also, and I rescued her together with his lordship. She will be able to acquaint her uncle with the details of that and of the present state of affairs."

Swept thus from surprise to surprise, Captain Calverley could do no more than bow again.

"As for me," said Lord Julian, with intent to make Miss Bishop's departure free from all interference on the part of the buccaneers, "I shall remain aboard the *Arabella* until we reach Port Royal. My compliments to Colonel Bishop. Say that I look forward to making his acquaintance there."

CHAPTER XXII

HOSTILITIES

IN the great harbour of Port Royal, spacious enough to have given moorings to all the ships of all the navies of the world, the *Arabella* rode at anchor. Almost she had the air of a prisoner, for a quarter of a mile ahead, to starboard, rose the lofty, massive single round tower of the fort, whilst a couple of cables'-length astern, and to larboard, rode the six men-of-war that composed the Jamaica squadron.

Abeam with the *Arabella*, across the harbour, were the flat-fronted white buildings of that imposing city that came down to the very water's edge. Behind these the red roofs rose like terraces, marking the gentle slope upon which the city was built, dominated here by a turret, there by a spire, and behind these again a range of green hills with for ultimate background a sky that was like a dome of polished steel.

On a cane day-bed that had been set for him on the quarter-deck, sheltered from the dazzling, blistering sunshine by an improvised awning of brown sailcloth, lounged Peter Blood, a calf-bound, well-thumbed copy of Horace's Odes neglected in his hands.

From immediately below him came the swish of mops and the gurgle of water in the scuppers, for it was still early morning, and under the directions of Hayton, the bo'sun, the swabbers were at work in the waist and forecastle. Despite the heat and the stag-

nant air, one of the toilers found breath to croak a
ribald buccaneering ditty:

> "For we laid her board and board,
> And we put her to the sword,
> And we sank her in the deep blue sea.
> So it's heigh-ho, and heave-a-ho!
> Who'll sail for the Main with me?"

Blood fetched a sigh, and the ghost of a smile
played over his keen, lean, sun-tanned face. Then the
black brows came together above the vivid blue eyes,
and thought swiftly closed the door upon his immediate surroundings.

Things had not sped at all well with him in the past
fortnight since his acceptance of the King's commission. There had been trouble with Bishop from the
moment of landing. As Blood and Lord Julian had
stepped ashore together, they had been met by a man
who took no pains to dissemble his chagrin at the
turn of events and his determination to change it.
He awaited them on the mole, supported by a group
of officers.

"You are Lord Julian Wade, I understand," was
his truculent greeting. For Blood at the moment he
had nothing beyond a malignant glance.

Lord Julian bowed. "I take it I have the honour
to address Colonel Bishop, Deputy-Governor of Jamaica." It was almost as if his lordship were giving the Colonel a lesson in deportment. The Colonel accepted it, and belatedly bowed, removing his
broad hat. Then he plunged on.

"You have granted, I am told, the King's commission to this man." His very tone betrayed the bitterness of his rancour. "Your motives were no doubt

worthy ... your gratitude to him for delivering you from the Spaniards. But the thing itself is unthinkable, my lord. The commission must be cancelled."

"I don't think I understand," said Lord Julian distantly.

"To be sure you don't, or you'd never ha' done it. The fellow's bubbled you. Why, he's first a rebel, then an escaped slave, and lastly a bloody pirate. I've been hunting him this year past."

"I assure you, sir, that I was fully informed of all. I do not grant the King's commission lightly."

"Don't you, by God! And what else do you call this? But as His Majesty's Deputy-Governor of Jamaica, I'll take leave to correct your mistake in my own way."

"Ah! And what way may that be?"

"There's a gallows waiting for this rascal here in Port Royal."

Blood would have intervened at that, but Lord Julian forestalled him.

"I see, sir, that you do not yet quite apprehend the circumstances. If it is a mistake to grant Captain Blood a commission, the mistake is not mine. I am acting upon the instructions of my Lord Sunderland; and with a full knowledge of all the facts, his lordship expressly designated Captain Blood for this commission if Captain Blood could be persuaded to accept it."

Colonel Bishop's mouth fell open in surprise and dismay.

"Lord Sunderland designated him?" he asked, amazed.

"Expressly."

His lordship waited a moment for a reply. None coming from the speechless Deputy-Governor, he asked a question: "Would you still venture to describe the matter as a mistake, sir? And dare you take the risk of correcting it?"

"I . . . I had not dreamed . . ."

"I understand, sir. Let me present Captain Blood."

Perforce Bishop must put on the best face he could command. But that it was no more than a mask for his fury and his venom was plain to all.

From that unpromising beginning matters had not improved; rather had they grown worse.

Blood's thoughts were upon this and other things as he lounged there on the day-bed. He had been a fortnight in Port Royal, his ship virtually a unit now in the Jamaica squadron. And when the news of it reached Tortuga and the buccaneers who awaited his return, the name of Captain Blood, which had stood so high among the Brethren of the Coast, would become a byword, a thing of execration, and before all was done his life might pay forfeit for what would be accounted a treacherous defection. And for what had he placed himself in this position? For the sake of a girl who avoided him so persistently and intentionally that he must assume that she still regarded him with aversion. He had scarcely been vouchsafed a glimpse of her in all this fortnight, although with that in view for his main object he had daily haunted her uncle's residence, and daily braved the unmasked hostility and baffled rancour in which Colonel Bishop held him. Nor was that the worst of it. He was allowed plainly to perceive that it was the graceful, elegant

young trifler from St. James's, Lord Julian Wade, to
whom her every moment was devoted. And what
chance had he, a desperate adventurer with a record
of outlawry, against such a rival as that, a man of
parts, moreover, as he was bound to admit?

You conceive the bitterness of his soul. He beheld
himself to be as the dog in the fable that had dropped
the substance to snatch at a delusive shadow.

He sought comfort in a line on the open page before him:

"levius fit patientia quicquid corrigere est nefas."

Sought it, but hardly found it.

A boat that had approached unnoticed from the
shore came scraping and bumping against the great
red hull of the *Arabella*, and a raucous voice sent up
a hailing shout. From the ship's belfry two silvery
notes rang clear and sharp, and a moment or two later
the bo'sun's whistle shrilled a long wail.

The sounds disturbed Captain Blood from his disgruntled musings. He rose, tall, active, and arrestingly elegant in a scarlet, gold-laced coat that adver-
tised his new position, and slipping the slender volume into his pocket, advanced to the carved rail of
the quarter-deck, just as Jeremy Pitt was setting foot
upon the companion.

"A note for you from the Deputy-Governor," said
the master shortly, as he proffered a folded sheet.

Blood broke the seal, and read. Pitt, loosely clad
in shirt and breeches, leaned against the rail the while
and watched him, unmistakable concern imprinted
on his fair, frank countenance.

Blood uttered a short laugh, and curled his lip.

"It is a very peremptory summons," he said, and passed the note to his friend.

The young master's grey eyes skimmed it. Thoughtfully he stroked his golden beard.

"You'll not go?" he said, between question and assertion.

"Why not? Haven't I been a daily visitor at the fort . . . ?"

"But it'll be about the Old Wolf that he wants to see you. It gives him a grievance at last. You know, Peter, that it is Lord Julian alone has stood between Bishop and his hate of you. If now he can show that . . ."

"What if he can?" Blood interrupted carelessly. "Shall I be in greater danger ashore than aboard, now that we've but fifty men left, and they lukewarm rogues who would as soon serve the King as me? Jeremy, dear lad, the *Arabella*'s a prisoner here, bedad, 'twixt the fort there and the fleet yonder. Don't be forgetting that."

Jeremy clenched his hands. "Why did ye let Wolverstone and the others go?" he cried, with a touch of bitterness. "You should have seen the danger."

"How could I in honesty have detained them? It was in the bargain. Besides, how could their staying have helped me?" And as Pitt did not answer him: "Ye see?" he said, and shrugged. "I'll be getting my hat and cane and sword, and go ashore in the cock-boat. See it manned for me."

"Ye're going to deliver yourself into Bishop's hands," Pitt warned him.

"Well, well, maybe he'll not find me quite so easy

to grasp as he imagines. There's a thorn or two left on me." And with a laugh Blood departed to his cabin.

Jeremy Pitt answered the laugh with an oath. A moment he stood irresolute where Blood had left him. Then slowly, reluctance dragging at his feet, he went down the companion to give the order for the cock-boat.

"If anything should happen to you, Peter," he said, as Blood was going over the side, "Colonel Bishop had better look to himself. These fifty lads may be lukewarm at present, as you say, but — sink me! — they'll be anything but lukewarm if there's a breach of faith."

"And what should be happening to me, Jeremy? Sure, now, I'll be back for dinner, so I will."

Blood climbed down into the waiting boat. But laugh though he might, he knew as well as Pitt that in going ashore that morning he carried his life in his hands. Because of this, it may have been that when he stepped on to the narrow mole, in the shadow of the shallow outer wall of the fort through whose crenels were thrust the black noses of its heavy guns, he gave order that the boat should stay for him at that spot. He realized that he might have to retreat in a hurry.

Walking leisurely, he skirted the embattled wall, and passed through the great gates into the court-yard. Half-a-dozen soldiers lounged there, and in the shadow cast by the wall, Major Mallard, the Com-mandant, was slowly pacing. He stopped short at sight of Captain Blood, and saluted him, as was his due, but the smile that lifted the officer's stiff mostachos was grimly sardonic. Peter Blood's attention, however, was elsewhere.

On his right stretched a spacious garden, beyond which rose the white house that was the residence of the Deputy-Governor. In that garden's main avenue, that was fringed with palm and sandalwood, he had caught sight of Miss Bishop alone. He crossed the courtyard with suddenly lengthened stride.

"Good-morning to ye, ma'am," was his greeting as he overtook her; and hat in hand now, he added on a note of protest: "Sure, it's nothing less than uncharitable to make me run in this heat."

"Why do you run, then?" she asked him coolly, standing slim and straight before him, all in white and very maidenly save in her unnatural composure. "I am pressed," she informed him. "So you will forgive me if I do not stay."

"You were none so pressed until I came," he protested, and if his thin lips smiled, his blue eyes were oddly hard.

"Since you perceive it, sir, I wonder that you trouble to be so insistent."

That crossed the swords between them, and it was against Blood's instincts to avoid an engagement.

"Faith, you explain yourself after a fashion," said he. "But since it was more or less in your service that I donned the King's coat, you should suffer it to cover the thief and pirate."

She shrugged and turned aside, in some resentment and some regret. Fearing to betray the latter, she took refuge in the former. "I do my best," said she.

"So that ye can be charitable in some ways!" He laughed softly. "Glory be, now, I should be thankful for so much. Maybe I'm presumptuous. But I can't forget that when I was no better than a slave in your uncle's household in Barbados, ye used me with a certain kindness."

"Why not? In those days you had some claim upon my kindness. You were just an unfortunate gentleman then."

"And what else would you be calling me now?"

"Hardly unfortunate. We have heard of your good fortune on the seas — how your luck has passed into a byword. And we have heard other things: of your good fortune in other directions."

She spoke hastily, the thought of Mademoiselle d'Ogeron in her mind. And instantly would have recalled the words had she been able. But Peter Blood swept them lightly aside, reading into them none of her meaning, as she feared he would.

"Aye — a deal of lies, devil a doubt, as I could prove to you."

"I cannot think why you should trouble to put yourself on your defence," she discouraged him.

"So that ye may think less badly of me than you do."

"What I think of you can be a very little matter to you, sir."

This was a disarming stroke. He abandoned combat for expostulation.

"Can ye say that now? Can ye say that, beholding me in this livery of a service I despise? Didn't ye tell me that I might redeem the past? It's little enough I am concerned to redeem the past save only in your eyes. In my own I've done nothing at all that I am ashamed of, considering the provocation I received."

Her glance faltered, and fell away before his own that was so intent.

"I . . . I can't think why you should speak to me like this," she said, with less than her earlier assurance.

"Ah, now, can't ye, indeed?" he cried. "Sure, then, I'll be telling ye."

"Oh, please." There was real alarm in her voice. "I realize fully what you did, and I realize that partly, at least, you may have been urged by consideration for myself. Believe me, I am very grateful. I shall always be grateful."

"But if it's also your intention always to think of me as a thief and a pirate, faith, ye may keep your gratitude for all the good it's like to do me."

A livelier colour crept into her cheeks. There was a perceptible heave of the slight breast that faintly swelled the flimsy bodice of white silk. But if she resented his tone and his words, she stifled her resent- ment. She realized that perhaps she had, herself, pro- voked his anger. She honestly desired to make amends.

"You are mistaken," she began. "It isn't that."

But they were fated to misunderstand each other. Jealousy, that troubler of reason, had been over-busy with his wits as it had with hers.

"What is it, then?" quoth he, and added the ques- tion: "Lord Julian?"

She started, and stared at him blankly indignant now.

"Och, be frank with me," he urged her, unpardon- ably. "'Twill be a kindness, so it will."

For a moment she stood before him with quickened breathing, the colour ebbing and flowing in her cheeks. Then she looked past him, and tilted her chin forward.

"You ... you are quite insufferable," she said. "I beg that you will let me pass."

He stepped aside, and with the broad feathered hat which he still held in his hand, he waved her on towards the house.

"I'll not be detaining you any longer, ma'am. After all, the cursed thing I did for nothing can be undone. Ye'll remember afterwards that it was your hardness drove me."

She moved to depart, then checked, and faced him again. It was she now who was on her defence, her voice quivering with indignation.

"You take that tone! You dare to take that tone!" she cried, astounding him by her sudden vehemence. "You have the affrontery to upbraid me because I will not take your hands when I know how they are stained; when I know you for a murderer and worse?"

He stared at her open-mouthed.

"A murderer — I?" he said at last.

"Must I name your victims? Did you not murder Levasseur?"

"Levasseur?" He smiled a little. "So they've told you about that!"

"Do you deny it?"

"I killed him, it is true. I can remember killing another man in circumstances that were very similar. That was in Bridgetown on the night of the Spanish raid. Mary Traill would tell you of it. She was present."

He clapped his hat on his head with a certain abrupt fierceness, and strode angrily away, before she could answer or even grasp the full significance of what he had said.

CHAPTER XXIII

HOSTAGES

PETER BLOOD stood in the pillared portico of Government House, and with unseeing eyes that were laden with pain and anger, stared out across the great harbour of Port Royal to the green hills rising from the farther shore and the ridge of the Blue Mountains beyond, showing hazily through the quivering heat.

He was aroused by the return of the negro who had gone to announce him, and following now this slave, he made his way through the house to the wide piazza behind it, in whose shade Colonel Bishop and my Lord Julian Wade took what little air there was.

"So ye've come," the Deputy-Governor hailed him, and followed the greeting by a series of grunts of vague but apparently ill-humoured import.

He did not trouble to rise, not even when Lord Julian, obeying the instincts of finer breeding, set him the example. From under scowling brows the wealthy Barbados planter considered his sometime slave, who, hat in hand, leaning lightly upon his long beribboned cane, revealed nothing in his countenance of the anger which was being steadily nourished by this cavalier reception.

At last, with scowling brow and in self-sufficient tones, Colonel Bishop delivered himself.

"I have sent for you, Captain Blood, because of certain news that has just reached me. I am informed that yesterday evening a frigate left the harbour having on board your associate Wolverstone and a hundred men of the hundred and fifty that were serving under you. His lordship and I shall be glad to have your explanation of how you came to permit that departure."

"Permit?" quoth Blood. "I ordered it."

The answer left Bishop speechless for a moment. Then:

"You ordered it?" he said in accents of unbelief, whilst Lord Julian raised his eyebrows. "'Swounds! Perhaps you'll explain yourself? Whither has Wolverstone gone?"

"To Tortuga. He's gone with a message to the officers commanding the other four ships of the fleet that is awaiting me there, telling them what's happened and why they are no longer to expect me."

Bishop's great face seemed to swell and its high colour to deepen. He swung to Lord Julian.

"You hear that, my lord? Deliberately he has let Wolverstone loose upon the seas again — Wolverstone, the worst of all that gang of pirates after himself. I hope your lordship begins at last to perceive the folly of granting the King's commission to such a man as this against all my counsels. Why, this thing is . . . it's just mutiny . . . treason! By God! It's matter for a court-martial."

"Will you cease your blather of mutiny and treason and courts-martial?" Blood put on his hat, and sat down unbidden. "I have sent Wolverstone to inform Hagthorpe and Christian and Yberville and the rest of my lads that they've one clear month in which to follow my example, quit piracy, and get back to their boucans or their logwood, or else sail out of the Caribbean Sea. That's what I've done."

"But the men?" his lordship interposed in his level, cultured voice. "This hundred men that Wolverstone has taken with him?"

"They are those of my crew who have no taste for King James's service, and have preferred to seek work of other kinds. It was in our compact, my lord, that there should be no constraining of my men."

"I don't remember it," said his lordship, with sincerity.

Blood looked at him in surprise. Then he shrugged. "Faith, I'm not to blame for your lordship's poor memory. I say that it was so; and I don't lie. I've never found it necessary. In any case ye couldn't have supposed that I should consent to anything different."

And then the Deputy-Governor exploded.

"You have given those damned rascals in Tortuga this warning so that they may escape! That is what you have done. That is how you abuse the commission that has saved your own neck!"

Peter Blood considered him steadily, his face impassive.

"I will remind you," he said at last, very quietly, "that the object in view was — leaving out of account your own appetites which, as every one knows, are just those of a hangman — to rid the Caribbean of buccaneers. Now, I've taken the most effective way of accomplishing that object. The knowledge that I've entered the King's service should in itself go far towards disbanding the fleet of which I was until lately the admiral."

"I see!" sneered the Deputy-Governor malevolently. "And if it does not?"

"It will be time enough then to consider what else is to be done."

Lord Julian forestalled a fresh outburst on the part of Bishop.

"It is possible," he said, "that my Lord Sunderland will be satisfied, provided that the solution is such as you promise."

It was a courteous, conciliatory speech. Urged by friendliness towards Blood and understanding of the difficult position in which the buccaneer found himself, his lordship was disposed to take his stand upon the letter of his instructions. Therefore he now held out a friendly hand to help him over the latest and most difficult obstacle which Blood himself had enabled Bishop to place in the way of his redemption. Unfortunately the last person from whom Peter Blood desired assistance at that moment was this young nobleman, whom he regarded with the jaundiced eyes of jealousy.

"Anyway," he answered, with a suggestion of defiance and more than a suggestion of a sneer, "it's the most ye should expect from me, and certainly it's the most ye'll get."

His lordship frowned, and dabbed his lips with a handkerchief.

"I don't think that I quite like the way you put it. Indeed, upon reflection, Captain Blood, I am sure that I do not."

"I am sorry for that, so I am," said Blood impudently. "But there it is. I'm not on that account concerned to modify it."

His lordship's pale eyes opened a little wider. Languidly he raised his eyebrows.

"Ah!" he said. "You're a prodigiously uncivil fellow. You disappoint me, sir. I had formed the notion that you might be a gentleman."

"And that's not your lordship's only mistake," Bishop cut in. "You made a worse when you gave him the King's commission, and so sheltered the rascal from the gallows I had prepared for him in Port Royal."

"Aye — but the worst mistake of all in this matter of commissions," said Blood to his lordship, "was the one that made this greasy slaver Deputy-Governor of Jamaica instead of its hangman, which is the office for which he's by nature fitted."

"Captain Blood!" said his lordship sharply in reproof. "Upon my soul and honour, sir, you go much too far. You are . . ."

But here Bishop interrupted him. He had heaved himself to his feet, at last, and was venting his fury in unprintable abuse. Captain Blood, who had also risen, stood apparently impassive, for the storm to spend itself. When at last this happened, he addressed himself quietly to Lord Julian, as if Colonel Bishop had not spoken.

"Your lordship was about to say?" he asked, with challenging smoothness.

But his lordship had by now recovered his habitual composure, and was again disposed to be conciliatory. He laughed and shrugged.

"Faith! here's a deal of unnecessary heat," said he. "And God knows this plaguey climate provides enough of that. Perhaps, Colonel Bishop, you are a little uncompromising; and you, sir, are certainly a deal too peppery. I have said, speaking on behalf of my Lord Sunderland, that I am content to await the result of your experiment."

But Bishop's fury had by now reached a stage in which it was not to be restrained.

"Are you, indeed?" he roared. "Well, then, I am not. This is a matter in which your lordship must allow me to be the better judge. And, anyhow, I'll take the risk of acting on my own responsibility."

Lord Julian abandoned the struggle. He smiled wearily, shrugged, and waved a hand in implied resignation. The Deputy-Governor stormed on.

"Since my lord here has given you a commission, I can't regularly deal with you out of hand for piracy as you deserve. But you shall answer before a court-martial for your action in the matter of Wolverstone, and take the consequences."

"I see," said Blood. "Now we come to it. And it's yourself as Deputy-Governor will preside over that same court-martial. So that ye can wipe off old scores by hanging me, it's little ye care how ye do it!" He laughed, and added: "Præmonitus, præmunitus."

"What shall that mean?" quoth Lord Julian sharply.

"I had imagined that your lordship would have had some education."

He was at pains, you see, to be provocative.

"It's not the literal meaning I am asking, sir," said Lord Julian, with frosty dignity. "I want to know what you desire me to understand?"

"I'll leave your lordship guessing," said Blood. "And I'll be wishing ye both a very good day." He swept off his feathered hat, and made them a leg very elegantly.

"Before you go," said Bishop, "and to save you from any idle rashness, I'll tell you that the Harbour-Master and the Commandant have their orders. You don't leave Port Royal, my fine gallows bird. Damme, I mean to provide you with permanent moorings here, in Execution Dock."

Peter Blood stiffened, and his vivid blue eyes stabbed the bloated face of his enemy. He passed his long cane into his left hand, and with his right thrust negligently into the breast of his doublet, he swung to Lord Julian, who was thoughtfully frowning.

"Your lordship, I think, promised me immunity from this."

"What I may have promised," said his lordship, "your own conduct makes it difficult to perform." He rose. "You did me a service, Captain Blood, and I had hoped that we might be friends. But since you prefer to have it otherwise..." He shrugged, and waved a hand towards the Deputy-Governor.

Blood completed the sentence in his own way:

"Ye mean that ye haven't the strength of character to resist the urgings of a bully." He was apparently at his ease, and actually smiling. "Well, well — as I said before — præmonitus, præmunitus. I'm afraid that ye're no scholar, Bishop, or ye'd know that it means forewarned, forearmed."

"Forewarned? Ha!" Bishop almost snarled. "The warning comes a little late. You do not leave this house." He took a step in the direction of the doorway, and raised his voice. "Ho there..." he was beginning to call.

Then with a sudden audible catch in his breath, he stopped short. Captain Blood's right hand had re-emerged from the breast of his doublet, bringing with it a long pistol with silver mountings richly chased, which he levelled within a foot of the Deputy-Governor's head.

"And forearmed," said he. "Don't stir from where you are, my lord, or there may be an accident."

And my lord, who had been moving to Bishop's assistance, stood instantly arrested. Chap-fallen, with much of his high colour suddenly departed, the Deputy-Governor was swaying on unsteady legs. Peter Blood considered him with a grimness that increased his panic.

"I marvel that I don't pistol you without more ado, ye fat blackguard. If I don't, it's for the same reason that once before I gave ye your life when it was forfeit. Ye're not aware of the reason, to be sure; but it may comfort ye to know that it exists. At the same time I'll warn ye not to put too heavy a strain on my generosity, which resides at the moment in my trigger-finger. Ye mean to hang me, and since that's the worst that can happen to me anyway, you'll realize that I'll not boggle at increasing the account by spilling your nasty blood." He cast his cane from him, thus disengaging his left hand. "Be good enough to give me your arm, Colonel Bishop. Come, come, man, your arm."

Under the compulsion of that sharp tone, those resolute eyes, and that gleaming pistol, Bishop obeyed without demur. His recent foul volubility was stemmed. He could not trust himself to speak. Captain Blood tucked his left arm through the Deputy-

Governor's proffered right. Then he thrust his own right hand with its pistol back into the breast of his doublet.

"Though invisible, it's aiming at ye none the less, and I give you my word of honour that I'll shoot ye dead upon the very least provocation, whether that provocation is yours or another's. Ye'll bear that in mind, Lord Julian. And now, ye greasy hangman, step out as brisk and lively as ye can, and behave as naturally as ye may, or it's the black stream of Cocytus ye'll be contemplating." Arm in arm they passed through the house, and down the garden, where Arabella lingered, awaiting Peter Blood's return.

Consideration of his parting words had brought her first turmoil of mind, then a clear perception of what might be indeed the truth of the death of Levasseur. She perceived that the particular inference drawn from it might similarly have been drawn from Blood's deliverance of Mary Traill. When a man so risks his life for a woman, the rest is easily assumed. For the men who will take such risks without hope of personal gain are few. Blood was of those few, as he had proved in the case of Mary Traill.

It needed no further assurances of his to convince her that she had done him a monstrous injustice. She remembered words he had used — words overheard aboard his ship (which he had named the *Arabella*) on the night of her deliverance from the Spanish admiral; words he had uttered when she had approved his acceptance of the King's commission; the words he had spoken to her that very morning, which had but served to move her indignation. All these as-

sumed a fresh meaning in her mind, delivered now from its unwarranted preconceptions.

Therefore she lingered there in the garden, awaiting his return that she might make amends; that she might set a term to all misunderstanding. In impatience she awaited him. Yet her patience, it seemed, was to be tested further. For when at last he came, it was in company — unusually close and intimate company — with her uncle. In vexation she realized that explanations must be postponed. Could she have guessed the extent of that postponement, vexation would have been changed into despair.

He passed, with his companion, from that fragrant garden into the courtyard of the fort. Here the Commandant, who had been instructed to hold himself in readiness with the necessary men against the need to effect the arrest of Captain Blood, was amazed by the curious spectacle of the Deputy-Governor of Jamaica strolling forth arm in arm and apparently on the friendliest terms with the intended prisoner. For as they went, Blood was chatting and laughing briskly.

They passed out of the gates unchallenged, and so came to the mole where the cock-boat from the *Arabella* was waiting. They took their places side by side in the stern sheets, and were pulled away together, always very close and friendly, to the great red ship where Jeremy Pitt so anxiously awaited news.

You conceive the master's amazement to see the Deputy-Governor come toiling up the entrance ladder, with Blood following very close behind him.

"Sure, I walked into a trap, as ye feared, Jeremy," Blood hailed him. "But I walked out again, and fetched the trapper with me. He loves his life, does this fat rascal."

Colonel Bishop stood in the waist, his great face blenched to the colour of clay, his mouth loose, almost afraid to look at the sturdy ruffians who lounged about the shot-rack on the main hatch.

Blood shouted an order to the bo'sun, who was leaning against the forecastle bulkhead.

"Throw me a rope with a running noose over the yardarm there, against the need of it. Now, don't be alarming yourself, Colonel, darling. It's no more than a provision against your being unreasonable, which I am sure ye'll not be. We'll talk the matter over whiles we are dining, for I trust ye'll not refuse to honour my table by your company."

He led away the will-less, cowed bully to the great cabin. Benjamin, the negro steward, in white drawers and cotton shirt, made haste by his command to serve dinner.

Colonel Bishop collapsed on the locker under the stern ports, and spoke now for the first time.

"May I ask wha ... what are your intentions?" he quavered.

"Why, nothing sinister, Colonel. Although ye deserve nothing less than that same rope and yardarm, I assure you that it's to be employed only as a last resource. Ye've said his lordship made a mistake when he handed me the commission which the Secretary of State did me the honour to design for me. I'm disposed to agree with you; so I'll take to the sea again. Cras ingens iterabimus æquor. It's the fine Latin scholar ye'll be when I've done with ye. I'll be getting back to Tortuga and my buccaneers, who at least are honest, decent fellows. So I've fetched ye aboard as a hostage."

"My God!" groaned the Deputy-Governor. "Ye ... ye never mean that ye'll carry me to Tortuga!"

Blood laughed outright. "Oh, I'd never serve ye such a bad turn as that. No, no. All I want is that ye ensure my safe departure from Port Royal. And, if ye're reasonable, I'll not even trouble you to swim for it this time. Ye've given certain orders to your Harbour-Master, and others to the Commandant of your plaguey fort. Ye'll be so good as to send for them both aboard here, and inform them in my presence that the *Arabella* is leaving this afternoon on the King's service and is to pass out unmolested. And so as to make quite sure of their obedience, they shall go a little voyage with us, themselves. Here's what you require. Now write — unless you prefer the yard-arm."

Colonel Bishop heaved himself up in a pet. "You constrain me with violence ..." he was beginning.

Blood smoothly interrupted him.

"Sure, now, I am not constraining you at all. I'm giving you a perfectly free choice between the pen and the rope. It's a matter for yourself entirely."

Bishop glared at him; then shrugging heavily, he took up the pen and sat down at the table. In an unsteady hand he wrote that summons to his officers. Blood despatched it ashore; and then bade his unwilling guest to table.

"I trust, Colonel, your appetite is as stout as usual."

The wretched Bishop took the seat to which he was commanded. As for eating, however, that was not easy to a man in his position; nor did Blood press him. The Captain, himself, fell to with a good appetite. But before he was midway through the meal came Hayton to inform him that Lord Julian Wade had just come aboard, and was asking to see him instantly.

"I was expecting him," said Blood. "Fetch him in."

Lord Julian came. He was very stern and dignified. His eyes took in the situation at a glance, as Captain Blood rose to greet him.

"It's mighty friendly of you to have joined us, my lord."

"Captain Blood," said his lordship with asperity, "I find your humour a little forced. I don't know what may be your intentions; but I wonder do you realize the risks you are running."

"And I wonder does your lordship realize the risk to yourself in following us aboard as I had counted that you would."

"What shall that mean, sir?"

Blood signalled to Benjamin, who was standing behind Bishop.

"Set a chair for his lordship. Hayton, send his lordship's boat ashore. Tell them he'll not be returning yet awhile."

"What's that?" cried his lordship. "Blister me! D'ye mean to detain me? Are ye mad?"

"Better wait, Hayton, in case his lordship should turn violent," said Blood. "You, Benjamin, you heard the message. Deliver it."

"Will you tell me what you intend, sir?" demanded his lordship, quivering with anger.

"Just to make myself and my lads here safe from Colonel Bishop's gallows. I've said that I trusted to your gallantry not to leave him in the lurch, but to follow him hither, and there's a note from his hand gone ashore to summon the Harbour-Master and the Commandant of the fort. Once they are aboard, I shall have all the hostages I need for our safety."

"You scoundrel!" said his lordship through his teeth.

"Sure, now, that's entirely a matter of the point of view," said Blood. "Ordinarily it isn't the kind of name I could suffer any man to apply to me. Still, considering that ye willingly did me a service once, and that ye're likely unwillingly to do me another now, I'll overlook your discourtesy, so I will."

His lordship laughed. "You fool," he said. "Do you dream that I came aboard your pirate ship without taking my measures? I informed the Commandant of exactly how you had compelled Colonel Bishop to accompany you. Judge now whether he or the Harbour-Master will obey the summons, or whether you will be allowed to depart as you imagine."

Blood's face became grave. "I'm sorry for that," said he.

"I thought you would be," answered his lordship.

"Oh, but not on my own account. It's the Deputy-Governor there I'm sorry for. D'ye know what ye've done? Sure, now, ye've very likely hanged him."

"My God!" cried Bishop in a sudden increase of panic.

"If they so much as put a shot across my bows, up goes their Deputy-Governor to the yardarm. Your only hope, Colonel, lies in the fact that I shall send

them word of that intention. And so that you may
mend as far as you can the harm you have done, it's
yourself shall bear them the message, my lord."

"I'll see you damned before I do," fumed his lordship.

"Why, that's unreasonable and unreasoning. But
if ye insist, why, another messenger will do as well,
and another hostage aboard — as I had originally intended — will make my hand the stronger."

Lord Julian stared at him, realizing exactly what
he had refused.

"You'll think better of it now that ye understand?"
quoth Blood.

"Aye, in God's name, go, my lord," spluttered
Bishop, "and make yourself obeyed. This damned
pirate has me by the throat."

His lordship surveyed him with an eye that was
not by any means admiring. "Why, if that is your
wish . . ." he began. Then he shrugged, and turned
again to Blood.

"I suppose I can trust you that no harm will come
to Colonel Bishop if you are allowed to sail?"

"You have my word for it," said Blood. "And also
that I shall put him safely ashore again without delay."

Lord Julian bowed stiffly to the cowering Deputy-
Governor. "You understand, sir, that I do as you
desire," he said coldly.

"Aye, man, aye!" Bishop assented hastily.

"Very well." Lord Julian bowed again and took
his departure. Blood escorted him to the entrance
ladder at the foot of which still swung the *Arabella's*
own cock-boat.

"It's good-bye, my lord," said Blood. "And there's another thing." He proffered a parchment that he had drawn from his pocket. "It's the commission. Bishop was right when he said it was a mistake."

Lord Julian considered him, and considering him his expression softened.

"I am sorry," he said sincerely.

"In other circumstances . . ." began Blood. "Oh, but there! Ye'll understand. The boat's waiting."

Yet with his foot on the first rung of the ladder, Lord Julian hesitated.

"I still do not perceive — blister me if I do! — why you should not have found some one else to carry your message to the Commandant, and kept me aboard as an added hostage for his obedience to your wishes."

Blood's vivid eyes looked into the other's that were clear and honest, and he smiled, a little wistfully. A moment he seemed to hesitate. Then he explained himself quite fully.

"Why shouldn't I tell you? It's the same reason that's been urging me to pick a quarrel with you so that I might have the satisfaction of slipping a couple of feet of steel into your vitals. When I accepted your commission, I was moved to think it might redeem me in the eyes of Miss Bishop — for whose sake, as you may have guessed, I took it. But I have discovered that such a thing is beyond accomplishment. I should have known it for a sick man's dream. I have discovered also that if she's choosing you, as I believe she is, she's choosing wisely between us, and that's why I'll not have your life risked by keeping you aboard whilst the message goes by another who might bungle it. And now perhaps ye'll understand."

Lord Julian stared at him bewildered. His long, aristocratic face was very pale.

"My God!" he said. "And you tell me this?"

"I tell you because . . . Oh, plague on it! — so that ye may tell her; so that she may be made to realize that there's something of the unfortunate gentleman left under the thief and pirate she accounts me, and that her own good is my supreme desire. Knowing that, she may . . . faith, she may remember me more kindly — if it's only in her prayers. That's all, my lord."

Lord Julian continued to look at the buccaneer in silence. In silence, at last, he held out his hand; and in silence Blood took it.

"I wonder whether you are right," said his lord-ship, "and whether you are not the better man."

"Where she is concerned see that you make sure that I am right. Good-bye to you."

Lord Julian wrung his hand in silence, went down the ladder, and was pulled ashore. From the distance he waved to Blood, who stood leaning on the bul-warks watching the receding cock-boat.

The *Arabella* sailed within the hour, moving lazily before a sluggish breeze. The fort remained silent and there was no movement from the fleet to hinder her departure. Lord Julian had carried the message effectively, and had added to it his own personal commands.

CHAPTER XXIV

WAR

FIVE miles out at sea from Port Royal, whence the details of the coast of Jamaica were losing their sharpness, the *Arabella* hove to, and the sloop she had been towing was warped alongside.

Captain Blood escorted his compulsory guest to the head of the ladder. Colonel Bishop, who for two hours and more had been in a state of mortal anxiety, breathed freely at last; and as the tide of his fears receded, so that of his deep-rooted hate of this audacious buccaneer resumed its normal flow. But he practised circumspection. If in his heart he vowed that once back in Port Royal there was no effort he would spare, no nerve he would not strain, to bring Peter Blood to final moorings in Execution Dock, at least he kept that vow strictly to himself.

Peter Blood had no illusions. He was not, and never would be, the complete pirate. There was not another buccaneer in all the Caribbean who would have denied himself the pleasure of stringing Colonel Bishop from the yardarm, and by thus finally stifling the vindictive planter's hatred have increased his own security. But Blood was not of these. Moreover, in the case of Colonel Bishop there was a particular reason for restraint. Because he was Arabella Bishop's uncle, his life must remain sacred to Captain Blood.

And so the Captain smiled into the sallow, bloated

face and the little eyes that fixed him with a malevolence not to be dissembled.

"A safe voyage home to you, Colonel, darling,"
said he in valediction, and from his easy, smiling
manner you would never have dreamt of the pain he
carried in his breast. "It's the second time ye've
served me for a hostage. Ye'll be well advised to
avoid a third. I'm not lucky to you, Colonel, as you
should be perceiving."

Jeremy Pitt, the master, lounging at Blood's elbow,
looked darkly upon the departure of the Deputy-
Governor. Behind them a little mob of grim, stalwart, sun-tanned buccaneers were restrained from
cracking Bishop like a flea only by their submission
to the dominant will of their leader. They had learnt
from Pitt while yet in Port Royal of their Captain's
danger, and whilst as ready as he to throw over the
King's service which had been thrust upon them, yet
they resented the manner in which this had been rendered necessary, and they marvelled now at Blood's
restraint where Bishop was concerned. The Deputy-
Governor looked round and met the lowering hostile
glances of those fierce eyes. Instinct warned him that
his life at that moment was held precariously, that an
injudicious word might precipitate an explosion of
hatred from which no human power could save him.
Therefore he said nothing. He inclined his head in
silence to the Captain, and went blundering and
stumbling in his haste down that ladder to the sloop
and its waiting negro crew.

They pushed off the craft from the red hull of the
Arabella, bent to their sweeps, then, hoisting sail,
headed back for Port Royal, intent upon reaching it

before darkness should come down upon them. And Bishop, the great bulk of him huddled in the stern sheets, sat silent, his black brows knitted, his coarse lips pursed, malevolence and vindictiveness so whelming now his recent panic that he forgot his near escape of the yardarm and the running noose.

On the mole at Port Royal, under the low, embattled wall of the fort, Major Mallard and Lord Julian waited to receive him, and it was with infinite relief that they assisted him from the sloop.

Major Mallard was disposed to be apologetic.

"Glad to see you safe, sir," said he. "I'd have sunk Blood's ship in spite of your excellency's being aboard but for your own orders by Lord Julian, and his lordship's assurance that he had Blood's word for it that no harm should come to you so that no harm came to him. I'll confess I thought it rash of his lordship to accept the word of a damned pirate . . ."

"I have found it as good as another's," said his lordship, cropping the Major's too eager eloquence. He spoke with an unusual degree of that frosty dignity he could assume upon occasion. The fact is that his lordship was in an exceedingly bad humour. Having written jubilantly home to the Secretary of State that his mission had succeeded, he was now faced with the necessity of writing again to confess that this success had been ephemeral. And because Major Mallard's crisp mostachios were lifted by a sneer at the notion of a buccaneer's word being acceptable, he added still more sharply: "My justification is here in the person of Colonel Bishop safely returned. As against that, sir, your opinion does not weigh for very much. You should realize it."

"Oh, as your lordship says." Major Mallard's manner was tinged with irony. "To be sure, here is the Colonel safe and sound. And out yonder is Captain Blood, also safe and sound, to begin his piratical ravages all over again."

"I do not propose to discuss the reasons with you, Major Mallard."

"And, anyway, it's not for long," growled the Colonel, finding speech at last. "No, by ..." He emphasized the assurance by an unprintable oath. "If I spend the last shilling of my fortune and the last ship of the Jamaica fleet, I'll have that rascal in a hempen necktie before I rest. And I'll not be long about it." He had empurpled in his angry vehemence, and the veins of his forehead stood out like whipcord. Then he checked.

"You did well to follow Lord Julian's instructions," he commended the Major. With that he turned from him, and took his lordship by the arm. "Come, my lord. We must take order about this, you and I."

They went off together, skirting the redoubt, and so through courtyard and garden to the house where Arabella waited anxiously. The sight of her uncle brought her infinite relief, not only on his own account, but on account also of Captain Blood.

"You took a great risk, sir," she gravely told Lord Julian after the ordinary greetings had been exchanged.

But Lord Julian answered her as he had answered Major Mallard. "There was no risk, ma'am."

She looked at him in some astonishment. His long, aristocratic face wore a more melancholy, pensive air than usual. He answered the enquiry in her glance:

"So that Blood's ship were allowed to pass the fort,
no harm could come to Colonel Bishop. Blood pledged
me his word for that."

A faint smile broke the set of her lips, which hitherto
had been wistful, and a little colour tinged her cheeks.
She would have pursued the subject, but the Deputy-
Governor's mood did not permit it. He sneered and
snorted at the notion of Blood's word being good for
anything, forgetting that he owed to it his own preservation at that moment.

At supper, and for long thereafter, he talked of
nothing but Blood — of how he would lay him by the
heels, and what hideous things he would perform upon
his body. And as he drank heavily the while, his
speech became increasingly gross and his threats increasingly horrible; until in the end Arabella withdrew, white-faced and almost on the verge of tears.
It was not often that Bishop revealed himself to his
niece. Oddly enough, this coarse, overbearing planter
went in a certain awe of that slim girl. It was as if she
had inherited from her father the respect in which he
had always been held by his brother.

Lord Julian, who began to find Bishop disgusting
beyond endurance, excused himself soon after, and
went in quest of the lady. He had yet to deliver the
message from Captain Blood, and this, he thought,
would be his opportunity. But Miss Bishop had re-
tired for the night, and Lord Julian must curb his
impatience — it amounted by now to nothing less —
until the morrow.

Very early next morning, before the heat of the day
came to render the open intolerable to his lordship, he
espied her from his window moving amid the azaleas

in the garden. It was a fitting setting for one who was
still as much a delightful novelty to him in womanhood as was the azalea among flowers. He hurried
forth to join her, and when, aroused from her pensiveness, she had given him a good-morrow, smiling and
frank, he explained himself by the announcement that
he bore her a message from Captain Blood.

He observed her little start and the slight quiver
of her lips, and observed thereafter not only her pallor and the shadowy rings about her eyes, but also
that unusually wistful air which last night had escaped his notice.

They moved out of the open to one of the terraces,
where a pergola of orange-trees provided a shaded
sauntering space that was at once cool and fragrant.
As they went, he considered her admiringly, and marvelled at himself that it should have taken him so long
fully to realize her slim, unusual grace, and to find
her, as he now did, so entirely desirable, a woman
whose charm must irradiate all the life of a man, and
touch its commonplaces into magic.

He noted the sheen of her red-brown hair, and how
gracefully one of its heavy ringlets coiled upon her
slender, milk-white neck. She wore a gown of shimmering grey silk, and a scarlet rose, fresh-gathered,
was pinned at her breast like a splash of blood. Always thereafter when he thought of her it was as he
saw her at that moment, as never, I think, until that
moment had he seen her.

In silence they paced on a little way into the green
shade. Then she paused and faced him.

"You said something of a message, sir," she re-
minded him, thus betraying some of her impatience.

He fingered the ringlets of his periwig, a little embarrassed how to deliver himself, considering how he should begin.

"He desired me," he said at last, "to give you a message that should prove to you that there is still something left in him of the unfortunate gentleman that . . . that . . . for which once you knew him."

"That is not now necessary," said she very gravely.

He misunderstood her, of course, knowing nothing of the enlightenment that yesterday had come to her.

"I think . . . nay, I know that you do him an injustice," said he.

Her hazel eyes continued to regard him.

"If you will deliver the message, it may enable me to judge."

To him, this was confusing. He did not immediately answer. He found that he had not sufficiently considered the terms he should employ, and the matter, after all, was of an exceeding delicacy, demanding delicate handling. It was not so much that he was concerned to deliver a message as to render it a vehicle by which to plead his own cause. Lord Julian, well versed in the lore of womankind and usually at his ease with ladies of the beau-monde, found himself oddly constrained before this frank and unsophisticated niece of a colonial planter.

They moved on in silence and as if by common consent towards the brilliant sunshine where the pergola was intersected by the avenue leading upwards to the house. Across this patch of light fluttered a gorgeous butterfly, that was like black and scarlet velvet and large as a man's hand. His lordship's brooding eyes followed it out of sight before he answered.

"It is not easy. Stab me, it is not. He was a man
who deserved well. And amongst us we have marred
his chances: your uncle, because he could not forget
his rancour; you, because ... because having told
him that in the King's service he would find his redemption of what was past, you would not afterwards
admit to him that he was so redeemed. And this, although concern to rescue you was the chief motive of
his embracing that same service."

She turned her shoulder to him so that he should
not see her face.

"I know. I know now," she said softly. Then
after a pause she added the question: "And you?
What part has your lordship had in this — that you
should incriminate yourself with us?"

"My part?" Again he hesitated, then plunged
recklessly on, as men do when determined to perform
a thing they fear. "If I understood him aright, if he
understood aright, himself, my part, though entirely
passive, was none the less effective. I implore you
to observe that I but report his own words. I say
nothing for myself." His lordship's unusual nervous-
ness was steadily increasing. "He thought, then —
so he told me — that my presence here had contributed to his inability to redeem himself in your sight;
and unless he were so redeemed, then was redemption
nothing."

She faced him fully, a frown of perplexity bringing
her brows together above her troubled eyes.

"He thought that you had contributed?" she
echoed. It was clear she asked for enlightenment.
He plunged on to afford it her, his glance a little
scared, his cheeks flushing.

"Aye, and he said so in terms which told me something that I hope above all things, and yet dare not believe, for, God knows, I am no coxcomb, Arabella. He said . . . But first let me tell you how I was placed. I had gone aboard his ship to demand the instant surrender of your uncle whom he held captive. He laughed at me. Colonel Bishop should be a hostage for his safety. By rashly venturing aboard his ship, I afforded him in my own person yet another hostage as valuable at least as Colonel Bishop. Yet he bade me depart; not from the fear of consequences, for he is above fear, nor from any personal esteem for me whom he confessed that he had come to find detestable; and this for the very reason that made him concerned for my safety."

"I do not understand," she said, as he paused. "Is not that a contradiction in itself?"

"It seems so only. The fact is, Arabella, this unfortunate man has the . . . the temerity to love you."

She cried out at that, and clutched her breast whose calm was suddenly disturbed. Her eyes dilated as she stared at him.

"I . . . I've startled you," said he, with concern. "I feared I should. But it was necessary so that you may understand."

"Go on," she bade him.

"Well, then: he saw in me one who made it impossible that he should win you — so he said. Therefore he could with satisfaction have killed me. But because my death might cause you pain, because your happiness was the thing that above all things he desired, he surrendered that part of his guarantee of safety which my person afforded him. If his departure should be hindered, and I should lose my life in what might follow, there was the risk that ... that you might mourn me. That risk he would not take. Him you deemed a thief and a pirate, he said, and added that — I am giving you his own words always — if in choosing between us two, your choice, as he believed, would fall on me, then were you in his opinion choosing wisely. Because of that he bade me leave his ship, and had me put ashore."

She looked at him with eyes that were aswim with tears. He took a step towards her, a catch in his breath, his hand held out.

"Was he right, Arabella? My life's happiness hangs upon your answer."

But she continued silently to regard him with those tear-laden eyes, without speaking, and until she spoke he dared not advance farther.

A doubt, a tormenting doubt beset him. When presently she spoke, he saw how true had been the instinct of which that doubt was born, for her words revealed the fact that of all that he had said the only thing that had touched her consciousness and absorbed it from all other considerations was Blood's conduct as it regarded herself.

"He said that!" she cried. "He did that! Oh!" She turned away, and through the slender, clustering trunks of the bordering orange-trees she looked out across the glittering waters of the great harbour to the distant hills. Thus for a little while, my lord standing stiffly, fearfully, waiting for fuller revelation of her mind. At last it came, slowly, deliberately, in a voice that at moments was half suffocated. "Last night when my uncle displayed his rancour and his evil rage, it began to be borne in upon me that such vindictiveness can belong only to those who have wronged. It is the frenzy into which men whip themselves to justify an evil passion. I must have known then, if I had not already learnt it, that I had been too credulous of all the unspeakable things attributed to Peter Blood. Yesterday I had his own explanation of that tale of Levasseur that you heard in St. Nicholas. And now this . . . this but gives me confirmation of his truth and worth. To a scoundrel such as I was too readily brought to believe him, the act of which you have just told me would have been impossible."

"That is my own opinion," said his lordship gently.

"It must be. But even if it were not, that would now weigh for nothing. What weighs — oh, so heavily and bitterly — is the thought that but for the words in which yesterday I repelled him, he might have been saved. If only I could have spoken to him again before he went! I waited for him; but my uncle was with him, and I had no suspicion that he was going away again. And now he is lost — back at his outlawry and piracy, in which ultimately he will be taken and destroyed. And the fault is mine — mine!"

"What are you saying? The only agents were your uncle's hostility and his own obstinacy which would not study compromise. You must not blame yourself for anything."

She swung to him with some impatience, her eyes aswim in tears. "You can say that, and in spite of his message, which in itself tells how much I was to blame! It was my treatment of him, the epithets I cast at him that drove him. So much he has told you. I know it to be true."

"You have no cause for shame," said he. "As for your sorrow — why, if it will afford you solace — you may still count on me to do what man can to rescue him from this position."

She caught her breath.

"You will do that!" she cried with sudden eager hopefulness. "You promise?" She held out her hand to him impulsively. He took it in both his own.

"I promise," he answered her. And then, retaining still the hand she had surrendered to him — "Arabella," he said very gently, "there is still this other matter upon which you have not answered me"

"This other matter?" Was he mad, she wondered. Could any other matter signify in such a moment.

"This matter that concerns myself, and all my future, oh, so very closely. This thing that Blood believed, that prompted him . . . that . . . that you are not indifferent to me." He saw the fair face change colour and grow troubled once more.

"Indifferent to you?" said she. "Why, no. We have been good friends; we shall continue so, I hope, my lord."

"Friends! Good friends?" He was between dismay and bitterness. "It is not your friendship only that I ask, Arabella. You heard what I said, what I reported. You will not say that Peter Blood was wrong?"

Gently she sought to disengage her hand, the trouble in her face increasing. A moment he resisted; then, realizing what he did, he set her free.

"Arabella!" he cried on a note of sudden pain.

"I have friendship for you, my lord. But only friendship."

His castle of hopes came clattering down about
him, leaving him a little stunned. As he had said, he
was no coxcomb. Yet there was something that he
did not understand. She confessed to friendship, and
it was in his power to offer her a great position, one to
which she, a colonial planter's niece, however wealthy,
could never have aspired even in her dreams. This
she rejected, yet spoke of friendship. Peter Blood had
been mistaken, then. How far had he been mistaken?
Had he been as mistaken in her feelings towards himself as he obviously was in her feelings towards his
lordship? In that case... His reflections broke
short. To speculate was to wound himself in vain.
He must know. Therefore he asked her with grim
frankness:

"Is it Peter Blood?"

"Peter Blood?" she echoed. At first she did not
understand the purport of his question. When understanding came, a flush suffused her face.

"I do not know," she said, faltering a little.

This was hardly a truthful answer. For, as if an
obscuring veil had suddenly been rent that morning,
she was permitted at last to see Peter Blood in his true
relations to other men, and that sight, vouchsafed her
twenty-four hours too late, filled her with pity and
regret and yearning.

Lord Julian knew enough of women to be left in no
further doubt. He bowed his head so that she might
not see the anger in his eyes, for as a man of honour
he took shame in that anger which as a human being
he could not repress.

And because Nature in him was stronger — as it is
in most of us — than training, Lord Julian from that

moment began, almost in spite of himself, to practise something that was akin to villainy. I regret to chronicle it of one for whom — if I have done him any sort of justice — you should have been conceiving some esteem. But the truth is that the lingering remains of the regard in which he had held Peter Blood were choked by the desire to supplant and destroy a rival. He had passed his word to Arabella that he would use his powerful influence on Blood's behalf. I deplore to set it down that not only did he forget his pledge, but secretly set himself to aid and abet Arabella's uncle in the plans he laid for the trapping and undoing of the buccaneer. He might reasonably have urged — had he been taxed with it — that he conducted himself precisely as his duty demanded. But to that he might have been answered that duty with him was but the slave of jealousy in this.

When the Jamaica fleet put to sea some few days later, Lord Julian sailed with Colonel Bishop in Vice-Admiral Craufurd's flagship. Not only was there no need for either of them to go, but the Deputy-Governor's duties actually demanded that he should remain ashore, whilst Lord Julian, as we know, was a useless man aboard a ship. Yet both set out to hunt Captain Blood, each making of his duty a pretext for the satisfaction of personal aims; and that common purpose became a link between them, binding them in a sort of friendship that must otherwise have been impossible between men so dissimilar in breeding and in aspirations.

The hunt was up. They cruised awhile off Hispaniola, watching the Windward Passage, and suffering the discomforts of the rainy season which had now set in. But they cruised in vain, and after a month of it, returned empty-handed to Port Royal, there to find awaiting them the most disquieting news from the Old World.

The megalomania of Louis XIV had set Europe in a blaze of war. The French legionaries were ravaging the Rhine provinces, and Spain had joined the nations leagued to defend themselves from the wild ambitions of the King of France. And there was worse than this: there were rumours of civil war in England, where the people had grown weary of the bigoted tyranny of King James. It was reported that William of Orange had been invited to come over.

Weeks passed, and every ship from home brought additional news. William had crossed to England, and in March of that year 1689 they learnt in Jamaica that he had accepted the crown and that James had thrown himself into the arms of France for rehabilitation.

To a kinsman of Sunderland's this was disquieting news, indeed. It was followed by letters from King William's Secretary of State informing Colonel Bishop that there was war with France, and that in view of its effect upon the Colonies a Governor-General was coming out to the West Indies in the person of Lord Willoughby, and that with him came a squadron under the command of Admiral van der Kuylen to reënforce the Jamaica fleet against eventualities.

Bishop realized that this must mean the end of his supreme authority, even though he should continue in Port Royal as Deputy-Governor. Lord Julian, in the lack of direct news to himself, did not know what it might mean to him. But he had been very close and

confidential with Colonel Bishop regarding his hopes
of Arabella, and Colonel Bishop more than ever, now
that political events put him in danger of being re-
tired, was anxious to enjoy the advantages of having
a man of Lord Julian's eminence for his relative.

They came to a complete understanding in the
matter, and Lord Julian disclosed all that he knew.

"There is one obstacle in our path," said he. "Captain Blood. The girl is in love with him."

"Ye're surely mad!" cried Bishop, when he had
recovered speech.

"You are justified of the assumption," said his
lordship dolefully. "But I happen to be sane, and to
speak with knowledge."

"With knowledge?"

"Arabella herself has confessed it to me."

"The brazen baggage! By God, I'll bring her to
her senses." It was the slave-driver speaking, the
man who governed with a whip.

"Don't be a fool, Bishop." His lordship's contempt did more than any argument to calm the Colonel. "That's not the way with a girl of Arabella's
spirit. Unless you want to wreck my chances for all
time, you'll hold your tongue, and not interfere at all."

"Not interfere? My God, what, then?"

"Listen, man. She has a constant mind. I don't
think you know your niece. As long as Blood lives,
she will wait for him."

"Then with Blood dead, perhaps she will come to
her silly senses."

"Now you begin to show intelligence," Lord Julian
commended him. "That is the first essential step."

"And here is our chance to take it." Bishop warmed

to a sort of enthusiasm. "This war with France re-
moves all restrictions in the matter of Tortuga. We
are free to invest it in the service of the Crown. A
victory there and we establish ourselves in the favour
of this new government."

"Ah!" said Lord Julian, and he pulled thoughtfully
at his lip.

"I see that you understand." Bishop laughed
coarsely. "Two birds with one stone, eh? We'll hunt
this rascal in his lair, right under the beard of the King
of France, and we'll take him this time, if we reduce
Tortuga to a heap of ashes."

On that expedition they sailed two days later —
which would be some three months after Blood's departure — taking every ship of the fleet, and several
lesser vessels as auxiliaries. To Arabella and the
world in general it was given out that they were going
to raid French Hispaniola, which was really the only
expedition that could have afforded Colonel Bishop
any sort of justification for leaving Jamaica at all at
such a time. His sense of duty, indeed, should have
kept him fast in Port Royal; but his sense of duty
was smothered in hatred — that most fruitless and
corruptive of all the emotions. In the great cabin of
Vice-Admiral Craufurd's flagship, the *Imperator*, the
Deputy-Governor got drunk that night to celebrate
his conviction that the sands of Captain Blood's career
were running out.

CHAPTER XXV

MEANWHILE, some three months before Colonel Bishop set out to reduce Tortuga, Captain Blood, bearing hell in his soul, had blown into its rockbound harbour ahead of the winter gales, and two days ahead of the frigate in which Wolverstone had sailed from Port Royal a day before him.

In that snug anchorage he found his fleet awaiting him — the four ships which had been separated in that gale off the Lesser Antilles, and some seven hundred men composing their crews. Because they had been beginning to grow anxious on his behalf, they gave him the greater welcome. Guns were fired in his honour and the ships made themselves gay with bunting. The town, aroused by all this noise in the harbour, emptied itself upon the jetty, and a vast crowd of men and women of all creeds and nationalities collected there to be present at the coming ashore of the great buccaneer.

Ashore he went, probably for no other reason than to obey the general expectation. His mood was taciturn; his face grim and sneering. Let Wolverstone arrive, as presently he would, and all this hero-worship would turn to execration.

His captains, Hagthorpe, Christian, and Yberville, were on the jetty to receive him, and with them were some hundreds of his buccaneers. He cut short their greetings, and when they plagued him with questions of where he had tarried, he bade them await the coming of Wolverstone, who would satisfy their curiosity to a surfeit. On that he shook them off, and shouldered his way through that heterogeneous throng that was composed of bustling traders of several nations — English, French, and Dutch — of planters and of seamen of various degrees, of buccaneers who were legitimate boucan-hunters from Hispaniola and buccaneers who were frankly pirates, of lumbermen and Indians, of fruit-selling half-castes, negro slaves, some doll-tearsheets and dunghill-queans from the Old World, and all the other types of the human family that converted the quays of Cayona into a disreputable image of Babel.

Winning clear at last, and after difficulties, Captain Blood took his way alone to the fine house of M. d'Ogeron, there to pay his respects to his friends, the Governor and the Governor's family.

At first the buccaneers jumped to the conclusion that Wolverstone was following with some rare prize of war, but gradually from the reduced crew of the *Arabella* a very different tale leaked out to stem their satisfaction and convert it into perplexity. Partly out of loyalty to their captain, partly because they perceived that if he was guilty of defection they were guilty with him, and partly because being simple, sturdy men of their hands, they were themselves in the main a little confused as to what really had happened, the crew of the *Arabella* practised reticence with their brethren in Tortuga during those two days before Wolverstone's arrival. But they were not reticent enough to prevent the circulation of certain uneasy rumours and extravagant stories of discreditable adventures — discreditable, that is, from the buccaneering point of view — of which Captain Blood had been guilty.

But that Wolverstone came when he did, it is possible that there would have been an explosion. When, however, the Old Wolf cast anchor in the bay two days later, it was to him all turned for the explanation they were about to demand of Blood.

Now Wolverstone had only one eye; but he saw a deal more with that one eye than do most men with two; and despite his grizzled head — so picturesquely swathed in a green and scarlet turban — he had the sound heart of a boy, and in that heart much love for Peter Blood.

The sight of the *Arabella* at anchor in the bay had at first amazed him as he sailed round the rocky headland that bore the fort. He rubbed his single eye clear of any deceiving film and looked again. Still he could not believe what it saw. And then a voice at his elbow — the voice of Dyke, who had elected to sail with him — assured him that he was not singular in his bewilderment.

"In the name of Heaven, is that the *Arabella* or is it the ghost of her?"

The Old Wolf rolled his single eye over Dyke, and opened his mouth to speak. Then he closed it again without having spoken; closed it tightly. He had a great gift of caution, especially in matters that he did not understand. That this was the *Arabella* he could no longer doubt. That being so, he must think before he spoke. What the devil should the *Arabella* be doing here, when he had left her in Jamaica? And was Captain Blood aboard and in command, or had the remainder of her hands made off with her, leaving the Captain in Port Royal?

Dyke repeated his question. This time Wolverstone answered him.

"Ye've two eyes to see with, and ye ask me, who's only got one, what it is ye see!"

"But I see the *Arabella*."

"Of course, since there she rides. What else was you expecting?"

"Expecting?" Dyke stared at him, open-mouthed. "Was you expecting to find the *Arabella* here?"

Wolverstone looked him over in contempt, then laughed and spoke loud enough to be heard by all around him.

"Of course. What else?" And he laughed again, a laugh that seemed to Dyke to be calling him a fool. On that Wolverstone turned to give his attention to the operation of anchoring.

Anon when ashore he was beset by questioning buccaneers, it was from their very questions that he gathered exactly how matters stood, and perceived that either from lack of courage or other motive Blood, himself, had refused to render any account of his doings since the *Arabella* had separated from her sister ships. Wolverstone congratulated himself upon the discretion he had used with Dyke.

"The Captain was ever a modest man," he explained to Hagthorpe and those others who came crowding round him. "It's not his way to be sounding his own praises. Why, it was like this. We fell in with old Don Miguel, and when we'd scuttled him we took aboard a London pimp sent out by the Secretary of State to offer the Captain the King's commission if so be him'd quit piracy and be o' good behaviour. The Captain damned his soul to hell for answer. And then we fell in wi' the Jamaica fleet and that grey old devil Bishop in command, and there was a sure end to Captain Blood and to every mother's son of us all. So I goes to him, and 'accept this poxy commission,' say I; 'turn King's man and save your neck and ours.' He took me at my word, and the London pimp gave him the King's commission on the spot, and Bishop all but choked hisself with rage when he was told of it. But happened it had, and he was forced to swallow it. We were King's men all, and so into Port Royal we sailed along o' Bishop. But Bishop didn't trust us. He knew too much. But for his lordship, the fellow from London, he'd ha' hanged the Captain, King's commission and all. Blood would ha' slipped out o' Port Royal again that same night. But that hound Bishop had passed the word, and the fort kept a sharp lookout. In the end, though it took a fortnight, Blood bubbled him. He sent me and most o' the men off in a frigate that I bought for the voyage. His game — as he'd secretly told me — was to follow and give chase. Whether that's the game he played or not I can't tell ye; but here he is afore me as I'd expected he would be."

There was a great historian lost in Wolverstone. He had the right imagination that knows just how far it is safe to stray from the truth and just how far to colour it so as to change its shape for his own purposes.

Having delivered himself of his decoction of fact and falsehood, and thereby added one more to the exploits of Peter Blood, he enquired where the Captain might be found. Being informed that he kept his ship, Wolverstone stepped into a boat and went aboard, to report himself, as he put it.

In the great cabin of the *Arabella* he found Peter Blood alone and very far gone in drink — a condition in which no man ever before remembered to have seen him. As Wolverstone came in, the Captain raised bloodshot eyes to consider him. A moment they sharpened in their gaze as he brought his visitor into focus. Then he laughed, a loose, idiot laugh, that yet somehow was half a sneer.

"Ah! The Old Wolf!" said he. "Got here at last, eh? And whatcher gonnerdo wi' me, eh?" He hiccoughed resoundingly, and sagged back loosely in his chair.

Old Wolverstone stared at him in sombre silence. He had looked with untroubled eye upon many a hell of devilment in his time, but the sight of Captain Blood in this condition filled him with sudden grief. To express it he loosed an oath. It was his only expression for emotion of all kinds. Then he rolled forward, and dropped into a chair at the table, facing the Captain.

"My God, Peter, what's this?"

"Rum," said Peter. "Rum, from Jamaica." He pushed bottle and glass towards Wolverstone.

Wolverstone disregarded them.

"I'm asking you what ails you?" he bawled.

"Rum," said Captain Blood again, and smiled. "Jus' rum. I answer all your queshons. Why donjerr answer mine? Whatcher gonerdo wi' me?"

"I've done it," said Wolverstone. "Thank God, ye had the sense to hold your tongue till I came. Are ye sober enough to understand me?"

"Drunk or sober, allus 'derstand you."

"Then listen." And out came the tale that Wolverstone had told. The Captain steadied himself to grasp it.

"It'll do as well asertruth," said he when Wolverstone had finished. "And . . . oh, no marrer! Much obliged to ye, Old Wolf — faithful Old Wolf! But was it worthertrouble? I'm norrer pirate now; never a pirate again. 'S finished!" He banged the table, his eyes suddenly fierce.

"I'll come and talk to you again when there's less rum in your wits," said Wolverstone, rising. "Meanwhile ye'll please to remember the tale I've told, and say nothing that'll make me out a liar. They all believes me, even the men as sailed wi' me from Port Royal. I've made 'em. If they thought as how you'd taken the King's commission in earnest, and for the purpose o' doing as Morgan did, ye guess what would follow."

"Hell would follow," said the Captain. "An' tha's all I'm fit for."

"Ye're maudlin," Wolverstone growled. "We'll talk again to-morrow."

They did; but to little purpose, either that day or on any day thereafter while the rains — which set in that night — endured. Soon the shrewd Wolverstone discovered that rum was not what ailed Blood. Rum was in itself an effect, and not by any means the cause of the Captain's listless apathy. There was a canker eating at his heart, and the Old Wolf knew enough to make a shrewd guess of its nature. He cursed all things that daggled petticoats, and, knowing his world, waited for the sickness to pass.

But it did not pass. When Blood was not dicing or drinking in the taverns of Tortuga, keeping company that in his saner days he had loathed, he was shut up in his cabin aboard the *Arabella*, alone and uncommunicative. His friends at Government House, bewildered at this change in him, sought to reclaim him. Mademoiselle d'Ogeron, particularly distressed, sent him almost daily invitations, to few of which he responded.

Later, as the rainy season approached its end, he was sought by his captains with proposals of remunerative raids on Spanish settlements. But to all he manifested an indifference which, as the weeks passed and the weather became settled, begot first impatience and then exasperation. Christian, who commanded the *Clotho*, came storming to him one day, upbraiding him for his inaction, and demanding that he should take order about what was to do.

"Go to the devil!" Blood said, when he had heard him out.

Christian departed fuming, and on the morrow the *Clotho* weighed anchor and sailed away, setting an example of desertion from which the loyalty of Blood's other captains would soon be unable to restrain their men.

Sometimes Blood asked himself why had he come back to Tortuga at all. Held fast in bondage by the thought of Arabella and her scorn of him for a thief and a pirate, he had sworn that he had done with buccaneering. Why, then, was he here? That question he would answer with another: Where else was he to go? Neither backward nor forward could he move, it seemed.

He was degenerating visibly, under the eyes of all. He had entirely lost the almost foppish concern for his appearance, and was grown careless and slovenly in his dress. He allowed a black beard to grow on cheeks that had ever been so carefully shaven; and the long, thick black hair, once so sedulously curled, hung now in a lank, untidy mane about a face that was changing from its vigorous swarthiness to an unhealthy sallow, whilst the blue eyes, that had been so vivid and compelling, were now dull and lack-lustre.

Wolverstone, the only one who held the clue to this degeneration, ventured once — and once only — to beard him frankly about it.

"Lord, Peter! Is there never to be no end to this?" the giant had growled. "Will you spend your days moping and swilling 'cause a white-faced ninny in Port Royal'll have none o' ye? 'Sblood and 'Ounds! If ye wants the wench, why the plague doesn't ye go and fetch her?"

The blue eyes glared at him from under the jet-black eyebrows, and something of their old fire began to kindle in them. But Wolverstone went on heedlessly.

"I'll be nice wi' a wench as long as niceness be the key to her favour. But sink me now if I'd rot myself in rum on account of anything that wears a petticoat. That's not the Old Wolf's way. If there's no other expedition'll tempt you, why not Port Royal? What a plague do it matter if it is an English settlement? It's commanded by Colonel Bishop, and there's no lack of rascals in your company'd follow you to hell if it meant getting Colonel Bishop by the throat. It could be done, I tell you. We've but to spy the chance when the Jamaica fleet is away. There's enough plunder in the town to tempt the lads, and there's the wench for you. Shall I sound them on't?"

Blood was on his feet, his eyes blazing, his livid face distorted. "Ye'll leave my cabin this minute, so ye will, or, by Heaven, it's your corpse'll be carried out of it. Ye mangy hound, d'ye dare come to me with such proposals?"

He fell to cursing his faithful officer with a virulence the like of which he had never yet been known to use. And Wolverstone, in terror before that fury, went out without another word. The subject was not raised again, and Captain Blood was left to his idle abstraction.

But at last, as his buccaneers were growing desperate, something happened, brought about by the Captain's friend M. d'Ogeron. One sunny morning the Governor of Tortuga came aboard the *Arabella*, accompanied by a chubby little gentleman, amiable of countenance, amiable and self-sufficient of manner.

"My Captain," M. d'Ogeron delivered himself, "I bring you M. de Cussy, the Governor of French Hispaniola, who desires a word with you."

Out of consideration for his friend, Captain Blood pulled the pipe from his mouth, shook some of the rum out of his wits, and rose and made a leg to M. de Cussy.

"Serviteur!" said he.

M. de Cussy returned the bow and accepted a seat on the locker under the stern windows.

"You have a good force here under your command, my Captain," said he.

"Some eight hundred men."

"And I understand they grow restive in idleness."

"They may go to the devil when they please."

M. de Cussy took snuff delicately. "I have something better than that to propose," said he.

"Propose it, then," said Blood, without interest.

M. de Cussy looked at M. d'Ogeron, and raised his eyebrows a little. He did not find Captain Blood encouraging. But M. d'Ogeron nodded vigorously with pursed lips, and the Governor of Hispaniola propounded his business.

"News has reached us from France that there is war with Spain."

"That is news, is it?" growled Blood.

"I am speaking officially, my Captain. I am not alluding to unofficial skirmishes, and unofficial predatory measures which we have condoned out here. There is war — formally war — between France and Spain in Europe. It is the intention of France that this war shall be carried into the New World. A fleet is coming out from Brest under the command of M. le Baron de Rivarol for that purpose. I have letters from him desiring me to equip a supplementary squadron and raise a body of not less than a thousand men to reënforce him on his arrival. What I have come to propose to you, my Captain, at the suggestion of our good friend M. d'Ogeron, is, in brief, that you enrol your ships and your force under M. de Rivarol's flag."

Blood looked at him with a faint kindling of interest. "You are offering to take us into the French service?" he asked. "On what terms, monsieur?"

"With the rank of Capitaine de Vaisseau for yourself, and suitable ranks for the officers serving under you. You will enjoy the pay of that rank, and you

-will be entitled, together with your men, to one-tenth share in all prizes taken."

"My men will hardly account it generous. They will tell you that they can sail out of here to-morrow, disembowel a Spanish settlement, and keep the whole of the plunder."

"Ah, yes, but with the risks attaching to acts of piracy. With us your position will be regular and official, and considering the powerful fleet by which M. de Rivarol is backed, the enterprises to be undertaken will be on a much vaster scale than anything you could attempt on your own account. So that the one tenth in this case may be equal to more than the whole in the other."

Captain Blood considered. This, after all, was not piracy that was being proposed. It was honourable employment in the service of the King of France.

"I will consult my officers," he said; and he sent for them.

They came and the matter was laid before them by M. de Cussy himself. Hagthorpe announced at once that the proposal was opportune. The men were grumbling at their protracted inaction, and would no doubt be ready to accept the service which M. de Cussy offered on behalf of France. Hagthorpe looked at Blood as he spoke. Blood nodded gloomy agreement. Emboldened by this, they went on to discuss the terms. Yberville, the young French filibuster, had the honour to point out to M. de Cussy that the share offered was too small. For one fifth of the prizes, the officers would answer for their men; not for less.

M. de Cussy was distressed. He had his instructions. It was taking a deal upon himself to exceed them. The buccaneers were firm. Unless M. de Cussy could make it one fifth there was no more to be said. M. de Cussy finally consenting to exceed his instructions, the articles were drawn up and signed that very day. The buccaneers were to be at Petit Goave by the end of January, when M. de Rivarol had announced that he might be expected.

After that followed days of activity in Tortuga, refitting the ships, boucanning meat, laying in stores. In these matters which once would have engaged all Captain Blood's attention, he now took no part. He continued listless and aloof. If he had given his consent to the undertaking, or, rather, allowed himself to be swept into it by the wishes of his officers — it was only because the service offered was of a regular and honourable kind, nowise connected with piracy, with which he swore in his heart that he had done for ever. But his consent remained passive. The service entered awoke no zeal in him. He was perfectly indifferent — as he told Hagthorpe, who ventured once to offer a remonstrance — whether they went to Petit Goave or to Hades, and whether they entered the service of Louis XIV or of Satan.

CHAPTER XXVI

M. DE RIVAROL

CAPTAIN BLOOD was still in that disgruntled mood when he sailed from Tortuga, and still in that mood when he came to his moorings in the bay of Petit Goave. In that same mood he greeted M. le Baron de Rivarol when this nobleman with his fleet of five men-of-war at last dropped anchor alongside the buccaneer ships, in the middle of February. The Frenchman had been six weeks on the voyage, he announced, delayed by unfavourable weather.

Summoned to wait on him, Captain Blood repaired to the Castle of Petit Goave, where the interview was to take place. The Baron, a tall, hawk-faced man of forty, very cold and distant of manner, measured Captain Blood with an eye of obvious disapproval. Of Hagthorpe, Yberville, and Wolverstone who stood ranged behind their captain, he took no heed whatever. M. de Cussy offered Captain Blood a chair.

"A moment, M. de Cussy. I do not think M. le Baron has observed that I am not alone. Let me present to you, sir, my companions: Captain Hagthorpe of the *Elizabeth*, Captain Wolverstone of the *Atropos*, and Captain Yberville of the *Lachesis*."

The Baron stared hard and haughtily at Captain Blood, then very distantly and barely perceptibly inclined his head to each of the other three. His manner implied plainly that he despised them and that he desired them at once to understand it. It had a curious effect upon Captain Blood. It awoke the devil in him, and it awoke at the same time his self-respect which of late had been slumbering. A sudden shame of his disordered, ill-kempt appearance made him perhaps the more defiant. There was almost a significance in the way he hitched his sword-belt round, so that the wrought hilt of his very serviceable rapier was brought into fuller view. He waved his captains to the chairs that stood about.

"Draw up to the table, lads. We are keeping the Baron waiting."

They obeyed him, Wolverstone with a grin that was full of understanding. Haughtier grew the stare of M. de Rivarol. To sit at table with these bandits placed him upon what he accounted a dishonouring equality. It had been his notion that — with the possible exception of Captain Blood — they should take his instructions standing, as became men of their quality in the presence of a man of his. He did the only thing remaining to mark a distinction between himself and them. He put on his hat.

"Ye're very wise now," said Blood amiably. "I feel the draught myself." And he covered himself with his plumed castor.

M. de Rivarol changed colour. He quivered visibly with anger, and was a moment controlling himself before venturing to speak. M. de Cussy was obviously very ill at ease.

"Sir," said the Baron frostily, "you compel me to remind you that the rank you hold is that of Capitaine de Vaisseau, and that you are in the presence of the General of the Armies of France by Sea and Land in America. You compel me to remind you further that there is a deference due from your rank to mine."

"I am happy to assure you," said Captain Blood, "that the reminder is unnecessary. I am by way of accounting myself a gentleman, little though I may look like one at present; and I should not account myself that were I capable of anything but deference to those whom nature or fortune may have placed above me, or to those who being placed beneath me in rank may labour under a disability to resent my lack of it." It was a neatly intangible rebuke. M. de Rivarol bit his lip. Captain Blood swept on without giving him time to reply: "Thus much being clear, shall we come to business?"

M. de Rivarol's hard eyes considered him a moment. "Perhaps it will be best," said he. He took up a paper. "I have here a copy of the articles into which you entered with M. de Cussy. Before going further, I have to observe that M. de Cussy has exceeded his instructions in admitting you to one fifth of the prizes taken. His authority did not warrant his going beyond one tenth."

"That is a matter between yourself and M. de Cussy, my General."

"Oh, no. It is a matter between myself and you."

"Your pardon, my General. The articles are signed. So far as we are concerned, the matter is closed. Also out of regard for M. de Cussy, we should not desire to be witnesses of the rebukes you may consider that he deserves."

"What I may have to say to M. de Cussy is no concern of yours."

"That is what I am telling you, my General."

"But — nom de Dieu! — it is your concern, I suppose, that we cannot award you more than one-tenth share." M. de Rivarol smote the table in exasperation. This pirate was too infernally skilful a fencer.

"You are quite certain of that, M. le Baron — that you cannot?"

"I am quite certain that I will not."

Captain Blood shrugged, and looked down his nose. "In that case," said he, "it but remains for me to present my little account for our disbursement, and to fix the sum at which we should be compensated for our loss of time and derangement in coming hither. That settled, we can part friends, M. le Baron. No harm has been done."

"What the devil do you mean?" The Baron was on his feet, leaning forward across the table.

"Is it possible that I am obscure? My French, perhaps, is not of the purest, but . . ."

"Oh, your French is fluent enough; too fluent at moments, if I may permit myself the observation. Now, look you here, M. le filibustier, I am not a man with whom it is safe to play the fool, as you may very soon discover. You have accepted service of the King of France — you and your men; you hold the rank and draw the pay of a Capitaine de Vaisseau, and these your officers hold the rank of lieutenants. These ranks carry obligations which you would do well to study, and penalties for failing to discharge them which you might study at the same time. They are something severe. The first obligation of an officer is obedience. I commend it to your attention. You are not to conceive yourselves, as you appear to be doing, my allies in the enterprises I have in view, but my subordinates. In me you behold a commander to

lead you, not a companion or an equal. You understand me, I hope."

"Oh, be sure that I understand," Captain Blood
laughed. He was recovering his normal self amazingly under the inspiring stimulus of conflict. The
only thing that marred his enjoyment was the reflection that he had not shaved. "I forget nothing, I assure you, my General. I do not forget, for instance, as
you appear to be doing, that the articles we signed
are the condition of our service; and the articles provide that we receive one-fifth share. Refuse us that,
and you cancel the articles; cancel the articles, and
you cancel our services with them. From that moment we cease to have the honour to hold rank in the
navies of the King of France."

There was more than a murmur of approval from
his three captains.

Rivarol glared at them, checkmated.

"In effect . . ." M. de Cussy was beginning timidly.

"In effect, monsieur, this is your doing," the Baron
flashed on him, glad to have some one upon whom he
could fasten the sharp fangs of his irritation. "You
should be broke for it. You bring the King's service
into disrepute; you force me, His Majesty's representative, into an impossible position."

"Is it impossible to award us the one-fifth share?"
quoth Captain Blood silkily. "In that case, there is
no need for heat or for injuries to M. de Cussy. M. de
Cussy knows that we would not have come for less.
We depart again upon your assurance that you cannot award us more. And things are as they would
have been if M. de Cussy had adhered rigidly to his
instructions. I have proved, I hope, to your satis-

faction, M. le Baron, that if you repudiate the articles you can neither claim our services nor hinder our departure — not in honour."

"Not in honour, sir? To the devil with your insolence! Do you imply that any course that were not in honour would be possible to me?"

"I do not imply it, because it would not be possible," said Captain Blood. "We should see to that. It is, my General, for you to say whether the articles are repudiated."

The Baron sat down. "I will consider the matter," he said sullenly. "You.shall be advised of my resolve."

Captain Blood rose, his officers rose with him. Captain Blood bowed.

"M. le Baron!" said he.

Then he and his buccaneers removed themselves from the august and irate presence of the General of the King's Armies by Land and Sea in America.

You conceive that there followed for M. de Cussy an extremely bad quarter of an hour. M. de Cussy, in fact, deserves your sympathy. His self-sufficiency was blown from him by the haughty M. de Rivarol, as down from a thistle by the winds of autumn. The General of the King's Armies abused him — this man who was Governor of Hispaniola — as if he were a lackey. M. de Cussy defended himself by urging the thing that Captain Blood had so admirably urged already on his behalf — that if the terms he had made with the buccaneers were not confirmed there was no harm done. M. de Rivarol bullied and browbeat him into silence.

Having exhausted abuse, the Baron proceeded to indignities. Since he accounted that M. de Cussy had

proved himself unworthy of the post he held, M. de
Rivarol took over the responsibilities of that post for
as long as he might remain in Hispaniola, and to give
effect to this he began by bringing soldiers from his
ships, and setting his own guard in M. de Cussy's
castle.

Out of this, trouble followed quickly. Wolverstone
coming ashore next morning in the picturesque garb
that he affected, his head swathed in a coloured handkerchief, was jeered at by an officer of the newly
landed French troops. Not accustomed to derision,
Wolverstone replied in kind and with interest. The
officer passed to insult, and Wolverstone struck him a
blow that felled him, and left him only the half of his
poor senses. Within the hour the matter was reported
to M. de Rivarol, and before noon, by M. de Rivarol's
orders, Wolverstone was under arrest in the castle.

The Baron had just sat down to dinner with M. de
Cussy when the negro who waited on them announced
Captain Blood. Peevishly M. de Rivarol bade him be
admitted, and there entered now into his presence a
spruce and modish gentleman, dressed with care and
sombre richness in black and silver, his swarthy, clear-
cut face scrupulously shaven, his long black hair in
ringlets that fell to a collar of fine point. In his right
hand the gentleman carried a broad black hat with a
scarlet ostrich-plume, in his left hand an ebony cane.
His stockings were of silk, a bunch of ribbons masked
his garters, and the black rosettes on his shoes were
finely edged with gold.

For a moment M. de Rivarol did not recognize him.
For Blood looked younger by ten years than yesterday. But the vivid blue eyes under their level black

brows were not to be forgotten, and they proclaimed him for the man announced even before he had spoken. His resurrected pride had demanded that he should put himself on an equality with the baron and advertise that equality by his exterior.

"I come inopportunely," he courteously excused himself. "My apologies. My business could not wait. It concerns, M. de Cussy, Captain Wolverstone of the *Lachesis*, whom you have placed under arrest."

"It was I who placed him under arrest," said M. de Rivarol.

"Indeed! But I thought that M. de Cussy was Governor of Hispaniola."

"Whilst I am here, monsieur, I am the supreme authority. It is as well that you should understand it."

"Perfectly. But it is not possible that you are aware of the mistake that has been made."

"Mistake, do you say?"

"I say mistake. On the whole, it is polite of me to use that word. Also it is expedient. It will save discussions. Your people have arrested the wrong man, M. de Rivarol. Instead of the French officer, who used the grossest provocation, they have arrested Captain Wolverstone. It is a matter which I beg you to reverse without delay."

M. de Rivarol's hawk-face flamed scarlet. His dark eyes bulged.

"Sir, you . . . you are insolent! But of an insolence that is intolerable!" Normally a man of the utmost self-possession, he was so rudely shaken now that he actually stammered.

"M. le Baron, you waste words. This is the New

World. It is not merely new; it is novel to one reared
amid the superstitions of the Old. That novelty you
have not yet had time, perhaps, to realize; therefore I
overlook the offensive epithet you have used. But
justice is justice in the New World as in the Old, and
injustice as intolerable here as there. Now justice
demands the enlargement of my officer and the arrest
and punishment of yours. That justice I invite you,
with submission, to administer."

"With submission?" snorted the Baron in furious
scorn.

"With the utmost submission, monsieur. But at
the same time I will remind M. le Baron that my buccaneers number eight hundred; your troops five hundred; and M. de Cussy will inform you of the interesting fact that any one buccaneer is equal in action
to at least three soldiers of the line. I am perfectly
frank with you, monsieur, to save time and hard
words. Either Captain Wolverstone is instantly set
at liberty, or we must take measures to set him at liberty ourselves. The consequences may be appalling.
But it is as you please, M. le Baron. You are the supreme authority. It is for you to say."

M. de Rivarol was white to the lips. In all his life
he had never been so bearded and defied. But he controlled himself.

"You will do me the favour to wait in the ante-
room, M. le Capitaine. I desire a word with M. de
Cussy. You shall presently be informed of my decision."

When the door had closed, the baron loosed his
fury upon the head of M. de Cussy.

"So, these are the men you have enlisted in the

King's service, the men who are to serve under me — men who do not serve, but dictate, and this before the enterprise that has brought me from France is even under way! What explanations do you offer me, M. de Cussy? I warn you that I am not pleased with you. I am, in fact, as you may perceive, exceedingly angry."

The Governor seemed to shed his chubbiness. He drew himself stiffly erect.

"Your rank, monsieur, does not give you the right to rebuke me; nor do the facts. I have enlisted for you the men that you desired me to enlist. It is not my fault if you do not know how to handle them better. As Captain Blood has told you, this is the New World."

"So, so!" M. de Rivarol smiled malignantly. "Not only do you offer no explanation, but you venture to put me in the wrong. Almost I admire your temerity. But there!" He waved the matter aside. He was supremely sardonic. "It is, you tell me, the New World, and — new worlds, new manners, I suppose. In time I may conform my ideas to this new world, or I may conform this new world to my ideas." He was menacing on that. "For the moment I must accept what I find. It remains for you, monsieur, who have experience of these savage by-ways, to advise me out of that experience how to act."

"M. le Baron, it was a folly to have arrested the buccaneer captain. It would be madness to persist. We have not the forces to meet force."

"In that case, monsieur, perhaps you will tell me what we are to do with regard to the future. Am I to submit at every turn to the dictates of this man

Blood? Is the enterprise upon which we are embarked to be conducted as he decrees? Am I, in short, the King's representative in America, to be at the mercy of these rascals?"

"Oh, by no means. I am enrolling volunteers here in Hispaniola, and I am raising a corps of negroes. I compute that when this is done we shall have a force of a thousand men, the buccaneers apart."

"But in that case why not dispense with them?"

"Because they will always remain the sharp edge of any weapon that we forge. In the class of warfare that lies before us they are so skilled that what Captain Blood has just said is not an overstatement. A buccaneer is equal to three soldiers of the line. At the same time we shall have a sufficient force to keep them in control. For the rest, monsieur, they have certain notions of honour. They will stand by their articles, and so that we deal justly with them, they will deal justly with us, and give no trouble. I have experience of them, and I pledge you my word for that."

M. de Rivarol condescended to be mollified. It was necessary that he should save his face, and in a degree the Governor afforded him the means to do so, as well as a certain guarantee for the future in the further force he was raising.

"Very well," he said. "Be so good as to recall this Captain Blood."

The Captain came in, assured and very dignified. M. de Rivarol found him detestable; but dissembled it.

"M. le Capitaine, I have taken counsel with M. le Gouverneur. From what he tells me, it is possible that a mistake has been committed. Justice, you may be sure, shall be done. To ensure it, I shall myself preside over a council to be composed of two of my senior officers, yourself and an officer of yours. This council shall hold at once an impartial investigation into the affair, and the offender, the man guilty of having given provocation, shall be punished."

Captain Blood bowed. It was not his wish to be extreme.

"Perfectly, M. le Baron. And now, sir, you have had the night for reflection in this matter of the articles. Am I to understand that you confirm or that you repudiate them?"

M. de Rivarol's eyes narrowed. His mind was full of what M. de Cussy had said — that these buccaneers must prove the sharp edge of any weapon he might forge. He could not dispense with them. He perceived that he had blundered tactically in attempting to reduce the agreed share. Withdrawal from a position of that kind is ever fraught with loss of dignity. But there were those volunteers that M. de Cussy was enrolling to strengthen the hand of the King's General. Their presence might admit anon of the reopening of this question. Meanwhile he must retire in the best order possible.

"I have considered that, too," he announced. "And whilst my opinion remains unaltered, I must confess that since M. de Cussy has pledged us, it is for us to fulfil the pledges. The articles are confirmed, sir."

Captain Blood bowed again. In vain M. de Rivarol looked searchingly for the least trace of a smile of triumph on those firm lips. The buccaneer's face remained of the utmost gravity.

Wolverstone was set at liberty that afternoon, and

his assailant sentenced to two months' detention. Thus harmony was restored. But it had been an unpromising beginning, and there was more to follow shortly of a similar discordant kind.

Blood and his officers were summoned a week later to a council which sat to determine their operations against Spain. M. de Rivarol laid before them a project for a raid upon the wealthy Spanish town of Cartagena. Captain Blood professed astonishment. Sourly invited by M. de Rivarol to state his grounds for it, he did so with the utmost frankness.

"Were I General of the King's Armies in America," said he, "I should have no doubt or hesitation as to the best way in which to serve my royal master and the French nation. That which I think will be obvious to M. de Cussy, as it is to me, is that we should at once invade Spanish Hispaniola and reduce the whole of this fruitful and splendid island into the possession of the King of France."

"That may follow," said M. de Rivarol. "It is my wish that we begin with Cartagena."

"You mean, sir, that we are to sail across the Caribbean on an adventurous expedition, neglecting that which lies here at our very door. In our absence, a Spanish invasion of French Hispaniola is possible. If we begin by reducing the Spaniards here, that possibility will be removed. We shall have added to the Crown of France the most coveted possession in the West Indies. The enterprise offers no particular difficulty; it may be speedily accomplished, and once accomplished, it would be time to look farther afield. That would seem the logical order in which this campaign should proceed."

He ceased, and there was silence. M. de Rivarol sat back in his chair, the feathered end of a quill between his teeth. Presently he cleared his throat and asked a question.

"Is there anybody else who shares Captain Blood's opinion?"

None answered him. His own officers were overawed by him; Blood's followers naturally preferred Cartagena, because offering the greater chance of loot. Loyalty to their leader kept them silent.

"You seem to be alone in your opinion," said the Baron with his vinegary smile.

Captain Blood laughed outright. He had suddenly read the Baron's mind. His airs and graces and haughtiness had so imposed upon Blood that it was only now that at last he saw through them, into the fellow's peddling spirit. Therefore he laughed; there was really nothing else to do. But his laughter was charged with more anger even than contempt. He had been deluding himself that he had done with piracy. The conviction that this French service was free of any taint of that was the only consideration that had induced him to accept it. Yet here was this haughty, supercilious gentleman, who dubbed himself General of the Armies of France, proposing a plundering, thieving raid which, when stripped of its mean, transparent mask of legitimate warfare, was revealed as piracy of the most flagrant.

M. de Rivarol, intrigued by his mirth, scowled upon him disapprovingly.

"Why do you laugh, monsieur?"

"Because I discover here an irony that is supremely droll. You, M. le Baron, General of the King's Armies by Land and Sea in America, propose an enterprise of a purely buccaneering character; whilst I, the buccaneer, am urging one that is more concerned with upholding the honour of France. You perceive how droll it is."

M. de Rivarol perceived nothing of the kind. M. de Rivarol in fact was extremely angry. He bounded to his feet, and every man in the room rose with him — save only M. de Cussy, who sat on with a grim smile on his lips. He, too, now read the Baron like an open book, and reading him despised him.

"M. le filibustier," cried Rivarol in a thick voice, "it seems that I must again remind you that I am your superior officer."

"My superior officer! You! Lord of the World! Why, you are just a common pirate! But you shall hear the truth for once, and that before all these gentlemen who have the honour to serve the King of France. It is for me, a buccaneer, a sea-robber, to stand here and tell you what is in the interest of French honour and the French Crown. Whilst you, the French King's appointed General, neglecting this, are for spending the King's resources against an outlying settlement of no account, shedding French blood in seizing a place that cannot be held, only because it has been reported to you that there is much gold in Cartagena, and that the plunder of it will enrich you. It is worthy of the huckster who sought to haggle with us about our share, and to beat us down after the articles pledging you were already signed. If I am wrong — let M. de Cussy say so. If I am wrong, let me be proven wrong, and I will beg your pardon. Meanwhile, monsieur, I withdraw from this

council. I will have no further part in your delibera-
tions. I accepted the service of the King of France with
intent to honour that service. I cannot honour that
service by lending countenance to a waste of life and
resources in raids upon unimportant settlements, with
plunder for their only object. The responsibility for
such decisions must rest with you, and with you alone.
I desire M. de Cussy to report me to the Ministers of
France. For the rest, monsieur, it merely remains for
you to give me your orders. I await them aboard my
ship — and anything else, of a personal nature, that
you may feel I have provoked by the terms I have
felt compelled to use in this council. M. le Baron, I
have the honour to wish you good-day."

He stalked out, and his three captains — although
they thought him mad — rolled after him in loyal
silence.

M. de Rivarol was gasping like a landed fish. The
stark truth had robbed him of speech. When he recovered, it was to thank Heaven vigorously that the
council was relieved by Captain Blood's own act of
that gentleman's further participation in its delibera-
tions. Inwardly M. de Rivarol burned with shame
and rage. The mask had been plucked from him, and
he had been held up to scorn — he, the General of the
King's Armies by Sea and Land in America.

Nevertheless, it was to Cartagena that they sailed
in the middle of March. Volunteers and negroes had
brought up the forces directly under M. de Rivarol to
twelve hundred men. With these he thought he could
keep the buccaneer contingent in order and submis-
sive.

They made up an imposing fleet, led by M. de

Rivarol's flagship, the *Victorieuse*, a mighty vessel of eighty guns. Each of the four other French ships was at least as powerful as Blood's *Arabella*, which was of forty guns. Followed the lesser buccaneer vessels, the *Elizabeth*, *Lachesis*, and *Atropos*, and a dozen frigates laden with stores, besides canoes and small craft in tow.

Narrowly they missed the Jamaica fleet with Colonel Bishop, which sailed north for Tortuga two days after the Baron de Rivarol's southward passage.

CHAPTER XXVII

CARTAGENA

HAVING crossed the Caribbean in the teeth of contrary winds, it was not until the early days of April that the French fleet hove in sight of Cartagena, and M. de Rivarol summoned a council aboard his flagship to determine the method of assault.

"It is of importance, messieurs," he told them, "that we take the city by surprise, not only before it can put itself into a state of defence; but before it can remove its treasures inland. I propose to land a force sufficient to achieve this to the north of the city tonight after dark." And he explained in detail the scheme upon which his wits had laboured.

He was heard respectfully and approvingly by his officers, scornfully by Captain Blood, and indifferently by the other buccaneer captains present. For it must be understood that Blood's refusal to attend councils had related only to those concerned with determining the nature of the enterprise to be undertaken.

Captain Blood was the only one amongst them who knew exactly what lay ahead. Two years ago he had himself considered a raid upon the place, and he had actually made a survey of it in circumstances which he was presently to disclose.

The Baron's proposal was one to be expected from a commander whose knowledge of Cartagena was only such as might be derived from maps.

Geographically and strategically considered, it is a curious place. It stands almost four-square, screened east and north by hills, and it may be said to face south upon the inner of two harbours by which it is normally approached. The entrance to the outer harbour, which is in reality a lagoon some three miles across, lies through a neck known as the Boca Chica — or Little Mouth — and defended by a fort. A long strip of densely wooded land to westward acts here as a natural breakwater, and as the inner harbour is approached, another strip of land thrusts across at right angles from the first, towards the mainland on the east. Just short of this it ceases, leaving a deep but very narrow channel, a veritable gateway, into the secure and sheltered inner harbour. Another fort defends this second passage. East and north of Cartagena lies the mainland, which may be left out of account. But to the west and northwest this city, so well guarded on every other side, lies directly open to the sea. It stands back beyond a half-mile of beach, and besides this and the stout walls which fortify it, would appear to have no other defences. But those appearances are deceptive, and they had utterly deceived M. de Rivarol, when he devised his plan.

It remained for Captain Blood to explain the difficulties when M. de Rivarol informed him that the honour of opening the assault in the manner which he prescribed was to be accorded to the buccaneers.

Captain Blood smiled sardonic appreciation of the honour reserved for his men. It was precisely what he would have expected. For the buccaneers the dangers; for M. de Rivarol the honour, glory and profit of the enterprise.

"It is an honour which I must decline," said he quite coldly.

Wolverstone grunted approval and Hagthorpe nodded. Yberville, who as much as any of them resented the superciliousness of his noble compatriot, never wavered in loyalty to Captain Blood. The French officers — there were six of them present — stared their haughty surprise at the buccaneer leader, whilst the Baron challengingly fired a question at him.

"How? You decline it, sir? You decline to obey orders, do you say?"

"I understood, M. le Baron, that you summoned us to deliberate upon the means to be adopted."

"Then you understood amiss, M. le Capitaine. You are here to receive my commands. I have already deliberated, and I have decided. I hope you understand."

"Oh, I understand," laughed Blood. "But, I ask myself, do you?" And without giving the Baron time to set the angry question that was bubbling to his lips, he swept on: "You have deliberated, you say, and you have decided. But unless your decision rests upon a wish to destroy my buccaneers, you will alter it when I tell you something of which I have knowledge. This city of Cartagena looks very vulnerable on the northern side, all open to the sea as it apparently stands. Ask yourself, M. le Baron, how came the Spaniards who built it where it is to have been at such trouble to fortify it to the south, if from the north it is so easily assailable."

That gave M. de Rivarol pause.

"The Spaniards," Blood pursued, "are not quite the fools you are supposing them. Let me tell you,

messieurs, that two years ago I made a survey of
Cartagena as a preliminary to raiding it. I came hither
with some friendly trading Indians, myself disguised
as an Indian, and in that guise I spent a week in the
city and studied carefully all its approaches. On the
side of the sea where it looks so temptingly open to
assault, there is shoal water for over half a mile out—
far enough out, I assure you, to ensure that no ship
shall come within bombarding range of it. It is not
safe to venture nearer land than three quarters of a
mile."

"But our landing will be effected in canoes and piraguas and open boats," cried an officer impatiently.

"In the calmest season of the year, the surf will
hinder any such operation. And you will also bear in
mind that if landing were possible as you are suggest-
ing, that landing could not be covered by the ships'
guns. In fact, it is the landing parties would be in
danger from their own artillery."

"If the attack is made by night, as I propose, cov-
ering will be unnecessary. You should be ashore in
force before the Spaniards are aware of the intent."

"You are assuming that Cartagena is a city of the
blind, that at this very moment they are not conning
our sails and asking themselves who we are and what
we intend."

"But if they feel themselves secure from the north
as you suggest," cried the Baron impatiently, "that
very security will lull them."

"Perhaps. But, then, they are secure. Any attempt to land on this side is doomed to failure at the
hands of Nature."

"Nevertheless, we make the attempt," said the obstinate Baron, whose haughtiness would not allow him to yield before his officers.

"If you still choose to do so after what I have said, you are, of course, the person to decide. But I do not lead my men into fruitless danger."

"If I command you . . ." the Baron was beginning. But Blood unceremoniously interrupted him.

"M. le Baron, when M. de Cussy engaged us on your behalf, it was as much on account of our knowledge and experience of this class of warfare as on account of our strength. I have placed my own knowledge and experience in this particular matter at your disposal. I will add that I abandoned my own project of raiding Cartagena, not being in sufficient strength at the time to force the entrance of the harbour, which is the only way into the city. The strength which you now command is ample for that purpose."

"But whilst we are doing that, the Spaniards will have time to remove great part of the wealth this city holds. We must take them by surprise."

Captain Blood shrugged. "If this is a mere pirating raid, that, of course, is a prime consideration. It was with me. But if you are concerned to abate the pride of Spain and plant the Lilies of France on the forts of this settlement, the loss of some treasure should not really weigh for much."

M. de Rivarol bit his lip in chagrin. His gloomy eye smouldered as it considered the self-contained buccaneer.

"But if I command you to go — to make the attempt?" he asked. "Answer me, monsieur, let us know once for all where we stand, and who commands this expedition."

"Positively, I find you tiresome," said Captain Blood, and he swung to M. de Cussy, who sat there gnawing his lip, intensely uncomfortable. "I appeal to you, monsieur, to justify me to the General."

M. de Cussy started out of his gloomy abstraction. He cleared his throat. He was extremely nervous.

"In view of what Captain Blood has submitted . . ."

"Oh, to the devil with that!" snapped Rivarol. "It seems that I am followed by poltroons. Look you, M. le Capitaine, since you are afraid to undertake this thing, I will myself undertake it. The weather is calm, and I count upon making good my landing. If I do so, I shall have proved you wrong, and I shall have a word to say to you to-morrow which you may not like. I am being very generous with you, sir." He waved his hand regally. "You have leave to go."

It was sheer obstinacy and empty pride that drove him, and he received the lesson he deserved. The fleet stood in during the afternoon to within a mile of the coast, and under cover of darkness three hundred men, of whom two hundred were negroes — the whole of the negro contingent having been pressed into the undertaking — were pulled away for the shore in the canoes, piraguas, and ships' boats. Rivarol's pride compelled him, however much he may have disliked the venture, to lead them in person.

The first six boats were caught in the surf, and pounded into fragments before their occupants could extricate themselves. The thunder of the breakers and the cries of the shipwrecked warned those who followed, and thereby saved them from sharing the same fate. By the Baron's urgent orders they pulled away again out of danger, and stood about to pick up such survivors as contrived to battle towards them. Close upon fifty lives were lost in the adventure, together with half-a-dozen boats stored with ammunition and light guns.

The Baron went back to his flagship an infuriated, but by no means a wiser man. Wisdom — not even the pungent wisdom experience thrusts upon us — is not for such as M. de Rivarol. His anger embraced all things, but focussed chiefly upon Captain Blood. In some warped process of reasoning he held the buccaneer chiefly responsible for this misadventure. He went to bed considering furiously what he should say to Captain Blood upon the morrow.

He was awakened at dawn by the rolling thunder of guns. Emerging upon the poop in nightcap and slippers, he beheld a sight that increased his unreasonable and unreasoning fury. The four buccaneer ships under canvas were going through extraordinary manœuvres half a mile off the Boca Chica and little more than half a mile away from the remainder of the fleet, and from their flanks flame and smoke were belching each time they swung broadside to the great round fort that guarded that narrow entrance. The fort was returning the fire vigorously and viciously. But the buccaneers timed their broadsides with extraordinary judgment to catch the defending ordnance reloading; then as they drew the Spaniards' fire, they swung away again, not only taking care to be ever moving targets, but, further, to present no more than bow or stern to the fort, their masts in line, when the heaviest cannonades were to be expected.

Gibbering and cursing, M. de Rivarol stood there

and watched this action, so presumptuously undertaken by Blood on his own responsibility. The officers of the *Victorieuse* crowded round him, but it was
not until M. de Cussy came to join the group that he
opened the sluices of his rage. And M. de Cussy himself invited the deluge that now caught him. He had
come up rubbing his hands and taking a proper satisfaction in the energy of the men whom he had enlisted.

"Aha, M. de Rivarol!" he laughed. "He understands his business, eh, this Captain Blood. He'll
plant the Lilies of France on that fort before break-
fast."

The Baron swung upon him snarling. "He understands his business, eh? His business, let me tell you,
M. de Cussy, is to obey my orders, and I have not
ordered this. Par la Mordieu! When this is over I'll
deal with him for his damned insubordination."

"Surely, M. le Baron, he will have justified it if he
succeeds."

"Justified it! Ah, parbleu! Can a soldier ever justify acting without orders?" He raved on furiously,
his officers supporting him out of their detestation of
Captain Blood.

Meanwhile the fight went merrily on. The fort was
suffering badly. Yet for all their manoeuvring the
buccaneers were not escaping punishment. The starboard gunwale of the *Atropos* had been hammered
into splinters, and a shot had caught her astern in the
coach. The *Elizabeth* was badly battered about the
forecastle, and the *Arabella's* maintop had been shot
away, whilst towards the end of that engagement the
Lachesis came reeling out of the fight with a shattered
rudder, steering herself by sweeps.

The absurd Baron's fierce eyes positively gleamed with satisfaction.

"I pray Heaven they may sink all his infernal ships!" he cried in his frenzy.

But Heaven didn't hear him. Scarcely had he spoken than there was a terrific explosion, and half the fort went up in fragments. A lucky shot from the buccaneers had found the powder magazine.

It may have been a couple of hours later, when Captain Blood, as spruce and cool as if he had just come from a levee, stepped upon the quarter-deck of the *Victorieuse*, to confront M. de Rivarol, still in bedgown and nightcap.

"I have to report, M. le Baron, that we are in possession of the fort on Boca Chica. The standard of France is flying from what remains of its tower, and the way into the outer harbour is open to your fleet."

M. de Rivarol was compelled to swallow his fury, though it choked him. The jubilation among his officers had been such that he could not continue as he had begun. Yet his eyes were malevolent, his face pale with anger.

"You are fortunate, M. Blood, that you succeeded," he said. "It would have gone very ill with you had you failed. Another time be so good as to await my orders, lest you should afterwards lack the justification which your good fortune has procured you this morning."

Blood smiled with a flash of white teeth, and bowed.

"I shall be glad of your orders now, General, for pursuing our advantage. You realize that speed in striking is the first essential."

Rivarol was left gaping a moment. Absorbed in his

ridiculous anger, he had considered nothing, But he made a quick recovery. "To my cabin, if you please," he commanded peremptorily, and was turning to lead the way, when Blood arrested him. .

"With submission, my General, we shall be better here. You behold there the scene of our coming action. It is spread before you like a map." He waved his hand towards the lagoon, the country flanking it and the considerable city standing back from the beach. "If it is not a presumption in me to offer a suggestion..." He paused. M. de Rivarol looked at him sharply, suspecting irony. But the swarthy face was bland, the keen eyes steady.

"Let us hear your suggestion," he consented.

Blood pointed out the fort at the mouth of the inner harbour, which was just barely visible above the waving palms on the intervening tongue of land. He announced that its armament was less formidable than that of the outer fort, which they had reduced; but on the other hand, the passage was very much narrower than the Boca Chica, and before they could attempt to make it in any case, they must dispose of those defences. He proposed that the French ships should enter the outer harbour, and proceed at once to bombardment. Meanwhile, he would land three hundred buccaneers and some artillery on the eastern side of the lagoon, beyond the fragrant garden islands dense with richly bearing fruit-trees, and proceed simultaneously to storm the fort in the rear. Thus beset on both sides at once, and demoralized by the fate of the much stronger outer fort, he did not think the Spaniards would offer a very long resistance. Then it would be for M. de Rivarol to garrison the fort, whilst

Captain Blood would sweep on with his men, and seize the Church of Nuestra Señora de la Poupa, plainly visible on its hill immediately eastward of the town. Not only did that eminence afford them a valuable and obvious strategic advantage, but it commanded the only road that led from Cartagena to the interior, and once it were held there would be no further question of the Spaniards attempting to remove the wealth of the city.

That to M. de Rivarol was — as Captain Blood had judged that it would be — the crowning argument. Supercilious until that moment, and disposed for his own pride's sake to treat the buccaneer's suggestions with cavalier criticism, M. de Rivarol's manner suddenly changed. He became alert and brisk, went so far as tolerantly to commend Captain Blood's plan, and issued orders that action might be taken upon it at once.

It is not necessary to follow that action step by step. Blunders on the part of the French marred its smooth execution, and the indifferent handling of their ships led to the sinking of two of them in the course of the afternoon by the fort's gunfire. But by evening, owing largely to the irresistible fury with which the buccaneers stormed the place from the landward side, the fort had surrendered, and before dusk Blood and his men with some ordnance hauled thither by mules dominated the city from the heights of Nuestra Señora de la Poupa.

At noon on the morrow, shorn of defences and threatened with bombardment, Cartagena sent offers of surrender to M. de Rivarol.

Swollen with pride by a victory for which he took

the entire credit to himself, the Baron dictated his terms. He demanded that all public effects and office accounts be delivered up; that the merchants surrender all moneys and goods held by them for their correspondents; the inhabitants could choose whether they would remain in the city or depart; but those who went must first deliver up all their property, and those who elected to remain must surrender half, and become the subjects of France; religious houses and churches should be spared, but they must render accounts of all moneys and valuables in their possession.

Cartagena agreed, having no choice in the matter, and on the next day, which was the 5th of April, M. de Rivarol entered the city and proclaimed it now a French colony, appointing M. de Cussy its Governor. Thereafter he proceeded to the Cathedral, where very properly a Te Deum was sung in honour of the conquest. This by way of grace, whereafter M. de Rivarol proceeded to devour the city. The only detail in which the French conquest of Cartagena differed from an ordinary buccaneering raid was that under the severest penalties no soldier was to enter the house of any inhabitant. But this apparent respect for the persons and property of the conquered was based in reality upon M. de Rivarol's anxiety lest a doubloon should be abstracted from all the wealth that was pouring into the treasury opened by the Baron in the name of the King of France. Once the golden stream had ceased, he removed all restrictions and left the city in prey to his men, who proceeded further to pillage it of that part of their property which the inhabitants who became French subjects had been assured should remain inviolate. The plunder was enormous. In the course of four days over a hundred mules laden with gold went out of the city and down to the boats waiting at the beach to convey the treasure aboard the ships.

CHAPTER XXVIII

THE HONOUR OF M. DE RIVAROL

DURING the capitulation and for some time after, Captain Blood and the greater portion of his buccaneers had been at their post on the heights of Nuestra Señora de la Poupa, utterly in ignorance of what was taking place. Blood, although the man chiefly, if not solely, responsible for the swift reduction of the city, which was proving a veritable treasure-house, was not even shown the consideration of being called to the council of officers which with M. de Rivarol determined the terms of the capitulation.

This was a slight that at another time Captain Blood would not have borne for a moment. But at present, in his odd frame of mind, and its divorcement from piracy, he was content to smile his utter contempt of the French General. Not so, however, his captains, and still less his men. Resentment smouldered amongst them for a while, to flame out violently at the end of that week in Cartagena. It was only by undertaking to voice their grievance to the Baron that their captain was able for the moment to pacify them. That done, he went at once in quest of M. de Rivarol.

He found him in the offices which the Baron had set up in the town, with a staff of clerks to register the treasure brought in and to cast up the surrendered account-books, with a view to ascertaining precisely what were the sums yet to be delivered up. The

Baron sat there scrutinizing ledgers, like a city merchant, and checking figures to make sure that all was correct to the last peso. A choice occupation this for the General of the King's Armies by Sea and Land. He looked up irritated by the interruption which Captain Blood's advent occasioned.

"M. le Baron," the latter greeted him. "I must speak frankly; and you must suffer it. My men are on the point of mutiny."

M. de Rivarol considered him with a faint lift of the eyebrows.

"Captain Blood, I, too, will speak frankly; and you, too, must suffer it. If there is a mutiny, you and your captains shall be held personally responsible. The mistake you make is in assuming with me the tone of an ally, whereas I have given you clearly to understand from the first that you are simply in the position of having accepted service under me. Your proper apprehension of that fact will save the waste of a deal of words."

Blood contained himself with difficulty. One of these fine days, he felt, that for the sake of humanity he must slit the comb of this supercilious, arrogant cockerel.

"You may define our positions as you please," said he. "But I'll remind you that the nature of a thing is not changed by the name you give it. I am concerned with facts; chiefly with the fact that we entered into definite articles with you. Those articles provide for a certain distribution of the spoil. My men demand it. They are not satisfied."

"Of what are they not satisfied?" demanded the Baron.

"Of your honesty, M. de Rivarol."

A blow in the face could scarcely have taken the Frenchman more aback. He stiffened, and drew himself up, his eyes blazing, his face of a deathly pallor. The clerks at the tables laid down their pens, and awaited the explosion in a sort of terror.

For a long moment there was silence. Then the great gentleman delivered himself in a voice of concentrated anger. "Do you really dare so much, you and the dirty thieves that follow you? God's Blood! You shall answer to me for that word, though it entail a yet worse dishonour to meet you. Faugh!"

"I will remind you," said Blood, "that I am speaking not for myself, but for my men. It is they who are not satisfied, they who threaten that unless satisfaction is afforded them, and promptly, they will take it."

"Take it?" said Rivarol, trembling in his rage. "Let them attempt it, and ..."

"Now don't be rash. My men are within their rights, as you are aware. They demand to know when this sharing of the spoil is to take place, and when they are to receive the fifth for which their articles provide."

"God give me patience! How can we share the spoil before it has been completely gathered?"

"My men have reason to believe that it is gathered; and, anyway, they view with mistrust that it should all be housed aboard your ships, and remain in your possession. They say that hereafter there will be no ascertaining what the spoil really amounts to."

"But — name of Heaven! — I have kept books. They are there for all to see."

"They do not wish to see account-books. Few of them can read. They want to view the treasure itself. They know — you compel me to be blunt — that the accounts have been falsified. Your books show the spoil of Cartagena to amount to some ten million livres. The men know — and they are very skilled in these computations — that it exceeds the enormous total of forty millions. They insist that the treasure itself be produced and weighed in their presence, as is the custom among the Brethren of the Coast."

"I know nothing of filibuster customs." The gentleman was disdainful.

"But you are learning quickly."

"What do you mean, you rogue? I am a leader of armies, not of plundering thieves."

"Oh, but of course!" Blood's irony laughed in his eyes. "Yet, whatever you may be, I warn you that unless you yield to a demand that I consider just and therefore uphold, you may look for trouble, and it would not surprise me if you never leave Cartagena at all, nor convey a single gold piece home to France."

"Ah, pardieu! Am I to understand that you are threatening me?"

"Come, come, M. le Baron! I warn you of the trouble that a little prudence may avert. You do not know on what a volcano you are sitting. You do not know the ways of buccaneers. If you persist, Cartagena will be drenched in blood, and whatever the outcome the King of France will not have been well served."

That shifted the basis of the argument to less hostile ground. Awhile yet it continued, to be concluded at last by an ungracious undertaking from

M. de Rivarol to submit to the demands of the buccaneers. He gave it with an extreme ill-grace, and
only because Blood made him realize at last that to
withhold it longer would be dangerous. In an engagement, he might conceivably defeat Blood's followers.
But conceivably he might not. And even if he succeeded, the effort would be so costly to him in men
that he might not thereafter find himself in sufficient
strength to maintain his hold of what he had seized.

The end of it all was that he gave a promise at once
to make the necessary preparations, and if Captain
Blood and his officers would wait upon him on board
the *Victorieuse* to-morrow morning, the treasure
should be produced, weighed in their presence, and
their fifth share surrendered there and then into their
own keeping.

Among the buccaneers that night there was hilarity
over the sudden abatement of M. de Rivarol's
monstrous pride. But when the next dawn broke
over Cartagena, they had the explanation of it. The
only ships to be seen in the harbour were the *Arabella*
and the *Elizabeth* riding at anchor, and the *Atropos*
and the *Lachesis* careened on the beach for repair of
the damage sustained in the bombardment. The
French ships were gone. They had been quietly and
secretly warped out of the harbour under cover of
night, and three sails, faint and small, on the horizon
to westward was all that remained to be seen of them.
The absconding M. de Rivarol had gone off with the
treasure, taking with him the troops and mariners he
had brought from France. He had left behind him at
Cartagena not only the empty-handed buccaneers,
whom he had swindled, but also M. de Cussy and the

volunteers and negroes from Hispaniola, whom he had swindled no less.

The two parties were fused into one by their common fury, and before the exhibition of it the inhabitants of that ill-fated town were stricken with deeper terror than they had yet known since the coming of this expedition.

Captain Blood alone kept his head, setting a curb upon his deep chagrin. He had promised himself that before parting from M. de Rivarol he would present a reckoning for all the petty affronts and insults to which that unspeakable fellow — now proved a scoundrel — had subjected him.

"We must follow," he declared. "Follow and punish."

At first that was the general cry. Then came the consideration that only two of the buccaneer ships were seaworthy — and these could not accommodate the whole force, particularly being at the moment indifferently victualled for a long voyage. The crews of the *Lachesis* and *Atropos* and with them their captains, Wolverstone and Yberville, renounced the intention. After all, there would be a deal of treasure still hidden in Cartagena. They would remain behind to extort it whilst fitting their ships for sea. Let Blood and Hagthorpe and those who sailed with them do as they pleased.

Then only did Blood realize the rashness of his proposal, and in attempting to draw back he almost precipitated a battle between the two parties into which that same proposal had now divided the buccaneers. And meanwhile those French sails on the horizon were growing less and less. Blood was re-

duced to despair. If he went off now, Heaven knew
what would happen to the town, the temper of those
whom he was leaving being what it was. Yet if he
remained, it would simply mean that his own and
Hagthorpe's crews would join in the saturnalia and
increase the hideousness of events now inevitable.
Unable to reach a decision, his own men and Hagthorpe's took the matter off his hands, eager to give
chase to Rivarol. Not only was a dastardly cheat to
be punished, but an enormous treasure was to be won
by treating as an enemy this French commander who,
himself, had so villainously broken the alliance.

When Blood, torn as he was between conflicting
considerations, still hesitated, they bore him almost
by main force aboard the *Arabella*.

Within an hour, the water-casks at least replen-
ished and stowed aboard, the *Arabella* and the *Elizabeth* put to sea upon that angry chase.

"When we were well at sea, and the *Arabella's*
course was laid," writes Pitt, in his log, "I went to
seek the Captain knowing him to be in great trouble
of mind over these events. I found him sitting alone
in his cabin, his head in his hands, torment in the
eyes that stared straight before him, seeing nothing."

"What now, Peter?" cried the young Somerset
mariner. "Lord, man, what is there here to fret you?
Surely 'tisn't the thought of Rivarol!"

"No," said Blood thickly. And for once he was
communicative. It may well be that he must vent
the thing that oppressed him or be driven mad by it.
And Pitt, after all, was his friend and loved him, and,
so, a proper man for confidences. "But if she knew!
If she knew! O God! I had thought to have done

with piracy; thought to have done with it for ever. Yet here have I been committed by this scoundrel to the worst piracy that ever I was guilty of. Think of Cartagena! Think of the hell those devils will be making of it now! And I must have that on my soul!"

"Nay, Peter — 'tisn't on your soul; but on Rivarol's. It is that dirty thief who has brought all this about. What could you have done to prevent it?"

"I would have stayed if it could have availed."

"It could not, and you know it. So why repine?"

"There is more than that to it," groaned Blood. "What now? What remains? Loyal service with the English was made impossible for me. Loyal service with France has led to this; and that is equally impossible hereafter. What remains, then? Piracy? I have done with it. Egad, if I am to live clean, I believe the only thing is to go and offer my sword to the King of Spain."

But something remained — the last thing that he could have expected — something towards which they were rapidly sailing over the tropical, sunlit sea. All this against which he now inveighed so bitterly was but a necessary stage in the shaping of his odd destiny.

Setting a course for Hispaniola, since they judged that thither must Rivarol go to refit before attempting to cross to France, the *Arabella* and the *Elizabeth* ploughed briskly northward with a moderately favourable wind for two days and nights without ever catching a glimpse of their quarry. The third dawn brought with it a haze which circumscribed their range of vision to something between two and three miles, and deepened their growing vexation and their apprehension that M. de Rivarol might escape them altogether.

Their position then — according to Pitt's log — was approximately 75° 30' W. Long. by 17° 45' N. Lat., so that they had Jamaica on their larboard beam some thirty miles to westward, and, indeed, away to the northwest, faintly visible as a bank of clouds, appeared the great ridge of the Blue Mountains whose peaks were thrust into the clear upper air above the low-lying haze. The wind, to which they were sailing very close, was westerly, and it bore to their ears a booming sound which in less experienced ears might have passed for the breaking of surf upon a lee shore.

"Guns!" said Pitt, who stood with Blood upon the quarter-deck. Blood nodded, listening.

"Ten miles away, perhaps fifteen — somewhere off Port Royal, I should judge," Pitt added. Then he looked at his captain. "Does it concern us?" he asked.

"Guns off Port Royal...that should argue Colonel Bishop at work. And against whom should he be in action but against friends of ours? I think it may concern us. Anyway, we'll stand in to investigate. Bid them put the helm over."

Close-hauled they tacked aweather, guided by the sound of combat, which grew in volume and definition as they approached it. Thus for an hour, perhaps. Then, as, telescope to his eye, Blood raked the haze, expecting at any moment to behold the battling ships, the guns abruptly ceased.

They held to their course, nevertheless, with all

hands on deck, eagerly, anxiously scanning the sea ahead. And presently an object loomed into view, which soon defined itself for a great ship on fire. As the *Arabella* with the *Elizabeth* following closely raced nearer on their northwesterly tack, the outlines of the blazing vessel grew clearer. Presently her masts stood out sharp and black above the smoke and flames, and through his telescope Blood made out plainly the pennon of St. George fluttering from her maintop.

"An English ship!" he cried.

He scanned the seas for the conqueror in the battle of which this grim evidence was added to that of the sounds they had heard, and when at last, as they drew closer to the doomed vessel, they made out the shadowy outlines of three tall ships, some three or four miles away, standing in toward Port Royal, the first and natural assumption was that these ships must belong to the Jamaica fleet, and that the burning vessel was a defeated buccaneer, and because of this they sped on to pick up the three boats that were standing away from the blazing hulk. But Pitt, who through the telescope was examining the receding squadron, observed things apparent only to the eye of the trained mariner, and made the incredible announcement that the largest of these three vessels was Rivarol's *Victorieuse*.

They took in sail and hove to as they came up with the drifting boats, laden to capacity with survivors. And there were others adrift on some of the spars and wreckage with which the sea was strewn, who must be rescued.

CHAPTER XXIX

THE SERVICE OF KING WILLIAM

ONE of the boats bumped alongside the *Arabella*, and up the entrance ladder came first a slight, spruce little gentleman in a coat of mulberry satin laced with gold, whose wizened, yellow, rather peevish face was framed in a heavy black periwig. His modish and costly apparel had nowise suffered by the adventure through which he had passed, and he carried himself with the easy assurance of a man of rank. Here, quite clearly, was no buccaneer. He was closely followed by one who in every particular, save that of age, was his physical opposite, corpulent in a brawny, vigorous way, with a full, round, weather-beaten face whose mouth was humourous and whose eyes were blue and twinkling. He was well dressed without fripperies, and bore with him an air of vigorous authority.

As the little man stepped from the ladder into the waist, whither Captain Blood had gone to receive him, his sharp, ferrety dark eyes swept the uncouth ranks of the assembled crew of the *Arabella*.

"And where the devil may I be now?" he demanded irritably. "Are you English, or what the devil are you?"

"Myself, I have the honour to be Irish, sir. My name is Blood — Captain Peter Blood, and this is my ship the *Arabella*, all very much at your service."

"Blood!" shrilled the little man. "'Odd's blood! A

pirate!" He swung to the Colossus who followed him
— "A damned pirate, van der Kuylen. Rend my
vitals, but we're come from Scylla to Charybdis."

"So?" said the other gutturally, and again, "So?"
Then the humour of it took him, and he yielded to it.

"Damme! What's to laugh at, you porpoise?"
spluttered mulberry-coat. "A fine tale this'll make at
home! Admiral van der Kuylen first loses his fleet in
the night, then has his flagship fired under him by a
French squadron, and ends all by being captured by a
pirate. I'm glad you find it matter for laughter. Since
for my sins I happen to be with you, I'm damned if
I do."

"There's a misapprehension, if I may make so bold
as to point it out," put in Blood quietly. "You are
not captured, gentlemen; you are rescued. When you
realize it, perhaps it will occur to you to acknowledge
the hospitality I am offering you. It may be poor, but
it is the best at my disposal."

The fierce little gentleman stared at him. "Damme!
Do you permit yourself to be ironical?" he disap-
proved him, and possibly with a view to correcting
any such tendency, proceeded to introduce himself.
"I am Lord Willoughby, King William's Governor-
General of the West Indies, and this is Admiral van
der Kuylen, commander of His Majesty's West
Indian fleet, at present mislaid somewhere in this
damned Caribbean Sea."

"King William?" quoth Blood, and he was conscious that Pitt and Dyke, who were behind him, now
came edging nearer, sharing his own wonder. "And
who may be King William, and of what may he be
King?"

"What's that?" In a wonder greater than his own, Lord Willoughby stared back at him. At last: "I am alluding to His Majesty King William III — William of Orange — who, with Queen Mary, has been ruling England for two months and more."

There was a moment's silence, until Blood realized what he was being told.

"D'ye mean, sir, that they've roused themselves at home, and kicked out that scoundrel James and his gang of ruffians?"

Admiral van der Kuylen nudged his lordship, a humourous twinkle in his blue eyes.

"His bolitics are fery sound, I dink," he growled.

His lordship's smile brought lines like gashes into his leathery cheeks. "'Slife! Hadn't you heard? Where the devil have you been at all?"

"Out of touch with the world for the last three months," said Blood.

"Stab me! You must have been. And in that three months the world has undergone some changes." Briefly he added an account of them. King James was fled to France, and living under the protection of King Louis, wherefore, and for other reasons, England had joined the league against her, and was now at war with France. That was how it happened that the Dutch Admiral's flagship had been attacked by M. de Rivarol's fleet that morning, from which it clearly followed that in his voyage from Cartagena, the Frenchman must have spoken some ship that gave him the news.

After that, with renewed assurances that aboard his ship they should be honourably entreated, Captain Blood led the Governor-General and the Admiral to his cabin, what time the work of rescue went on. The news he had received had set Blood's mind in a turmoil. If King James was dethroned and banished, there was an end to his own outlawry for his alleged share in an earlier attempt to drive out that tyrant. It became possible for him to return home and take up his life again at the point where it was so unfortunately interrupted four years ago. He was dazzled by the prospect so abruptly opened out to him. The thing so filled his mind, moved him so deeply, that he must afford it expression. In doing so, he revealed of himself more than he knew or intended to the astute little gentleman who watched him so keenly the while.

"Go home, if you will," said his lordship, when Blood paused. "You may be sure that none will harass you on the score of your piracy, considering what it was that drove you to it. But why be in haste? We have heard of you, to be sure, and we know of what you are capable upon the seas. Here is a great chance for you, since you declare yourself sick of piracy. Should you choose to serve King William out here during this war, your knowledge of the West Indies should render you a very valuable servant to His Majesty's Government, which you would not find ungrateful. You should consider it. Damme, sir, I repeat: it is a great chance you are given."

"That your lordship gives me," Blood amended, "I am very grateful. But at the moment, I confess, I can consider nothing but this great news. It alters the shape of the world. I must accustom myself to view it as it now is, before I can determine my own place in it."

Pitt came in to report that the work of rescue was
at an end, and the men picked up — some forty-five
in all — safe aboard the two buccaneer ships. He
asked for orders. Blood rose.

"I am negligent of your lordship's concerns in my
consideration of my own. You'll be wishing me to
land you at Port Royal."

"At Port Royal?" The little man squirmed wrathfully on his seat. Wrathfully and at length he informed Blood that they had put into Port Royal last
evening to find its Deputy-Governor absent. "He
had gone on some wild-goose chase to Tortuga after
buccaneers, taking the whole of the fleet with him."

Blood stared in surprise a moment; then yielded to
laughter.

"He went, I suppose, before news reached him of
the change of government at home, and the war with
France?"

"He did not," snapped Willoughby. "He was informed of both, and also of my coming before he set
out."

"Oh, impossible!"

"So I should have thought. But I have the information from a Major Mallard whom I found in
Port Royal, apparently governing in this fool's absence."

"But is he mad, to leave his post at such a time?"
Blood was amazed.

"Taking the whole fleet with him, pray remember,
and leaving the place open to French attack. That is
the sort of Deputy-Governor that the late Government thought fit to appoint: an epitome of its misrule,
damme! He leaves Port Royal unguarded save by a

ramshackle fort that can be reduced to rubble in an hour. Stab me! It's unbelievable!"

The lingering smile faded from Blood's face. "Is Rivarol aware of this?" he cried sharply.

It was the Dutch Admiral who answered him. "Vould he go dere if he were not? M. de Rivarol he take some of our men prisoners. Berhabs dey dell him. Berhabs he make dem tell. Id is a great obbordunidy."

His lordship snarled like a mountain-cat. "That rascal Bishop shall answer for it with his head if there's any mischief done through this desertion of his post. What if it were deliberate, eh? What if he is more knave than fool? What if this is his way of serving King James, from whom he held his office?"

Captain Blood was generous. "Hardly so much. It was just vindictiveness that urged him. It's myself he's hunting at Tortuga, my lord. But, I'm thinking that while he's about it, I'd best be looking after Jamaica for King William." He laughed, with more mirth than he had used in the last two months.

"Set a course for Port Royal, Jeremy, and make all speed. We'll be level yet with M. de Rivarol, and wipe off some other scores at the same time."

Both Lord Willoughby and the Admiral were on their feet.

"But you are not equal to it, damme!" cried his lordship. "Any one of the Frenchman's three ships is a match for both yours, my man."

"In guns — aye," said Blood, and he smiled. "But there's more than guns that matter in these affairs. If your lordship would like to see an action fought at sea as an action should be fought, this is your opportunity."

Both stared at him. "But the odds!" his lordship insisted. "Id is imbossible," said van der Kuylen, shaking his great head. "Seamanship is imbordand. Bud guns is guns."

"If I can't defeat him, I can sink my own ships in the channel, and block him in until Bishop gets back from his wild-goose chase with his squadron, or until your own fleet turns up."

"And what good will that be, pray?" demanded Willoughby.

"I'll be after telling you. Rivarol is a fool to take this chance, considering what he's got aboard. He carried in his hold the treasure plundered from Cartagena, amounting to forty million livres." They jumped at the mention of that colossal sum. "He has gone into Port Royal with it. Whether he defeats me or not, he doesn't come out of Port Royal with it again, and sooner or later that treasure shall find its way into King William's coffers, after, say, one fifth share shall have been paid to my buccaneers. Is that agreed, Lord Willoughby?"

His lordship stood up, and shaking back the cloud of lace from his wrist, held out a delicate white hand.

"Captain Blood, I discover greatness in you," said he.

"Sure it's your lordship has the fine sight to perceive it," laughed the Captain.

"Yes, yes! Bud how vill you do id?" growled van der Kuylen.

"Come on deck, and it's a demonstration I'll be giving you before the day's much older."

CHAPTER XXX

THE LAST FIGHT OF THE ARABELLA

"VHY do you vait, my friend?" growled van der Kuylen.

"Aye — in God's name!" snapped Willoughby.

It was the afternoon of that same day, and the two buccaneer ships rocked gently with idly flapping sails under the lee of the long spit of land forming the great natural harbour of Port Royal, and less than a mile from the straits leading into it, which the fort commanded. It was two hours and more since they had brought up thereabouts, having crept thither unobserved by the city and by M. de Rivarol's ships, and all the time the air had been aquiver with the roar of guns from sea and land, announcing that battle was joined between the French and the defenders of Port Royal. That long, inactive waiting was straining the nerves of both Lord Willoughby and van der Kuylen.

"You said you vould show us zome vine dings. Vhere are dese vine dings?"

Blood faced them, smiling confidently. He was arrayed for battle, in back-and-breast of black steel. "I'll not be trying your patience much longer. Indeed, I notice already a slackening in the fire. But it's this way, now: there's nothing at all to be gained by precipitancy, and a deal to be gained by delaying, as I shall show you, I hope."

Lord Willoughby eyed him suspiciously. "Ye think

that in the meantime Bishop may come back or Admiral van der Kuylen's fleet appear?"

"Sure, now, I'm thinking nothing of the kind. What I'm thinking is that in this engagement with the fort M. de Rivarol, who's a lubberly fellow, as I've reason to know, will be taking some damage that may make the odds a trifle more even. Sure, it'll be time enough to go forward when the fort has shot its bolt."

"Aye, aye!" The sharp approval came like a cough from the little Governor-General. "I perceive your object, and I believe ye're entirely right. Ye have the qualities of a great commander, Captain Blood. I beg your pardon for having misunderstood you."

"And that's very handsome of your lordship. Ye see, I have some experience of this kind of action, and whilst I'll take any risk that I must, I'll take none that I needn't. But . . ." He broke off to listen. "Aye, I was right. The fire's slackening. It'll mean the end of Mallard's resistance in the fort. Ho there, Jeremy!"

He leaned on the carved rail and issued orders crisply. The bo'sun's pipe shrilled out, and in a moment the ship that had seemed to slumber there, awoke to life. Came the padding of feet along the decks, the creaking of blocks and the hoisting of sail. The helm was put over hard, and in a moment they were moving, the *Elizabeth* following, ever in obedience to the signals from the *Arabella*, whilst Ogle the gunner, whom he had summoned, was receiving Blood's final instructions before plunging down to his station on the main deck.

Within a quarter of an hour they had rounded the

head, and stood in to the harbour mouth, within saker shot of Rivarol's three ships, to which they now abruptly disclosed themselves.

Where the fort had stood they now beheld a smoking rubbish heap, and the victorious Frenchman with the lily standard trailing from his mastheads was sweeping forward to snatch the rich prize whose defences he had shattered.

Blood scanned the French ships, and chuckled. The *Victorieuse* and the *Medusa* appeared to have taken no more than a few scars; but the third ship, the *Baleine,* listing heavily to larboard so as to keep the great gash in her starboard well above water, was out of account.

"You see!" he cried to van der Kuylen, and without waiting for the Dutchman's approving grunt, he shouted an order: "Helm, hard-a-port!"

The sight of that great red ship with her gilt beakhead and open ports swinging broadside on must have given check to Rivarol's soaring exultation. Yet before he could move to give an order, before he could well resolve what order to give, a volcano of fire and metal burst upon him from the buccaneers, and his decks were swept by the murderous scythe of the broadside. The *Arabella* held to her course, giving place to the *Elizabeth*, which, following closely, executed the same manœuvre. And then whilst still the Frenchmen were confused, panic-stricken by an attack that took them so utterly by surprise, the *Arabella* had gone about, and was returning in her tracks, presenting now her larboard guns, and loosing her second broadside in the wake of the first. Came yet another broadside from the *Elizabeth* and then the *Arabella's* trumpeter sent a call across the water, which Hagthorpe perfectly understood.

"On, now, Jeremy!" cried Blood. "Straight into them before they recover their wits. Stand by, there! Prepare to board! Hayton ... the grapnels! And pass the word to the gunner in the prow to fire as fast as he can load."

He discarded his feathered hat, and covered himself with a steel head-piece, which a negro lad brought him. He meant to lead this boarding-party in person. Briskly he explained himself to his two guests. "Boarding is our only chance here. We are too heavily outgunned."

Of this the fullest demonstration followed quickly. The Frenchmen having recovered their wits at last, both ships swung broadside on, and concentrating upon the *Arabella* as the nearer and heavier and therefore more immediately dangerous of their two opponents, volleyed upon her jointly at almost the same moment.

Unlike the buccaneers, who had fired high to cripple their enemies above decks, the French fired low to smash the hull of their assailant. The *Arabella* rocked and staggered under that terrific hammering, although Pitt kept her headed towards the French so that she should offer the narrowest target. For a moment she seemed to hesitate, then she plunged forward again, her beak-head in splinters, her forecastle smashed, and a gaping hole forward, that was only just above the water-line. Indeed, to make her safe from bilging, Blood ordered a prompt jettisoning of the forward guns, anchors, and water-casks and whatever else was movable.

Meanwhile, the Frenchmen going about, gave the like reception to the *Elizabeth*. The *Arabella*, indifferently served by the wind, pressed forward to come to grips. But before she could accomplish her object, the *Victorieuse* had loaded her starboard guns again, and pounded her advancing enemy with a second broadside at close quarters. Amid the thunder of cannon, the rending of timbers, and the screams of maimed men, the half-wrecked *Arabella* plunged and reeled into the cloud of smoke that concealed her prey, and then from Hayton went up the cry that she was going down by the head.

Blood's heart stood still. And then in that very moment of his despair, the blue and gold flank of the *Victorieuse* loomed through the smoke. But even as he caught that enheartening glimpse he perceived, too, how sluggish now was their advance, and how with every second it grew more sluggish. They must sink before they reached her.

Thus, with an oath, opined the Dutch Admiral, and from Lord Willoughby there was a word of blame for Blood's seamanship in having risked all upon this gambler's throw of boarding.

"There was no other chance!" cried Blood, in broken-hearted frenzy. "If ye say it was desperate and foolhardy, why, so it was; but the occasion and the means demanded nothing less. I fail within an ace of victory."

But they had not yet completely failed. Hayton himself, and a score of sturdy rogues whom his whistle had summoned, were crouching for shelter amid the wreckage of the forecastle with grapnels ready. Within seven or eight yards of the *Victorieuse*, when their way seemed spent, and their forward deck already awash under the eyes of the jeering, cheering Frenchmen, those men leapt up and forward, and hurled their grapnels across the chasm. Of the four they flung, two reached the Frenchman's decks, and fastened there. Swift as thought itself, was then the action of those sturdy, experienced buccaneers. Unhesitatingly all threw themselves upon the chain of one of those grapnels, neglecting the other, and heaved upon it with all their might to warp the ships together. Blood, watching from his own quarter-deck, sent out his voice in a clarion call:

"Musketeers to the prow!"

The musketeers, at their station at the waist, obeyed him with the speed of men who know that in obedience is the only hope of life. Fifty of them dashed forward instantly, and from the ruins of the forecastle they blazed over the heads of Hayton's men, mowing down the French soldiers who, unable to dislodge the irons, firmly held where they had deeply bitten into the timbers of the *Victorieuse*, were themselves preparing to fire upon the grapnel crew.

Starboard to starboard the two ships swung against each other with a jarring thud. By then Blood was down in the waist, judging and acting with the hurricane speed the occasion demanded. Sail had been lowered by slashing away the ropes that held the yards. The advance guard of boarders, a hundred strong, was ordered to the poop, and his grapnel-men were posted, and prompt to obey his command at the very moment of impact. As a result, the foundering *Arabella* was literally kept afloat by the half-dozen grapnels that in an instant moored her firmly to the *Victorieuse.*

Willoughby and van der Kuylen on the poop had watched in breathless amazement the speed and precision with which Blood and his desperate crew had gone to work. And now he came racing up, his bugler sounding the charge, the main host of the buccaneers following him, whilst the vanguard, led by the gunner Ogle, who had been driven from his guns by water in the gun-deck, leapt shouting to the prow of the *Victorieuse,* to whose level the high poop of the water-logged *Arabella* had sunk. Led now by Blood himself, they launched themselves upon the French like hounds upon the stag they have brought to bay. After them went others, until all had gone, and none but Willoughby and the Dutchman were left to watch the fight from the quarter-deck of the abandoned *Arabella.*

For fully half-an-hour that battle raged aboard the Frenchman. Beginning in the prow, it surged through the forecastle to the waist, where it reached a climax of fury. The French resisted stubbornly, and they had the advantage of numbers to encourage them. But for all their stubborn valour, they ended by being pressed back and back across the decks that were dangerously canted to starboard by the pull of the water-logged *Arabella.* The buccaneers fought with the desperate fury of men who know that retreat is impossible, for there was no ship to which they could retreat, and here they must prevail and make the *Victorieuse* their own, or perish.

And their own they made her in the end, and at a cost of nearly half their numbers. Driven to the

quarter-deck, the surviving defenders, urged on by
the infuriated Rivarol, maintained awhile their desperate resistance. But in the end, Rivarol went down
with a bullet in his head, and the French remnant,
numbering scarcely a score of whole men, called for
quarter.

Even then the labours of Blood's men were not at
an end. The *Elizabeth* and the *Medusa* were tight-
locked, and Hagthorpe's followers were being driven
back aboard their own ship for the second time.
Prompt measures were demanded. Whilst Pitt and
his seamen bore their part with the sails, and Ogle
went below with a gun-crew, Blood ordered the grapnels to be loosed at once. Lord Willoughby and the
Admiral were already aboard the *Victorieuse*. As they
swung off to the rescue of Hagthorpe, Blood, from the
quarter-deck of the conquered vessel, looked his last
upon the ship that had served him so well, the ship
that had become to him almost as a part of himself. A
moment she rocked after her release, then slowly and
gradually settled down, the water gurgling and eddy-
ing about her topmasts, all that remained visible to
mark the spot where she had met her death.

As he stood there, above the ghastly shambles in
the waist of the *Victorieuse*, some one spoke behind
him. "I think, Captain Blood, that it is necessary I
should beg your pardon for the second time. Never
before have I seen the impossible made possible by
resource and valour, or victory so gallantly snatched
from defeat."

He turned, and presented to Lord Willoughby a
formidable front. His head-piece was gone, his breast-
plate dinted, his right sleeve a rag hanging from his

shoulder about a naked arm. He was splashed from
head to foot with blood, and there was blood from a
scalp-wound that he had taken matting his hair and
mixing with the grime of powder on his face to render
him unrecognizable.

But from that horrible mask two vivid eyes looked
out preternaturally bright, and from those eyes two
tears had ploughed each a furrow through the filth of
his cheeks.

CHAPTER XXXI

ʹHIS EXCELLENCY THE GOVERNOR

WHEN the cost of that victory came to be counted, it was found that of three hundred and twenty buccaneers who had left Cartagena with Captain Blood, a bare hundred remained sound and whole. The *Elizabeth* had suffered so seriously that it was doubtful if she could ever again be rendered seaworthy, and Hagthorpe, who had so gallantly commanded her in that last action, was dead. Against this, on the other side of the account, stood the facts that, with a far inferior force and by sheer skill and desperate valour, Blood's buccaneers had saved Jamaica from bombardment and pillage, and they had captured the fleet of M. de Rivarol, and seized for the benefit of King William the splendid treasure which she carried.

It was not until the evening of the following day that van der Kuylen's truant fleet of nine ships came to anchor in the harbour of Port Royal, and its officers, Dutch and English, were made acquainted with their Admiral's true opinion of their worth.

Six ships of that fleet were instantly refitted for sea. There were other West Indian settlements demanding the visit of inspection of the new Governor-General, and Lord Willoughby was in haste to sail for the Antilles.

"And meanwhile," he complained to his Admiral, "I am detained here by the absence of this fool of a Deputy-Governor."

"So?" said van der Kuylen. "But vhy should dad dedain you?"

"That I may break the dog as he deserves, and appoint his successor in some man gifted with a sense of where his duty lies, and with the ability to perform it."

"Aha! But id is not necessary you remain for dat. And meandime de Vrench vill haf deir eye on Barbados, vhich is nod vell defended. You haf here chust de man you vant. He will require no insdrucshons, dis one. He vill know how to make Port Royal safe, bedder nor you or me."

"You mean Blood?"

"Of gourse. Could any man be bedder? You haf seen vhad he can do."

"You think so, too, eh? Egad! I had thought of it; and, rip me, why not? He's a better man than Morgan, and Morgan was made Governor."

Blood was sent for. He came, spruce and debonnair once more, having exploited the resources of Port Royal so to render himself. He was a trifle dazzled by the honour proposed to him, when Lord Willoughby made it known. It was so far beyond anything that he had dreamed, and he was assailed by doubts of his capacity to undertake so onerous a charge.

"Damme!" snapped Willoughby, "Should I offer it unless I were satisfied of your capacity? If that's your only objection . . ."

"It is not, my lord. I had counted upon going home, so I had. I am hungry for the green lanes of England." He sighed. "There will be apple-blossoms in the orchards of Somerset."

"Apple-blossoms!" His lordship's voice shot up like a rocket, and cracked on the word. "What the devil . . . ? Apple-blossoms!" He looked at van der Kuylen.

The Admiral raised his brows and pursed his heavy lips. His eyes twinkled humourously in his great face. "So!" he said. "Fery boedical!"

My lord wheeled fiercely upon Captain Blood. "You've a past score to wipe out, my man!" he admonished him. "You've done something towards it, I confess; and you've shown your quality in doing it. That's why I offer you the governorship of Jamaica in His Majesty's name — because I account you the fittest man for the office that I have seen."

Blood bowed low. "Your lordship is very good. But . . ."

"Tchah! There's no 'but' to it. If you want your past forgotten, and your future assured, this is your chance. And you are not to treat it lightly on account of apple-blossoms or any other damned sentimental nonsense. Your duty lies here, at least for as long as the war lasts. When the war's over, you may get back to Somerset and cider or your native Ireland and its potheen; but until then you'll make the best of Jamaica and rum."

Van der Kuylen exploded into laughter. But from Blood the pleasantry elicited no smile. He remained solemn to the point of glumness. His thoughts were on Miss Bishop, who was somewhere here in this very house in which they stood, but whom he had not seen since his arrival. Had she but shown him some compassion . . .

And then the rasping voice of Willoughby cut in again, upbraiding him for his hesitation, pointing out to him his incredible stupidity in trifling with such a golden opportunity as this. He stiffened and bowed.

"My lord, you are in the right. I am a fool. But don't be accounting me an ingrate as well. If I have hesitated, it is because there are considerations with which I will not trouble your lordship."

"Apple-blossoms, I suppose?" sniffed his lordship.

This time Blood laughed, but there was still a lingering wistfulness in his eyes.

"It shall be as you wish — and very gratefully, let me assure your lordship. I shall know how to earn His Majesty's approbation. You may depend upon my loyal service."

"If I didn't, I shouldn't offer you this governorship."

Thus it was settled. Blood's commission was made out and sealed in the presence of Mallard, the Commandant, and the other officers of the garrison, who looked on in round-eyed astonishment, but kept their thoughts to themselves.

"Now ve can aboud our business go," said van der Kuylen.

"We sail to-morrow morning," his lordship announced.

Blood was startled.

"And Colonel Bishop?" he asked.

"He becomes your affair. You are now the Governor. You will deal with him as you think proper on his return. Hang him from his own yardarm. He deserves it."

"Isn't the task a trifle invidious?" wondered Blood.

"Very well. I'll leave a letter for him. I hope he'll like it."

Captain Blood took up his duties at once. There was much to be done to place Port Royal in a proper state of defence, after what had happened there. He made an inspection of the ruined fort, and issued instructions for the work upon it, which was to be started immediately. Next he ordered the careening of the three French vessels that they might be rendered seaworthy once more. Finally, with the sanction of Lord Willoughby, he marshalled his buccaneers and surrendered to them one fifth of the captured treasure, leaving it to their choice thereafter either to depart or to enrol themselves in the service of King William.

A score of them elected to remain, and amongst these were Jeremy Pitt, Ogle, and Dyke, whose outlawry, like Blood's, had come to an end with the downfall of King James. They were — saving old Wolverstone, who had been left behind at Cartagena — the only survivors of that band of rebels-convict who had left Barbados over three years ago in the *Cinco Llagas*.

On the following morning, whilst van der Kuylen's fleet was making finally ready for sea, Blood sat in the spacious whitewashed room that was the Governor's office, when Major Mallard brought him word that Bishop's homing squadron was in sight.

"That is very well," said Blood. "I am glad he comes before Lord Willoughby's departure. The orders, Major, are that you place him under arrest the moment he steps ashore. Then bring him here to me. A moment." He wrote a hurried note. "That to Lord Willoughby aboard Admiral van der Kuylen's flagship."

Major Mallard saluted and departed. Peter Blood sat back in his chair and stared at the ceiling, frowning. Time moved on. Came a tap at the door, and an elderly negro slave presented himself. Would his excellency receive Miss Bishop?

His excellency changed colour. He sat quite still, staring at the negro a moment, conscious that his pulses were drumming in a manner wholly unusual to them. Then quietly he assented.

He rose when she entered, and if he was not as pale as she was, it was because his tan dissembled it. For a moment there was silence between them, as they stood looking each at the other. Then she moved forward, and began at last to speak, haltingly, in an unsteady voice, amazing in one usually so calm and deliberate.

"I . . . I . . . Major Mallard has just told me . . ."

"Major Mallard exceeded his duty," said Blood, and because of the effort he made to steady his voice it sounded harsh and unduly loud.

He saw her start, and stop, and instantly made amends. "You alarm yourself without reason, Miss Bishop. Whatever may lie between me and your uncle, you may be sure that I shall not follow the example he has set me. I shall not abuse my position to prosecute a private vengeance. On the contrary, I shall abuse it to protect him. Lord Willoughby's recommendation to me is that I shall treat him without mercy. My own intention is to send him back to his plantation in Barbados."

She came slowly forward now. "I . . . I am glad that you will do that. Glad, above all, for your own sake." She held out her hand to him.

He considered it critically. Then he bowed over it.

"I'll not presume to take it in the hand of a thief and a pirate," said he bitterly.

"You are no longer that," she said, and strove to smile.

"Yet I owe no thanks to you that I am not," he answered. "I think there's no more to be said, unless it be to add the assurance that Lord Julian Wade has also nothing to apprehend from me. That, no doubt, will be the assurance that your peace of mind requires?"

"For your own sake — yes. But for your own sake only. I would not have you do anything mean or dishonouring."

"Thief and pirate though I be?"

She clenched her hand, and made a little gesture of despair and impatience.

"Will you never forgive me those words?"

"I'm finding it a trifle hard, I confess. But what does it matter, when all is said?"

Her clear hazel eyes considered him a moment wistfully. Then she put out her hand again.

"I am going, Captain Blood. Since you are so generous to my uncle, I shall be returning to Barbados with him. We are not like to meet again — ever. Is it impossible that we should part friends? Once I wronged you, I know. And I have said that I am sorry. Won't you . . . won't you say 'good-bye'?"

He seemed to rouse himself, to shake off a mantle of deliberate harshness. He took the hand she proffered. Retaining it, he spoke, his eyes sombrely, wistfully considering her.

"You are returning to Barbados?" he said slowly. "Will Lord Julian be going with you?"

"Why do you ask me that?" she confronted him quite fearlessly.

"Sure, now, didn't he give you my message, or did he bungle it?"

"No. He didn't bungle it. He gave it me in your own words. It touched me very deeply. It made me see clearly my error and my injustice. I owe it to you that I should say this by way of amend. I judged too harshly where it was a presumption to judge at all."

He was still holding her hand. "And Lord Julian, then?" he asked, his eyes watching her, bright as sapphires in that copper-coloured face.

"Lord Julian will no doubt be going home to England. There is nothing more for him to do out here."

"But didn't he ask you to go with him?"

"He did. I forgive you the impertinence."

A wild hope leapt to life within him.

"And you? Glory be, ye'll not be telling me ye refused to become my lady, when . . ."

"Oh! You are insufferable!" She tore her hand free and backed away from him. "I should not have come . . . Good-bye!" She was speeding to the door.

He sprang after her, and caught her. Her face flamed, and her eyes stabbed him like daggers. "These are pirate's ways, I think! Release me!"

"Arabella!" he cried on a note of pleading. "Are ye meaning it? Must I release ye? Must I let ye go and never set eyes on ye again? Or will ye stay and make this exile endurable until we can go home together? Och, ye're crying now! What have I said to make ye cry, my dear?"

"I . . . I thought you'd never say it," she mocked him through her tears.

"Well, now, ye see there was Lord Julian, a fine figure of a . . ."

"There was never, never anybody but you, Peter."

They had, of course, a deal to say thereafter, so much, indeed, that they sat down to say it, whilst time sped on, and Governor Blood forgot the duties of his office. He had reached home at last. His odyssey was ended.

And meanwhile Colonel Bishop's fleet had come to anchor, and the Colonel had landed on the mole, a disgruntled man to be disgruntled further yet. He was accompanied ashore by Lord Julian Wade.

A corporal's guard was drawn up to receive him, and in advance of this stood Major Mallard and two others who were unknown to the Deputy-Governor: one slight and elegant, the other big and brawny.

Major Mallard advanced. "Colonel Bishop, I have orders to arrest you. Your sword, sir!"

Bishop stared, empurpling. "What the devil . . . ? Arrest me, d'ye say? Arrest me?"

"By order of the Governor of Jamaica," said the elegant little man behind Major Mallard. Bishop swung to him.

"The Governor? Ye're mad!" He looked from one to the other. "I am the Governor."

"You were," said the little man dryly. "But we've changed that in your absence. You're broke for abandoning your post without due cause, and thereby imperilling the settlement over which you had charge. It's a serious matter, Colonel Bishop, as you may find. Considering that you held your office from the Government of King James, it is even possible that a charge of treason might lie against you. It rests with your successor entirely whether ye're hanged or not."

Bishop rapped out an oath, and then, shaken by a sudden fear: "Who the devil may you be?" he asked.

"I am Lord Willoughby, Governor-General of His Majesty's colonies in the West Indies. You were informed, I think, of my coming."

The remains of Bishop's anger fell from him like a cloak. He broke into a sweat of fear. Behind him Lord Julian looked on, his handsome face suddenly white and drawn.

"But, my lord . . ." began the Colonel.

"Sir, I am not concerned to hear your reasons," his lordship interrupted him harshly. "I am on the point of sailing and I have not the time. The Governor will hear you, and no doubt deal justly by you." He waved to Major Mallard, and Bishop, a crumpled, broken man, allowed himself to be led away.

To Lord Julian, who went with him, since none deterred him, Bishop expressed himself when presently he had sufficiently recovered.

"This is one more item to the account of that scoundrel Blood," he said, through his teeth. "My God, what a reckoning there will be when we meet!"

Major Mallard turned away his face that he might conceal his smile, and without further words led him a prisoner to the Governor's house, the house that so long had been Colonel Bishop's own residence. He was left to wait under guard in the hall, whilst Major Mallard went ahead to announce him.

Miss Bishop was still with Peter Blood when Major Mallard entered. His announcement startled them back to realities.

. "You will be merciful with him. You will spare him all you can for my sake, Peter," she pleaded.

"To be sure I will," said Blood. "But I'm afraid the circumstances won't."

She effaced herself, escaping into the garden, and Major Mallard fetched the Colonel.

"His excellency the Governor will see you now," said he, and threw wide the door.

Colonel Bishop staggered in, and stood waiting.

. At the table sat a man of whom nothing was visible but the top of a carefully curled black head. Then his head was raised, and a pair of blue eyes solemnly regarded the prisoner. Colonel Bishop made a noise in his throat, and, paralyzed by amazement, stared into the face of his excellency the Deputy-Governor of Jamaica, which was the face of the man he had been hunting in Tortuga to his present undoing.

. The situation was best expressed to Lord Willoughby by van der Kuylen as the pair stepped aboard the Admiral's flagship.

"Id is fery boedigal!" he said, his blue eyes twinkling. "Cabdain Blood is fond of boedry — you remember de abble-blossoms. So? Ha, ha!"

CPSIA information can be obtained at www.ICGtesting.com
Printed in the USA
BVOW03s0042291013

334904BV00015B/540/P